Business in Emerging Lat

Business in Emerging Latin America provides students with a comprehensive overview of the business environment of this emerging, dynamic region.

Driven by expanding domestic markets and exports of natural resource commodities, Latin America has recently come into focus as an economic force in the international arena. The book begins at the macro level, focusing on the region's geopolitical, technological, social, competitive, and economic environments. It then moves to the micro level, illustrating that Latin America is a mosaic of countries with distinct cultures and political economies. This book aims to:

- Provide a comprehensive overview of the business environment in this region
- Identify major drivers of emerging market expansion
- Analyze the strategies of companies both within and outside of the region

The book includes examples and cases from across the region, as well as chapters on entrepreneurship, leadership, HRM, sustainability, income inequality, social responsibility, and transparency. Capturing the dynamism of this region, the book will appeal to students of international business who have a special interest in Latin America.

Fernando Robles is Professor of International Business and International Relations at the School of Business of The George Washington University, USA. His research and consulting experience is in global marketing and regional marketing strategies. He has published widely in academic and professional journals, and serves on the editorial boards of *Academia, Management Decision* and the *Journal of Asia Pacific Business*.

Nila M. Wiese is a Professor of International Business and Marketing and the Director of the Business Leadership Program at the University of Puget Sound, USA. Her teaching and research is in the areas of international business strategy, base of pyramid markets, and economic development in Latin America and other emerging economies. She has experience in banking and consulting and training with small businesses in Central America.

Gladys Torres-Baumgarten is Associate Professor of International Business at Ramapo College of New Jersey, USA. Her research interests focus on international marketing, as well as foreign direct investment issues in emerging markets with particular emphasis on Latin America and Africa. Her articles have appeared in marketing, management, and international business academic journals.

Business in Emerging Latin America

Fernando Robles, Nila M. Wiese,
and Gladys Torres-Baumgarten

Routledge
Taylor & Francis Group

NEW YORK AND LONDON

First published 2015
by Routledge
711 Third Avenue, New York, NY 10017

and by Routledge
2 Park Square, Milton Park, Abingdon, Oxon OX14 4RN

Routledge is an imprint of the Taylor & Francis Group, an informa business

Library of Congress Cataloging-in-Publication Data
Robles, Fernando.
Business in emerging latin america / Fernando Robles, Nila Wiese, Gladys
    Torres-Baumgarten.
       pages cm
    Includes bibliographical references and index.
  1. Business enterprises—Latin America.   2. Latin America—
Economic conditions—21st century.   3. Economic development—Latin
America.   4. Latin America—Commerce.   I. Wiese, Nila.   II. Torres-
Baumgarten, Gladys.   III. Title.
    HF3230.5.Z5R627   2014
    338.7098—dc23   2014000121

ISBN: 978-0-415-85906-6 (hbk)
ISBN: 978-0-415-85907-3 (pbk)
ISBN: 978-0-203-79794-5 (ebk)

Typeset in Minion
by Apex CoVantage, LLC

Printed and bound in the United States of America by Edwards Brothers
Malloy on sustainably sourced paper.

To Carol and Natalie for their quest for clarity of my ideas.
F.R.

To Ryan, Marisa, and Max, I missed you during all those weekends away.
N.W.

To Larry, Andrea, Derek, Jen, and Diana for all their support.
G.T-B.

Contents

PART IV
Challenges for the Future of Business in Latin America

Introduction

A book about the business environment in Latin America and the Caribbean is long overdue. After a long period of relative macroeconomic stability and sound economic growth, the region is enjoying prosperity, optimism, and progress. The main purpose of this book is to document this evolution and to provide a foundation to study business conditions and how firms react to the opportunities and challenges that this region offers.

To accomplish this purpose, we look first at the external factors affecting the region, focusing on the macroeconomic, competitive, and consumer environments. With this foundation in the key environmental factors, we explore in the second part of the book the business strategies and corporate culture of the region. The last part addresses future challenges and provides a glimpse of the future of business in Latin America.

Chapter 1 "sets the stage" for the book by reviewing Latin America's importance in the world economy. The recent economic history of the region is reviewed, as are the new trade and investment linkages that developed from 2000 to the present, most notably with China. The past decade has also seen marked increases in outward foreign direct investment flows by Latin American firms into new world regions—in both developing and developed markets alike.

Chapter 2 explores the impact of globalization on Latin America and how it continues to shape a polarized region. The new global economic order of stagnation in advanced developed economies and the growth and rising affluence in emerging countries is mirrored in Latin America. The region shows strong evidence of regional economic polarization, which creates structural economic and market differences in the two regional hubs: Brazil and Mexico. Chapter 2 provides a better understanding of the extent of regional polarization across different economic sectors and its impact on the business environment and strategies of firms in Latin America.

Chapter 3 reviews Latin American competitiveness in the world economy. The competitive landscape in Latin America has evolved significantly over the past 30 years. Formerly protected markets, which were dominated by a few large family groups and state-owned enterprises, have been replaced by open markets. Although large family-controlled domestic conglomerates still play an important role, there is now a stronger presence of multinational corporations from developed and emerging economies, as well as a more vibrant small and medium-size business sector. This dynamic competitive environment will require firms to leverage the unique opportunities offered by the region's macro-environment (e.g., abundant natural resources, growing consumer markets), while managing its many risks (e.g., regulatory bureaucracies, weak infrastructure). This chapter provides a better understanding of the competitive structure in Latin America and the drivers and barriers to competitiveness for firms operating in the region.

In Chapter 4, we look at Latin American consumers. Today's Latin American consumers look very much like any other consumers in developed countries. As the Latin American consumer market has grown in size and purchasing power, it has also become increasingly segmented and sophisticated, while remaining distinctive from other markets around the world. This chapter provides an overview of the size and growth of Latin American consumer markets and their current and evolving consumption patterns. Competing for this growing and increasingly affluent market will require that firms from inside and outside the region develop a deep understanding of consumers' characteristics and expectations.

As a follow-up to our discussion of consumer markets, in chapter 5 we discuss how firms should develop propositions that meet consumer values and build brands that resonate with these values. We also discuss how firms should position their brands in the marketplace to target particular market segments and utilize media to reach these consumers. The chapter ends with a discussion of two particular channels to reach these markets: grocery retailing and fast-food franchising.

Chapter 6 provides an overview of Latin American business culture and its influence on managerial behavior. Latin America's colonial legacy has created organizational and decision-making styles characterized by the concentration of power, multilevel hierarchical structures, strong networks of relationships, and paternalistic leadership. As a result, however, of the region's insertion into a globalized world, firms have adopted efficient and effective managerial systems. Business culture in the region is not homogeneous, and substantial differences exist across different countries. In particular, we explore business culture differences between two economic clusters, led by Brazil and Mexico, respectively. A solid grounding in Latin American business culture provides the foundation to elaborate on more specific managerial topics in the following chapter.

Chapter 7 covers managerial issues in the region. Competition for talent is now a reality for firms around the world, and the ability to recruit, develop, and retain skilled employees and effective leaders can be a significant source of competittive advantage. For Latin American organizations, acquiring this capability will be essential as they pursue global positioning. For foreign firms, the challenge will be understanding that in Latin America, culture is central to managing people. This chapter describes and analyzes issues related to leadership, organizational behavior, talent management, and negotiation, focusing on the influence of cultural norms and values in the management of organizations in the region. We argue that adopting culturally appropriate practices will have a direct impact on organizational performance.

The next two chapters take a more strategic view of the region. Chapter 8 analyzes how multinationals outside the region formulate their Latin American strategies. These firms bring formidable advantages to play in the region but also suffer from the disadvantages of not being native to Latin America. The examples provided in the chapter illustrate how multinationals assess the importance of opportunities in Latin America in relation to those in other emerging markets, allocate resources to build their presence in the region, identify key country markets in which to concentrate their investments, and adapt their global strategies to local managerial styles.

In chapter 9, we look at multinationals from the region. The chapter analyzes the evolution and competitiveness of Latin America–based firms that expanded intraregionally—"multilatinas"—and a few "global latinas," or Latin America-based firms that have a strong presence in at least one other world region outside Latin America. The chapter examines the historical and economic drivers that led to their creation, as well as their present competitiveness and prospects for growth in the years to come. In the final section of the chapter, we identify the sectors in which multilatina and global latina firms tend to predominate and their home-based advantages.

Chapter 10 turns its attention to small companies and the critical role of entrepreneurs in the creation of new businesses. Entrepreneurial spirit can be found in nearly every country across the globe, yet the challenges facing entrepreneurs vary greatly across countries, including within Latin America. The chapter addresses the nuances of being an entrepreneur in Latin America by first providing an overview of attitudes toward entrepreneurship in the region. Yet, as is noted in most if not all of the chapters of this book, in order to truly understand the entrepreneurial climate in the region, individual country differences must be taken into account. We distinguish between different types of entrepreneurial ventures and describe various programs that countries have implemented to attract new business ventures within their borders, with particular emphasis placed on a program aimed at attracting technology entrepreneurs. The chapter also looks at the interests and concerns of specific groups of entrepreneurs, including local entrepreneurs, entrepreneurs from outside the region, and women entrepreneurs. A final topic is social entrepreneurship.

As the book has shown, Latin America has emerged as a growing and stable regional market. Yet, challenges remain, primarily in the areas of natural-resource management, corruption, and poverty alleviation. Chapter 11 highlights the key challenges in Latin America's business environment and identifies windows of opportunity that these challenges may represent. We first focus on the importance of natural resources to the region's competitiveness and assess current efforts by firms and governments to engage in responsible resource management. Corruption represents a significant risk to potential foreign investors and is a major deterrent to growth for all firms operating in the region. We examine governmental and managerial responses to this challenge. Finally, issues of income inequality and poverty continue to represent social and political risk, but they also represent significant opportunities. We end the chapter by focusing our attention on corporate social responsibility as a strategically viable alternative for managing and leveraging these risks.

Chapter 12 looks to the region's prospects for future growth. The region is still poised for growth; however, the strides made in growth in gross domestic product (GDP) and prosperity at the consumer and firm levels from 2000 to 2008 will likely not be seen for quite some time. This chapter discusses some of the region's highly visible firms and describes the strategies that they will likely pursue while maneuvering through a more precarious economic climate.

Acknowledgments

In closing, we would like to recognize the support provided by our own institutions for the research and preparation of this book. The access to research material through the vast resources and databases of the library collections at our institutions was critical to compiling all of the information for the diverse topics covered in this book. Special thanks go to Merrill Silver and Tami Hulbert for their research and editorial help. We also acknowledge the encouragement and support received from Routledge, particularly our editorial assistant Manjula Raman and Sharon Golan at Taylor and Francis.

Finally, we acknowledge the immense support of our families during the process of manuscript preparation and the valuable editorial assistance of Carol and Natalie Robles, Ryan Wiese, and Larry Baumgarten.

Part I

The Emerging Latin American Region

1   The Economic Turnaround

Introduction

This chapter reviews the fundamental macroeconomic changes that Latin America has undergone since 2000 and also chronicles the new trade and political affiliations in the region. This chapter "sets the stage" for the rest of the book and also steps back to assess whether the growth experienced in the first decade of the 21st century is sustainable, an issue that will be discussed in greater detail in the last chapter of this book.

The first part of this chapter provides an overview of macroeconomic growth in the 21st century—for the region overall and for key individual countries. This section is then followed by a discussion on regional economic integration efforts and a section on the proliferation of bilateral and multilateral trade agreements between Latin American countries and other economic powers worldwide. The subsequent sections focus on the drivers of the growth that the region has experienced. The chapter closes with an assessment of the challenges that the region faces at present.

1.1   Latin America's Economic Performance from 2000 to the Present

As Latin America looks back on the first years of the 21st century, some will likely be satisfied with the progress that the region experienced over that time, while others will be quite disappointed. This underscores the significant heterogeneity in performance across individual Latin American countries during this period. From 2003 to 2008, Latin America experienced average gross domestic product (GDP) growth rates per year of about 6.6%, prompting some to refer to this prosperous time as the region's "Golden Years" (Talvi & Munyo, 2013). As pointed out, however, growth levels were uneven across Latin American countries. What accounts for this heterogeneity in performance within the region? At the 2013 conference on Latin America at the Wharton School of Business, Alberto Ramos, Goldman Sachs's head of the Latin American economic research team in the global investment division, indicated that Latin American countries can be classified into two distinct groups and that the economic performance of the countries will vary depending, in part, upon the group of which they are a part. He stated that Latin American countries are "bifurcating along two different paths, where one group is pursuing more orthodox, conventional policies and doing relatively well, while another group that is pursuing populist experiments has performance that is a little bit more complicated" (Universia Knowledge@Wharton, 2013). Chapter 2 provides additional insights on the economic polarization of the Latin American region. Countries such as Chile, Colombia, and Peru would be included in the first group, whereas countries such as Venezuela, Bolivia, and Argentina would be part of the second group. Others might fine-tune this grouping and argue that Latin American countries could be divided into three groups: first, those embracing free market ideals (such as Chile, Colombia, and Peru); second, those in which there is state-directed capitalism with a pivotal role for government in identifying and directing key industrial policies (such as Brazil); and third, the group with populist governments in which the government assumes the role of "the people's protector"—protecting the general population from the country's elite. In the countries of this latter group, the government acts as the "market," curbing inflation by setting price ceilings (or mandating price cuts) and enlisting the army or the national guard to enforce price controls with force. Venezuela under President Maduro in late 2013 is a prime example of this socioeconomic philosophy.

Table 1.1 summarizes key economic indicators for some of the Latin American countries. Data for the United States are provided as a frame of reference. Table 1.1 highlights the uneven growth dynamics across the region. Peru exhibited the highest GDP growth from 2010 to 2012, averaging 6.3% growth over that time frame. Peru was followed by Chile, Colombia and Mexico with average growth rates of 5.7%, 4.9% and 4.4%, respectively. Brazil's growth trailed somewhat, with an average GDP growth rate in that time frame equal to 3.71%;

Table 1.1 Key Economic Indicators for Pivotal Nations in Latin America, 2012

Country	Nominal GDP ($ Billions)	Real GDP Per Capita ($)	Population (Millions)	Average Annual GDP Real Change (2010–2012)	Inflation, GDP Deflator (% Change) 2009–2013	Current Account Balance ($ Billions)
U.S.	15,680.0	51,120	313.9	2.13	2.4	−440.4
Argentina	470.5	11,448	41.1	N/A	N/A	0.1
Brazil	2,253.0	11,630	198.7	3.71	5.3	−54.2
Chile	268.2	14,280	17.5	5.70	1.8	−9.5
Colombia	369.8	10,110	47.7	4.86	2.8	−11.9
Mexico	1,178.0	9,600	120.8	4.36	3.6	−11.4
Peru	197.0	5,880	30.0	6.30	1.8	−3.3
Venezuela	381.3	12,500	30.0	2.77	14.1	11.0

Source: World Bank (2012).

however, this figure is somewhat misleading; 2010 was an election year in Brazil, and during that politically sensitive year the government boosted spending and posted a 7.5% increase in GDP growth over the prior year; this was followed by 2.7% growth in 2011 and a paltry increase of 0.9% in 2012.

Another way of categorizing individual Latin American countries is by key trading partners. Mexico and the Central American countries trade more heavily with the United States than with any other major economic power. As a result, the economic performance of these countries is closely linked to US economic performance; it has been said that when the US economy catches cold, Mexico's economy sneezes. On the other hand, South American economies (such as those of Brazil and Argentina) have solidified their ties with China on trade and foreign direct investment, closely mirroring China's economic performance. The China-Latin America trade and investment relationship is explored in greater detail later in this chapter.

1.2   Latin America's Significance as a World Region

In 2013 Latin America and the Caribbean had approximately 600 million people. Latin America's total GDP in 2012 was US$5.34 trillion (World Bank, 2013b), representing 7% of total world GDP and a gross national income (GNI) per capita of US$9,000 for the region (World Bank, 2013b). Brazil is by far the largest economy. Argentina, Colombia, Chile, Mexico, Peru, and Venezuela are the next most important markets in terms of GDP contribution and per capita income. Some countries have become increasingly attractive for business (e.g., Chile, Mexico, Peru); others show signs of slow growth despite having attracted significant business attention because of their size (e.g., Brazil); others still have demonstrated an increasingly challenging business environment (e.g., Venezuela, and, and to a lesser degree, Argentina).

By 2025, the Latin American market is projected to be home to 661 million people with a GDP of US$15 trillion (Global Information, 2012). The size and growth of the Latin American economy translates into US$3.7 trillion in purchasing power for the region. Consumption per person in 2012 was US$6,360, and it is expected to reach US$11,100 by 2020 (Corpart, 2012). Latin America is a region of interest to many businesses because of its size, the long-term growth prospects, and its increasingly sophisticated consumers. The next section takes a closer look at the region's performance from 2000 to 2013.

1.3   Latin America's Progress in the 21st Century

GDP growth rates in Latin America averaged around 6.6% in the period 2003–2008; more recently GDP growth rates have paled by comparison, plummeting to about 3.7% for the region (2012–2013). The optimism that earlier growth rates generated has been tempered by the slower GDP growth of late. A greater concern is the significant heterogeneity in growth across individual countries in the region, with some countries, such as Brazil, dragging down the region's growth rates with its GDP growth of about 1% in 2012.

The regional growth seen in 2003–2008 was fueled by several factors: the rapid rise in demand for Latin America's natural and agricultural resources, along with corresponding price increases in these commodities; the growth of the middle class and parallel increases in consumption of durable goods (e.g., cars, appliances) and nondurable goods; the effectiveness of social programs that resulted in poverty alleviation, which in turn led to increased consumption and spending levels; and greater access to capital as a result of the increased investment flows in the region during that time. These factors not only contributed to GDP growth in the region but also contributed to the growth and enhanced competitiveness of many large Latin American firms.

Demand and Price for Latin America's Commodities

China experienced double-digit increases in its GDP for several years, coinciding roughly with Latin America's "Golden Years" of 2003–2008 (see in Table 1.2).

In Latin America, China found a reliable—and plentiful—source for many of the natural and agricultural resources it needed to fuel its economic growth. Exports of the region's oil, minerals, and metals increased significantly. Exports from Latin America to China tripled from 2000 to 2007, and commodities account for three-quarters of all exports from Latin America (Caulyt & Hamann, 2013). The increased demand for commodities, spurred in large part by China, led to price increases for these goods, but there was yet another source of pressure on commodity prices. The additional pressure on prices stemmed from speculative behavior on the part of investors interested in commodities futures. The ease of access to capital in many developed market regions (such as Europe, the United States, and Japan) following the 2008 financial crisis led to greater availability and liquidity of investment funds. These investment funds often included commodities in their portfolios, thus putting additional pressure on prices (Herrera, 2013). As a result, Latin America benefited from this global commodity boom.

Table 1.2 China's Year on Year GDP Growth, 2000–2012

2001	+ 8.4%	**2008**	+ 9.6%
2002	+ 8.3%	2009	+ 9.2%
2003	**+ 9.1%**	2010	+10.2%
2004	**+10.1%**	2011	+ 9.3%
2005	**+11.3%**	2012	+ 7.8%
2006	**+12.7%**		
2007	**+14.2%**		

Note: Latin America's "Golden Years" (2003–2008) are highlighted in bold.

Source: World Bank (2013c).

Growth of the Middle Class and Poverty Alleviation

The economic growth of the early 2000s was paralleled by social reforms in the region, many of which led to poverty alleviation (Beccaria, Maurizio, Fernández, Monsalvo, & Álvarez, 2012) and the growth of the middle class. Between 2003 and 2009, while income inequality widened in the world, the gap between rich and poor in Latin America narrowed. Latin America's middle class grew by 50% to nearly 50 million people (Ferreira, Messina, Rigolini, López-Calva, Lugo, & Vakis, 2013; World Bank, 2013a). In addition, the proportion of Latin Americans living in poverty fell from 44% to 30% over that same period. This new middle class spent heavily on durable and nondurable goods. Growth in consumer spending, however, slowed after the global financial crisis hit Latin America in 2009.

The demographic shifts described and the increases in Latin America's middle class occurred at the same time that the region was becoming a fuller participant in the globalized world through increased international trade, regional integration, and foreign investment. This socioeconomic shift occurred as the result of the favorable economic growth rates from 2000 to 2008, yet the sustainability of relatively high growth levels over the longer term may be questionable. The financial crisis resulted in declining world trade, largely because of the lack of credit availability (United Nations Economic Commission for Latin America and the Caribbean [ECLAC], 2013). As suggested previously, the impact of the global financial crisis on individual Latin American countries varied depending on who their large trading partner was.

In late 2008 and into 2009 for example, Mexico experienced a dramatic economic downturn: exports plummeted, and its economy contracted. Brazil and Argentina also experienced a decline in exports at the time, but the decline was mitigated by the fact that China's GDP growth was still projected to be about 7.5% for the year. In addition, the demand for agricultural exports is more inelastic than is the case for other natural resources, and, as a result, Brazilian and Argentine agricultural exports did not experience as pronounced a decline (ECLAC, 2013).

1.4   International Trade and Foreign Direct Investment

International trade and foreign direct investment are key drivers of economic growth. Until late in the 20th century Latin America was largely known for its policy of import substitution and protectionist measures, yet it underwent an attitudinal transformation toward trade and investment from 1980 to the present. During the past two or three decades the regional focus has been increasingly centered on trade liberalization, tariff reduction, regional economic integration, and formation of new trading alliances, contributing to unprecedented growth in international trade and foreign direct investment. This section provides an overview of international trade and foreign direct investment and then focuses on Latin America's new trading and investment alliances, forged largely since 2000.

World Trade

World trade reached $18.4 trillion in 2012. Of this total, the world merchandise trade was $13.7 trillion, the difference being the trade in services ($4.7 trillion). By comparison, in 2001, world merchandise trade was $6.18 trillion. Thus, in a decade alone, world merchandise trade has more than doubled in volume. Together, Europe and Asia account for nearly 70% of total world trade. By comparison, Latin America's share of world trade is small, suggesting that there is ample room for export expansion.

The growth in world trade is an impressive expansion, only interrupted by the 2008 global financial crisis. World merchandise trade before the 2008 crisis experienced robust average growth of 6% between 1990 and 2008 (World Trade Organization [WTO], 2012). This strong expansion was interrupted by the 2008 crisis, resulting in a contraction of world trade in 2009 of 5.4% followed by a rebound of almost 14% in 2010 and back to the normal 5 to 6% growth in subsequent years. With the advanced economies of Europe, the United States, and Japan struggling to recover, what are the sources of the growth in world trade? According to the World Bank, more than 50% of the emerging countries' trade is now with other emerging economies; such trade increased 37% in 2001 (World Bank, 2013b). This increase in what is referred to as "South-South trade" is driving economic growth in emerging markets following the global economic crisis.

Western Europe and Asia together accounted for nearly 70% of global trade in 2011 (see Table 1.3 for a regional breakout of world trade). Latin America accounted for only 4.5% of global trade, and while this is much lower than the figure for other world regions, the region's economies fared well during the 2008 financial crisis. This resilience in light of a difficult global economy suggests that the region has the potential to increase its share of global trade.

Foreign Direct Investment Trends and Latin America

The United Nation's Economic Commission on Latin America and the Caribbean (ECLAC) estimates that global foreign direct investment (FDI) in 2012 totaled $1.39 trillion, representing a 13% decline from the $1.61 trillion posted in 2011(ECLAC, 2013). Latin America received $173 billion in inward FDI (in US dollars), or 12% of global FDI flows in 2012. This marked the first time that the region had accounted for this large a portion of global FDI. Moreover, the year was also a landmark year for developing markets in that it was the first time that developing market FDI inflows surpassed developed market inflows. Developing market FDI accounted for 52% of FDI inflows. However, Latin America's record 12% of global FDI also suggests that there are other emerging market regions (namely Asia) that continue to attract a disproportionately

Table 1.3 World Exports by Region

Region	2000 Exports $ Billions	2000 Share of Total Exports %	2011 Exports $ Billions	2011 Share of Total Exports %	Increase in World Merchandise Trade 2011–2010 %
North America	1,058	17.1	2,922	16.5	2.76
Western Europe	2,441	39.4	6,881	39.0	2.81
Asia	1,649	26.7	5,132	29.0	3.11
South & Central America	359	5.8	748	4.5	2.08
CIS	271	4.3	529	3.0	1.95
Africa	145	2.4	538	3.0	3.7
Middle East	263	4.3	672	4.0	2.55
World	6,186	100	17,816	100.0	2.88

Source: World Trade Organization (2012).

higher amount of FDI than others. Latin America and Africa demonstrated their resilience in 2012 by posting year-on-year increases in inward FDI of 7% and 5.5%, respectively. By contrast, developed countries and regions, including the United States and Europe, experienced sharp declines in inward FDI (23% and 25%, respectively) from 2011 to 2012.

If the first half of 2013 is any indication, Latin America is expected to continue attracting FDI—much as it did in 2012. During the first six months of 2013, global inward FDI totaled $745 billion, and while inflows to developed countries continued to decline, approximately 60% of global inflows went to developing countries. Increases in FDI into developing countries were again fueled in large part by acquisitions in Latin America. Asia experienced a slight decline in FDI inflows during this time frame, yet, according to the United Nations Conference on Trade and Development (UNCTAD), the region continues to attract nearly half of the FDI to developing countries and about a quarter of global FDI flows (UNCTAD, 2013). UNCTAD further estimated that these patterns would continue into the second half of 2013 and into 2014. Therefore, for the foreseeable future, Latin America will remain an attractive target for FDI capital flows, even at a time when other world regions are experiencing declines (United States, Europe) or a tapering off from previous levels (Asia). This will further spur economic growth in the region, contribute to its resiliency, and solidify the interest in the region.

FDI Distribution by Country

There were marked differences in the distribution of the regional FDI total across individual countries in Latin America (See Table 1.4). Brazil received the greatest bulk of regional FDI flows in 2012, accounting for 38% of the region's annual total and receiving just over $66 billion in inward FDI. Chile received the region's second largest amount, or roughly $30 billion in 2012. Colombia, for the first time ever, recorded the region's third largest FDI inflows at approximately $16 billion. Mexico received approximately $13 billion in inward FDI in 2012, marking the lowest level of inward FDI over the past 13 years and representing a 35% decline in FDI inflows from the prior year's levels of $21 billion (ECLAC, 2012). The decline in FDI was likely due to variations that

Table 1.4 Inward Foreign Direct Investments Flows to Latin America, 2007–2012 ($ Millions)

Country	2007	2008	2009	2010	2011	2012
Argentina	6,473	9,726	4,017	7,848	9,882	12,551
Bahamas	1,623	1,512	873	1,148	1,533	1,094
Barbados	476	464	247	290	532	356
Belize	150	180	113	100	99	198
Bolivia	366	513	423	643	859	1060
Brazil	34,585	45,058	25,949	48,506	66,660	66,272
Chile	12,572	15,518	12,887	15,373	22,931	30,323
Colombia	9,049	10,620	7,137	6,758	13,438	15,823
Costa Rica	1,896	2,078	1,347	1,466	2,156	2,265
Dominican Republic	1,667	2,870	2,165	1,896	2,275	3,610
Ecuador	194	1,057	306	163	639	587
El Salvador	1,551	903	366	117	386	516
Guatemala	745	754	600	806	1,026	1,207
Guyana	152	168	208	270	215	231
Honduras	928	1006	509	969	1014	1059
Jamaica	867	1437	541	218	242	362
Mexico	31,380	27,853	16,561	21,372	21,504	12,659
Nicaragua	382	626	434	508	968	810
Panama	1,777	2,196	1,259	2,363	2,755	3,020
Paraguay	202	209	95	228	215	320
Peru	5,491	6,924	6,431	8,455	8,233	12,240
Suriname	−247	−231	−93	−248	70	70
Trinidad and Tobago	830	2,801	709	549	1831	2,527
Uruguay	1,329	2,106	1,529	2,289	2,505	2,710
Venezuela	1,505	1,741	−2,169	1,849	3,778	3,216

Source: United Nations Conference on Trade and Development (2013).

arise when large transactions appear in one year and not in subsequent years but also—at least in part—to concerns over crime in Mexico, leading some firms to be more conservative in expansion efforts.

FDI Source Countries

The previous section identified the key recipients of FDI in Latin America, but which countries are the primary providers of FDI into Latin America? During the 5 years between 2007 and 2011, the United States was the primary single source of FDI into the region, accounting for 22% of Latin American FDI inflows (ECLAC, 2012). The Netherlands and Spain each accounted for 10% of the inflows, with Latin American countries not far behind and accounting for 9% of the regional flows. Canada and Japan were also sources for FDI into Latin America, each accounting for about 4% of total FDI inflows. However, 40% of the inward flows in 2007–2011 were attributed to "Other [countries]." These flows are coming from locations such as Switzerland, Panama, Bermuda, the Cayman Islands, the Virgin Islands, other Caribbean islands, and Luxembourg. Some of the FDI derived from these source countries, such as Switzerland, is due to FDI undertaken by large multinational corporations (MNCs) such as Nestle or pharmaceutical companies such as Roche; but some of the flows originating in smaller locations may be related to MNCs seeking to establish corporate domiciles for tax or other reasons in intermediate small countries prior to the FDI reaching its final, intended destination. In cases such as this, it is difficult to determine what the original source of FDI is. This is further complicated by the fact that there are other countries in the region that either do not disclose information on this practice or provide incomplete data (ECLAC, 2012). For example, ECLAC estimates that much of the FDI originating from China into Latin America is in fact funneled through Peru and Venezuela, yet these countries do not report on this practice.

Despite the fact that it may, at times, be difficult to determine the original FDI source, the main investors into Latin America have remained fairly stable over the past six years. However, the proportion accounted by each of the source countries is shifting slightly (ECLAC, 2012). The United States, for example, accounted for a slightly greater portion of FDI inflows in 2012 than in the previous five years (24% versus 22%, respectively). Intraregional FDI increased to 14% in 2012 (from 9% in the previous five years), signaling greater investments by the region's multinationals. The other notable shift is with regard to Spanish investment in the region, which has declined since 2007. Between 2007 and 2011, Spain was responsible for 10% of the FDI into Latin America, in contrast to only 5% in 2012. This decrease reflects the economic difficulties that Spain is facing, prompting its firms to refrain or curtail international expansion into Latin America, or even to divest assets already within the region. With the United States being the exception, it appears that developed countries have continued to sell their assets in Latin America, which are acquired by Latin American firms.

Sectoral Concentration of FDI

Analysis of FDI flows into Latin America reveals that investments are concentrated in sectors that have historically attracted FDI, yet the relative importance of each sector varies over time and by country/region (ECLAC, 2012). An analysis of FDI inflows by destination of economic activity reveals several important trends. As of 2012, half of FDI inflows into South America (excluding Brazil), for example, go into natural-resource-related investments. By comparison, this proportion had averaged 42% during the earlier five-year period, 2007–2011. The countries most likely affected by this trend are Chile, Colombia, and Peru. The proportion of FDI going to services and manufacturing in these countries declined in 2012 vis-à-vis the prior five years.

The Brazilian sectors targeted by FDI have shifted over time. In the period between 2007 and 2011, approximately 23% of FDI went into natural resources, whereas this proportion was nearly cut in half by 2012, with only about 13% going to this sector. The proportion of FDI going into the manufacturing sector has remained virtually unchanged over the same time frame, at about 38%, and that continued to be the case through 2012. The services sector in Brazil experienced the largest gains: in 2007–2011, roughly 35% of FDI targeted this sector, whereas in 2012, nearly 50% of all FDI inflows into the country went to services.

Mexico has also undergone a sectoral shift in the industries attracting FDI. In 2012, the manufacturing sector experienced a significant shift, attracting 48% of FDI, in contrast with a more meager 35% of FDI in the five-year period between 2007 and 2011. These increases reflect the growing trend in favor of near-shoring, locating manufacturing closer to a key market, and renewed growth opportunities for Mexico and other Latin American countries. The increases in manufacturing costs in historically "low-cost production" sites (such as China) and the growing volatility in transportation costs have prompted producers to locate in slightly higher-cost production sites that are closer to their customers. The increases in labor costs are offset by lower transportation costs, and the reduction in the physical and cultural distance between a manufacturer and its customer base offers added market advantages. The practice of near-shoring bodes well for the Mexican economy as well as for other Latin American economies. As a result, the data suggest that Mexico's manufacturing sector is enjoying a resurgence as a preferred manufacturing site for the United States. Increases in FDI to the manufacturing sector have cut into the proportion of FDI inflows that are allocated to the services sector, as indicated by the 42% of the FDI inflows going to services in 2012, in contrast to the 55% of FDI the sector attracted during the previous five years. The proportion of natural-resource-related FDI has remained largely unchanged, accounting for about 10% of FDI in 2012 after staying at similar levels in the preceding five years.

Sectoral shifts are significant because the employment generated by various sectors can vary widely. For example, ECLAC (2012) estimates that commerce and construction generate the greatest number of jobs (seven new jobs for every $1 million invested), followed by the manufacturing and the services sectors (three jobs for every $1 million invested). In contrast, it is estimated that the mining sector generates only one job for every $2 million invested. Even within sectors there is a fair amount of variability in terms of the employment created. In the services sector, for example, there can be wide variability. Call centers are known to create 73 jobs for every $1 million invested. These are tenuous jobs because of the low barriers to entry, and investors may shift locations fairly easily. Tourism and personal services generate more employment than financial services and communications. As a result, policymakers must consider the employment implications of the foreign direct investment and recognize that not all FDI yields similar gains in employment.

Latin America's Trade Relationship with China

A bridge was built between Latin America and China in the 21st century, figuratively. For centuries, China and Latin America were distant from each other—both economically and culturally. In recent years, China and Latin America have forged a new economic relationship. From nonexistent economic exchanges in the 1990s, China has become the number one trading partner for Brazil, Chile, and Peru in the period 2000–2012. Three Latin American countries—Chile, Peru, and Costa Rica—have signed free-trade agreements with China. China is also the number one source of FDI in Brazil and Peru (ECLAC, 2012). Furthermore, China is becoming the main lending source for Latin America. A recent report indicates that since 2005, China has lent $86 billion, more than the combined loan commitments by the World Bank and Inter-American Development Bank—two traditional sources of development funds to the region—combined (Gallagher, 2013). The new role of China in Latin America is another example of the large global economic realignment. This new relationship brings great opportunities and risks to Latin America, which we will explore later. More important, this relationship has been asymmetrical. Few countries in the region have realigned to meet the opportunities with China; Argentina, Brazil, Chile, Peru, and to a certain extent Venezuela and Colombia are among these countries. This first group of Latin American countries has experienced solid economic growth during this period of increased economic engagement with China. In fact, this group of countries suffered less from the 2008 global financial crisis and recovered faster as a result of a continuing strong economic growth in China after the crisis. In contrast, other Latin American economies have suffered from China's efficient export competitiveness in manufactured goods. In addition, this group of countries, mostly Mexico and Central America, were not attractive to China's imports and/or investments. We analyze the trade and investment impacts of China in Latin America next.

The value of trade between China and Latin America has grown significantly from 2000 to the present. The value of Latin American exports to China was a mere $6.9 billion in 2000 (Thediplomat, 2013) but rose to $94 billion in 2011. Similarly, the region's imports from China were $5.3 billion in 2000, yet $139.7 billion in 2011–2012. In the more recent period of 2006–2011, Latin American exports to China grew at an annual rate of 33.5%, whereas imports grew 23.3%.

China has the faster-growing relationship with Latin America than with any other region, including other Asian economies. For comparison, in the same period of 2006–2013, the region's trade with the United States grew at 4.6% for exports and 8.4% for imports (ECLAC, 2012).

Latin American trade with China is highly concentrated in a few agricultural commodities, mining inputs, and oil. In general terms, Latin America exports primary commodities with little value added and imports manufactured goods. A few export commodities account for 74% of total Latin American exports to China: iron ore, soy grains, copper, and petroleum. Five Latin American countries account for 80% of these exports: Argentina, Brazil, Chile, Peru, and Venezuela (Econ South, 2011). Exports to China accounted for a peak of 23.2% total exports for Chile; 15.4% for Peru; 13.2% for Brazil; 6.6% for Argentina; and only 6% for Venezuela (ECLAC, 2012). With the exception of Costa Rica, for other countries in the region, China accounts for 3% or less of total exports. In the case of Mexico, China accounts for only 1% of total exports. Of the total exports of the region, China accounts for an average of 7.1%.

On the other hand, China is an importer source of manufactured goods, machinery, electronics, plastics and chemical products, appliances, and textiles (Econ South, 2011). In contrast to the patterns of exports, Chinese imports are more widely distributed in the region. Of total imports in 2009, China was the main supplier of 12.% of total imports in Argentina, 12.5% in Brazil, 14.6% in Chile and Peru, 13.9% in Mexico, and 11.9% in Colombia (ECLAC, 2012). The average for the region of imports from China was 11.9%.

These recent trends in trade between Latin America and China also represent risks for the region. One threat is the region's increasing negative trade balances with China. Whereas some Latin American countries have made advances in managing these balances with trade agreements with China, others fear that these trade imbalances will grow even further, resulting in the deindustrialization of their economies. Some Latin American countries, particularly Argentina and Brazil, have turned to protectionist measures to control further Chinese imports with antidumping investigations leading to countervailing tariffs (Shifter, 2012). Brazil imposed taxes on automobiles not assembled or manufactured in the country. Argentina and Brazil also moved to increase the common external tariff for Mercosur (or the "Common Market of the South," consisting primarily of Brazil, Argentina, Paraguay, Uruguay, and more recently, Venezuela. This trading bloc is explained in greater detail following the section on NAFTA under "Regional Economic Integration".) on a large number of manufactured products as a way to protect their industries. Other countries have opted to continue their support of free trade and open economies and to engage China either with trade agreements or as part of a promise of greater integration of Asian and Latin American economies under a more encompassing Pacific Alliance, which will further remove trade barriers among their members, including China, Mexico, Peru, Chile and Colombia (*Bloomberg Businessweek*, 2012).

There is an added risk stemming from Latin America's trade with China—volatility in the quantity and price of commodity exports, which are dependent on China's demand. China's recent decreases in demand for commodities have already put downward pressure on prices and threatened economic growth prospects in the region. Such a slowdown of exports already took place in 2012 and 2013. Mexico, Brazil, Chile, and Peru have decreased their exports to China significantly. With the exception of Mexico, which grew at 3.5% in 2012, it is not a coincidence that the economies of the other three have also slowed significantly to rates of about 1 to 2% (*Wall Street Journal*, 2013).

There is one other key driver fueling the region's growth, and that is the influx of foreign direct investment into the region. Not only have South-South investments have been pan-regional, but some Latin American firms are now expanding into new world regions, including new regions in the developing world such as Asia and Africa, as well as in the developed world. The following section focuses on foreign direct investment trends in Latin America and is followed by a section that takes a closer look at the newer investment relationships that have developed as a result of recent South-South and South-North FDI.

Latin America's Foreign Direct Investment Relationship with China

China's foreign direct investments have become another key driver of the new global economic order. In the years just prior to the 2008 global financial crisis, Chinese outward foreign direct investment (OFDI) flows grew from about 1% to 5% of total global FDI in 2010 (United States International Trade Commission [USITC], 2012). This places China as the fifth largest supplier of investment funds in the world in that year. The majority of this investment has been directed at Asia, Latin America, and Africa.

It is difficult to accurately assess the actual value of Chinese OFDI for two reasons. First, most if not all of Chinese OFDI goes first to tax-haven economies such as Hong Kong, the Cayman Islands, the British Virgin Islands, and Luxembourg; China's investments and other financial transactions to Latin America often originate in these tax havens. Second, China's MOFCOM (Minister of Finance and Commerce), which provides official data on OFDI Chinese transactions, underestimates the value of these transactions. One source indicates that the official figures underestimate the real investments by 40% (USITC, 2012).

Despite the difficulties in estimating Chinese FDI, the extent of China's investment in Latin America ranges widely depending on the sources used. Using private investment data sources and analysis of financial transactions, UNCTAD estimated that in 2010, the flow of Chinese investment in the region reached $15 billion (ECLAC, 2011). In contrast to this estimate and using official MOFCOM (Ministry of Commerce, People's Republic of China) data, UNCTAD estimated the Chinese OFDI to Latin America at $10.5 billion or 14% of total Chinese OFDI in that year (Latin American and Caribbean Economic System [SELA], 2012). Both sources estimate that more than 90% of that investment was in the Cayman Islands and the British Virgin Islands.

According to nonofficial sources, Brazil, Argentina, and Peru received the bulk of China's OFDI in 2010. About $9.5 billion went to Brazil, $5.5 billion to Argentina, and $84 million to Peru. The rest of Chinese investment in Latin America in 2010 was insignificant. The announced investments from China for 2011 totaled $22.7 billion. With Brazil still the number one destination with $9.8 billion, Peru moved to second place with $8.6 billion in investments announced, followed by Argentina's $3.5 billion (ECLAC, 2011).

Another source places the total cumulated China OFDI in Latin America at $50 billion between 2003 and 2010. This estimate was 27% higher than China's official MOFCOM data. Of the total OFDI in the period, 60% was in the form of greenfield investments (new projects) and 40% was in mergers and acquisitions (M&As). This split reflects China's preference for controlling its investments in Latin America. Some fully controlled Chinese investments, particularly mining in Peru, have aroused strong opposition to some labor practices and to a lack of concern with the environment (East Asia Forum, 2012). Of the total stocks of OFDI, the majority was in Brazil, with $18 billion worth of greenfield investments and $9 billion in M&As. Peru is the second recipient of total Chinese OFDI, with $5 billion of greenfield investments, followed by Argentina with $2 billion (USTIC, 2012).

China's OFDI to Latin America has been mostly in natural-resources-extractive activities and some manufacturing. Chinese OFDI in extractive industries have been mostly in oil (Argentina, Brazil, Colombia, Ecuador, and Venezuela) and mining ventures (Brazil, Chile, and Peru). The investments in manufacturing have gone to countries that can be used as a platform for Chinese manufacturers to export to nearby markets (Mexico to export to the United States, Uruguay to export to Brazil, Chery's car plant in Brazil).

The majority of China's OFDI in Latin America is carried out by state-owned companies that have followed China's long-term strategy to secure raw inputs needed to supply that country's immense manufacturing complex for its own domestic market and exports. Latin America's abundant natural resources complement this strategy very well.

Although direct investments are important to accomplish China's long-term strategy, lending to Latin American countries to develop extractive projects is another way to secure long-term supply contracts. As mentioned before, China has provided $86 billion in loans to the region to improve its infrastructure and for energy development (Gallagher, 2013).

1.5   Regional Economic Integration

Latin America has attempted to reduce trade barriers and to encourage regional economic integration in the past. Examples of this include the North American Free Trade Agreement (NAFTA) and Mercosur.

NAFTA went into effect on January 1, 1994. The agreement among the United States, Canada, and Mexico eliminated tariff barriers, instituted a reduction in nontariff barriers, and aimed to protect intellectual property rights. NAFTA now links 450 million people producing $17 trillion worth of goods and services. The benefits that accrued to the signing members with respect to trade have largely come to fruition, although analysts initially acknowledged that NAFTA's effects were difficult to measure as its implementation coincided with Mexico's peso crisis in 1994–1995 and also followed significant trade liberalization initiatives in the 1980s (World Bank, 2003).

US goods and services trade with NAFTA totaled $1.18 trillion in 2011. Exports totaled $559.6 billion. Imports totaled $621.3 billion. The US goods and services trade deficit with NAFTA partners was $61 billion in 2011 (Villarreal & Fergusson, 2013).

Total goods trade (two ways) in 2011 for the United States and its NAFTA partners amounted to $1,057.9 billion, where goods exports accounted for $478.3 billion and goods imports totaled $579.6 billion. In that same year, the US goods trade deficit with Mexico and Canada was $101.3 billion (Villarreal & Fergusson, 2013).

Services trade (exports and imports) in 2011 for the United States and its NAFTA partners totaled $123 billion, where services exports were $81.3 billion and imports were $41.7 billion. The US services trade surplus with NAFTA partners was $39.6 billion in 2011 (Villarreal & Fergusson, 2013).

In 2011, Canada and Mexico were the top two purchasers of US exports (Canada accounted for $336.9 billion and Mexico for $222.7 billion). US goods exports to NAFTA partners in 2011 were $559.6 billion. This figure represents a nearly 40% increase over 2009's total of $399.4 billion and is up 230% from 1993 (before NAFTA's implementation) (Villarreal & Fergusson, 2013).

Mercosur, originally envisioned as a common market, has fallen far short of its goals. As a common market, Mercosur would have likely reduced (or even eliminated) tariffs among its members, established a common tariff for nonmembers, and allowed for the free movement of the factors of production: labor and capital in this case. Uruguay's president Mujica was quoted as saying: "We cannot, we should not deceive ourselves—over the past few years Mercosur has been really stagnant, with growing difficulties for trading among its partners. More than a common market, it actually is nothing more than a bad customs union" (Haskel, 2013). Ordinarily, in a customs union, members agree upon a common tariff toward nonmember countries, in addition to reducing tariffs and nontariff barriers among member countries. In the case of Mercosur, average tariff rates among members remain at about 15%, underscoring the lack of progress that has been achieved since the trading bloc was first formed in 1991 (Mercosur, 2013).

Mercosur members include Brazil, Argentina, Uruguay, Paraguay, and Venezuela, but the organization has faced challenges to its integration goals, largely due to national interests and protectionist measures. These have impeded greater regional integration among its members. In June 2013, for example, Argentina expropriated a cargo and tourist railway concession from Brazil's train company, ALL (América Latina Logística), claiming noncompliance with contractual agreements. Uneven market performance—such as higher unemployment rates in Argentina than in Brazil, for example—has also complicated achievement of the trade bloc's original objectives.

As recently as March 2014, the European Union and Mercosur members, except Venezuela, expressed their interest in continuing negotiations in an effort to reach a joint EU/Mercosur agreement, , which would likely result in positive gains for both regions. Such an agreement would likely boost European exports to Latin America and open new markets for Latin American agricultural products, in particular. While similar negotiations began in 2000, Europe now sees a more promising market for its goods in Latin America's middle class. Europe's stagnation and Latin America's slower growth have likely prompted the renewed interest in these bilateral negotiations as well.

Chile, Mexico, Peru, and, more recently, Panama have taken part in trade negotiations for the Trans Pacific Partnership (TPP). This partnership would create a free-trade agreement among 12 Asia Pacific countries, including the United States, Canada, Australia, Japan, Malaysia, Singapore, Vietnam, New Zealand, and Brunei. It would aim to increase trade in goods and services through the removal of tariff and nontariff barriers to trade, encourage investment, and promote greater economic linkages among member countries. While there is great interest in the benefits that would accrue to TPP's signing members, there is also internal national opposition among potential members (e.g., the United States, Japan) and nonmembers, the most obvious one being China. In addition, there are some difficult negotiations on the forefront—for example, South Korea, Japan, and the United States have difficulty finding common ground with respect to agricultural products and automobiles. The TPP—if agreed upon—could potentially change the dynamics of trade between Latin America and other signing members, particularly if China is ultimately not included. However, these negotiations are not likely to be finalized in the near term.

1.6   Summary

After a long period of macroeconomic stability and growth, Latin America seems to be entering a turning point. At this juncture, Latin American economies are searching for new sources of growth. Each country is seeking to forge its own path to reignite its economy for the next decade. This reengineering effort is based on the structural transformations and accomplishments of the past decade. The following chapters provide a foundation to understand how the region's economies may move from their current plateau to the next level of economic and social transformation.

China has undeniably become a vital economic partner for Latin America, leading some to question the nature of this "South-South" relationship. The Sino-Latin American partnership has been very focused and aligned with China's long-term economic development strategy and has also been focused with respect to the countries and economic activities of interest. With such focused concentration through state-owned companies, China will continue to play a dominant role in extractive economic activities in Latin America. In addition, Latin American countries, which had relied on China's double-digit annual growth, will have to manage the reduced economic exchanges of this partnership.

The optimism that earlier growth rates generated has been tempered by slower GDP growth of late. GDP growth levels are likely to remain uneven across countries in Latin America. As a result, Latin America continues to be of regional and worldwide significance now that it has become entrenched in the globalized world. However, given that its long-term growth outlook has slowed relative to growth during the region's "golden years" (2000–2008), policymakers will have to find ways to encourage economic growth, while minimizing inflationary pressures.

References

Beccaria, L., Maurizio, R., Fernández, A. L., Monsalvo, P., & Álvarez, M. (2013). Urban poverty and labor markets dynamics in five Latin American countries: 2003–2008. *Journal of Economic Inequality, 11*, 555–580.

Bloomberg Businessweek. (2012). Latin America Pacific bloc rejects Brazil-led protectionism. Retrieved from www.businessweek.com/news/2012-06-06/latin-american-pacific-bloc-rejects-brazil-led-protectionism.

Caulyt, F., & Hamann, G. (2013). *China's influence in Latin America is increasing.* Retrieved from http://dw.de/chinas-influence-in-latin-america-is-increasing/a-17156409.

Corpart, G. (2012). The Latin American consumer of 2020. *Americas Market Intelligence.* Retrieved from http://americasmi.com/en_US/expertise/articles-trends/page/the-latin-american-consumer-of-2020.

East Asia Forum. (2012). China: Adapting investment to the Latin American experience. Retrieved from www.eastasiaforum.org/2012/07/14/china-adapting-to-the-latin-american-experience/.

ECLAC. (2011). *See* United Nations Economic Commission for Latin America and the Caribbean (2011).

ECLAC. (2012). *See* United Nations Economic Commission for Latin America and the Caribbean (2012).

ECLAC. (2013). *See* United Nations Economic Commission for Latin America and the Caribbean (2013).

Econ South. (2011). *Trade strengths ties between China and Latin America.* Retrieved from www.frbatlanta.org/pubs/econsouth/11q2_summary_trade.cfm.

Ferreira, F., Messina, J., Rigolini, J., López-Calva, L. F., Lugo, M. A., & Vakis, R. (2013). Economic mobility and the rise of the Latin American middle class. *World Bank, Latin American and Caribbean Studies.* Retrieved from http://siteresources.worldbank.org/EXTLACOFFICEOFCE/Resources/MobilityFlagshipOverviewEng.pdf.

Gallagher, K. (2013). Latin America playing a risky game by welcoming in the Chinese dragon. *The Guardian.* Retrieved from www.guardian.co.uk/global-development/poverty-matters/2013/may/30/latin-america-risky-chinese-dragon.

Global Information. (2012). *Mega trends in Latin America.* Retrieved from www.giiresearch.com/report/fs257433-mega-trends-latin-america-html.

Haskel, D. (2013). A trade pact left out in the cold. *Latin Trade,* April 4. Retrieved from http://latintrade.com/2013/04/a-trade-pact-left-out-in-the-cold.

Herrera, R. (2013). Latin America suffering from high commodity prices. *Buenos Aires Herald.* July 10. Retrieved from www.buenosairesherald.com/article/135680/latin-america-suffering-from-high-commodity-prices.

Latin American and Caribbean Economic System. (2012). *Relations between China and Latin America and the Caribbean in the current world economic situation.* SP/Di No. 10–12. Retrieved from www.sela.org/attach/258/default/Di_10–12-elations_between_China_LAC_in_the_current_world_ economic_situation.pdf.

Mercosur. (2013). Retrieved from www.mercosur.jp/english/about/.

SELA. (2012). *See* Latin American and Caribbean Economic System (2012).

Shifter, M. (2012). *The shifting landscape of Latin American regionalism.* Retrieved from www.thedialogue.org/PublicationFiles/Shifter-CurrentHistory.pdf.

Talvi, E., & Munyo, I. (2013). Latin America macroeconomic outlook, a global perspective: Are the golden years for Latin America over? *Brookings Global-CERES Economic & Social Policy in Latin America Initiative, 2013 Latin America Macroeconomic Outlook.* Retrieved from www.brookings.edu/research/opinions/2013/11/07-latin-america-growth-rate-talvi-munyo.

Thediplomat. (2013). *China and Latin America: Big business and big competition.* Retrieved from http://thediplomat.com/china-power/china-and-latin-america-big-business-and-big-competition/.

United Nations Economic Commission for Latin America and the Caribbean. (2011). *Foreign direct investment in Latin America and the Caribbean 2010.* Retrieved from www.eclac.org/publicaciones/xml/0/43290/2011–138-LIEI_2010-WEB_INGLES.pdf.

United Nations Economic Commission for Latin America and the Caribbean. (2012). *Foreign direct investment in Latin America and the Caribbean 2011.* Retrieved from www.cepal.org/noticias/paginas/1/33941/2013-371_PPT_FDI-2013.pdf.

United Nations Economic Commission for Latin America and the Caribbean. (2013). Latin America and the Caribbean in the World Economy: A sluggish post-crisis, mega trade negotiations and value chains: scope for regional action. Briefing paper. Retrieved from www.eclac.cl/publicaciones/xml/4/50844/2013-598_PII-BOOK-WEB.pdf

United Nations Conference on Trade and Development. (UNCTAD). (2013). *World investment report 2013.* Retrieved from http://unctad.org/en/PublicationsLibrary/wir2013_en.pdf.

Universia Knowledge@Wharton. (2013). *Investing in Latin America: Tremendous growth, but not without complications.* Retrieved from www.wharton.universia.net/index.cfm?fa=printArticle&ID=237&language=english.

United States International Trade Commission. (2012). *China's emerging role as a global source of FDI.* Retrieved from www.usitc.gov/publications/332/executive_briefings/EBOT_ChinaOFDI(HammerLin).pdf.

Villarreal, M. A., & Fergusson, I. (2013). NAFTA at 20: Overview and trade effects. Appendix: US merchandise trade with NAFTA partners. *Congressional Research Service.* Retrieved from www.fas.org/sgp/crs/row/R42965.pdf.

Wall Street Journal. (2013). Latin America boom starts to fade. Retrieved from http://online.wsj.com/article/SB10001424127887324682204578513462977983222.html.

World Bank. (2003). *Lessons from NAFTA for Latin America and the Caribbean.* Retrieved from http://web.worldbank.org/WBSITE/EXTERNAL/COUNTRIES/LACEXT/EXTLACOFFICEOFCE/0,,contentMDK:20393778~pagePK:64168445~piPK:64168309~theSitePK:870893,00.html.

World Bank. (2012). *Economic indicators.* Retrieved from http://data.worldbank.org/indicator.

World Bank. (2013a). *Growth in Latin America's middle classes.* Retrieved from www.worldbank.org/en/news/feature/2012/11/13/crecimiento-clase-media-america-latina.

World Bank. (2013b). *Latin America and Caribbean.* Retrieved from http://data.worldbank.org/region/latin-america-and-caribbean.

World Bank. (2013c). DATABANK. Retrieved from http://data.worldbank.org/indicator NY.GDP.MKTP.KD.ZG?order=wbapi_data_value_1998%20wbapi_data_value%20wbapi_data_value-last&sort=asc.

World Trade Organization (WTO). (2012). *World trade report 2012.* Retrieved from www.wto.org/english/res_e/statis_e/its2001_e/its01_toc_e.htm.

2 Economic Realignment and Regional Polarization

Introduction

The new global economic order of stagnation in advanced developed economies, as well as growth and rising affluence in emerging countries, is mirrored in Latin America. The region shows strong evidence of regional economic polarization. Economic polarization creates structural economic and market differences in the two regional hubs. Both groups share a legacy of issues that include poor educational systems, income inequality, weak infrastructure, a large informal sector, corruption, and obsolete legal and regulatory frameworks. The purpose of this chapter is to provide a better understanding of the extent of regional polarization across different economic sectors and its impact on the business environment and strategies of firms in Latin America. Alignment between firm strategy and the different business environments that emerged from polarization is a necessary condition for success. Such an alignment requires a configuration of firm strategic resources to respond to the increasing opportunities.

The chapter is organized into six sections. The first section describes the recent realignment of trade and investment patterns of Latin America with the rest of the world, which reveals increasing relations with other emerging economic regions and particularly with Asia. The second defines regional polarization. The third section describes the different macroeconomic environments in two clusters of economies in Latin America. The fourth section explains the different economic and social policies in two groups of economies in the region. The fifth section focuses on the polarization of foreign direct investments in two economic clusters. The next section introduces the concept that two economic clusters in the region have shaped different business environments and introduces the concept of matching strategies for each environmental contingency. The final section provides a summary of the chapter and highlights the key concepts of regional polarization.

2.1 Regional Realignment

The world economy has experienced a shift in economic power and political power over the past 15 years. The shift reflects the gradual decline in the economic power of Europe, Japan, and the United States and a surge of less-advanced emerging economies, particularly China's. The 2008 global financial crisis, which started in the developed world, has furthered this shift even more in recent years. As a result of the crisis, the advanced economies struggle with slow growth. In contrast, emerging economies have resumed growth after a short period of economic contraction. Although growth has not returned to the pace that preceded the 2008 crisis, the bulk of these countries have fully recovered. One study estimates that emerging economies will keep their pace of growth at the rate of 2.3 to 3.3 in 2013–2015 (World Bank, 2013). The majority of the sustained growth in the emerging economies comes from East Asia, a region led by China. The developed countries will achieve a modest 1.2% to 2.2% growth rate at the most, with Europe struggling from contraction to a very modest 1.5% in 2015. This prediction is an indication of the extent of the polarization of the world economy into high-income and low-growth countries and low-income and high-growth countries.

The polarity of the global economy extrapolates to Latin America. To a great extent, the polarization in the region is the result of the alignment of countries with either the advanced or the emerging world. Latin American economies aligned with Europe, the United States, and Japan have suffered from the stagnation of this group of advanced economies. The contrary is also true. Next, we explore the impact of a polarized world on Latin America as evidenced by shifting international trade and investment patterns.

Realignment of World Trade Patterns

World merchandise trade before the 2008 crisis had experienced a robust average growth of 6% between 1990 and 2008 (World Trade Organization [WTO], 2012a). This strong expansion of world trade was interrupted by the 2008 crisis, resulting in a contraction of world trade in 2009 of 5.4% followed by a rebound of almost 14% in 2010 and a return to the normal 5% to 6% in the following years. With the advanced economies of Europe, the United States, and Japan struggling to recover, what are the sources of this growth in world trade? According to the World Bank, more than 50% of the emerging countries' trade is now with other emerging economies, an increase from 37% in 2001 (World Bank, 2013). This increase of what is called South-South trade may be behind the economic growth in these economies after the crisis.

The shift of trade patterns is more clearly depicted in the destination of exports originating in a given region (see Table 2.1). Advanced countries are mostly focused on trading with each other. In 2011, about 65% of US merchandise trade was within North America (the United States, Canada, and Mexico) and Europe, an increase from 58% in 2000. In the case of Europe, 78% of merchandise trade was within Europe and/or the United States, no significant change from 78.6% in 2000 (World Trade Organization [WTO], 2012b).

The trade shift is evident for emerging economies. In Asia, more than 53% of merchandise trade is with other Asian economies. This increase in the share

Table 2.1 Regional Trade Patterns

Merchandise Exports From Region	Merchandise Exports Destination (% of total exports)											
	North America			Europe			Asia			South & Central America		
	2000	2005	2011	2000	2005	2011	2000	2005	2011	2000	2005	2011
North America	39.8	56	48	18.5	16	17	21.6	18	21	16.5	6	7
Europe	10.8	9	7	67.8	73	71	8.2	8	10	2.3	1	2
Asia	25.7	22	16	16.9	18	17	48.9	51	53	0.7	2	3
South & Central America	61.3	35	24	12.5	18	18	5.8	13	23	17.3	25	27
CIS	4.4	6	5	54.2	57	52	7.4	12	15	2.2	2	1
Africa	17.9	22	17	18.3	43	35	17.2	16	25	2.8	3	3
Middle East	15.6	12	9	16.9	15	13	47.9	48	53	1.1	1	1

Table 2.1 Regional Trade Patterns (continuation)

Merchandise Exports From Region	CIS			Africa			Middle East		
	2000	2005	2011	2000	2005	2011	2000	2005	2011
North America	0.6	0	1	1.1	1	2	1.9	2	3
Europe	5.3	2	4	2.4		3	2.5	1	2
Asia	0.9	2	4	1.3	2	3	2.5	3	4
South & Central America	0.8	1	1	0.8	2	3	0.8	2	2
CIS	26.6	18	20	1.1	1	2	2.6	3	3
Africa	0.7	0	0	7.6	9	13	1.4	2	4
Middle East	0.8	1	0	3.8	3	3	6.5	8	9

Source: World Trade Organization (2013b).

of intraregional trade in Asia stands in contrast to that of advanced economies, which was 33% in 2011, a drop from 42.6% in 2000.

The shift in merchandise patterns is even more evident in Latin America (defined as South and Central America in Table 2.1). In 2000, Latin American main merchandise export destinations were the advanced economies—74.8% of total exports. This reliance on advanced economies for their merchandise exports was reduced to 42% in 2011. The most significant change was exports to the United States, which accounted for 61.3% in 2000 and only 24% in 2011. Two export market destinations account for the bulk of the shift of Latin American exports. Merchandise of Latin American exports to Asia increased to 23% in 2011 from a mere 5.8% of total exports in 2000. Latin American exporters were also exporting more to other Latin American markets at the pace of 27% of their total exports—a jump from 17.3% in 2000.

The increased demand for Latin American primary commodities (agricultural and mining products) by emerging economies in Asia—in particular, China—has been an important contributor to the economic growth of Latin American commodity exporters. This new reliance on commodity exports presents the risks of dependence on low value-added exports, commodity price volatility, and the assumption that there will be sustainable imports of commodities by countries such as China. With the reduction of economic growth of key Asian economies, particularly China, Latin American commodity exports are also slowing down. Latin American countries with more diversified export markets and products are less vulnerable to the slowdown of world commodity markets. As Table 2.2 shows, agriculture, fuels, and mining commodities represent 70% of all commodity exports by the region, an increase from 62% in 2005 (WTO, 2012b). These two commodities have been increasing at the rates of 15% to 16% annually. Manufactured exports represent a minor component of Latin American trade with the world. The two strong power economies in the region, Brazil and Mexico, reflect significant differences in their structure of exports.

Table 2.2 Latin American Exports by Type of Product

Export Product	Value in $ billion 2011	Share in 2005	Share in 2011	Annual Percentage Growth 2005–2011
Agriculture	206	25	27	15
Fuels and mining	322	37	43	16
Manufactured	198	35	26	8
Total	726	100	100	

Source: World Trade Organization (2013b).

Brazil and Mexico had comparable 2011 export values, $256 billion in Brazil and $350 billion for Mexico. Both Brazil and Mexico suffered a contraction of their merchandise exports after the 2008 crisis; for 2009, Brazil contracted 23%, and Mexico contracted 21%. Both countries rebounded rapidly in 2010 with an annual increase of 32% for Brazil and 30% for Mexico. In 2011, Brazil did better with an annual increase of 27% over the previous year, while Mexico increased only 17% (WTO, 2012a).

Brazil and Mexico differed in the destination and structure of their merchandise exports. In 2011, about 20.6% of Brazil commodity exports went to Europe and 10% to the United States. Brazil's exports to emerging economies included 17% to China alone. About 26.7% of total Brazilian exports were agricultural products, 22% were fuels and mining products, and 27.5% were manufactured goods; other products such as textiles and clothing accounted for the rest.

In contrast, 5.5% of total merchandise exports in 2010 from Mexico were agricultural products, 12% fuels and mining, and 57.5% manufactured goods. In terms of destinations, Mexico exported 80% to the United States and 6.2% to Europe. A total of 86.2% of Mexican exports went to advanced economies. Only 8.3% of Mexico's commodity exports went to the rest of Latin America, and a mere 1.4% went to China.

Brazil and Mexico continued their export drive after the 2008 crisis but with two different strategies. Mexico focused on manufactured good exports to the advanced economies. Brazil, on the other hand, pursued a strategy of commodity exports to a more diversified mix of markets. Further in the chapter, we explore how these two export growth strategies have impacted the macroeconomic structures that have followed either the Mexican or Brazilian approach.

Realignment of Foreign Direct Investment

An analysis of the investment flows to different world regions reveals a similar pattern of realignment of the world economy (see Table 2.3). The direct investment flows in particular show the long-term impact of investments in assets geared toward generating productive activity. In the period 2007–2012, the average annual growth of foreign direct investment flows to advanced economies declined 18% to Europe and 5% in North America (United Nations Conference on Trade and Development [UNCTAD], 2013). Although the total value of foreign direct investment to these regions is large, the decline indicates the perception among investors of declining prospects in economies in North America and Europe. In contrast to these expectations, foreign companies are reorienting their commitments to emerging economies, particularly Asia, in addition to Latin America and Africa, as the primary attractors for investment.

Although FDI flows to Latin America are increasing at an average growth of 9.9%, this rate masks the vast differences between the northern and southern parts of the region. The South American economies experienced an average growth of 21.4% between 2007 and 2012, whereas the Central American

Table 2.3 Foreign Direct Investment Flows to World Regions

Region	FDI Stock in $ billions		Average Annual Growth % 2012/2000	FDI Flows in $ billions						Average growth of FDI Flows 2007–2012 %
	2000	2012		2007	2008	2009	2010	2011	2012	
World	7,511	22,812	16.9	2,002	1,816	1,216	1,408	1,651	1,350	−5.5
Europe	2,468	8,676	20.9	906	571	404	429	472	275	−18.3
EU	2350	7,805	19.3	859	545	359	379	441	258	−18
North America (Canada & US)	2,996	4,658	4.6	332	367	166	226	268	212	−5.2
Asia	1,108	4,779	27.6	364	396	324	400	436	406	3.2
China	193	832	27.5	83	108	95	114	123	121	8.8
Latin America & Caribbean	507	2,310	29.6	171	210	150	189	249	243	9.9
Central America	119	397	19.4	38	35	21	27	30	21	−7.6
Mexico	102	315	17.4	31	27	16	21	21	12	−13
South America	308	1,290	26.5	71	93	56	92	129	144	21.4
Brazil	122	702	39.6	34	45	25	48	66	65	23.1
Caribbean	78	623	66.4	61	81	72	70	90	77	6.6
CIS	54	754	108	78	106	63	69	88	82	5.1
Africa	153	629	25.9	51	58	52	43	47	50	0.3
Middle East	68.5	660	71.9	79.6	93	71	59	49	47	−8.9

Source: United Nations Conference on Trade and Development (2013).

region suffered a decline of 7.6% in the same period. Brazil, with the largest economy and internal market in South America, attracts the bulk of the FDI flows, with 30% of the total flows to Latin America or $65 billion in 2012. Brazil's immense natural resources, its favorable location for exporting to Asian markets, and its large domestic growth are very attractive to multinational companies. The promising growth of the domestic markets and abundant natural resources, coupled with a favorable world commodity crisis, are the central drivers of the surge of foreign investment to South America. Central and Mexico have suffered average annual declines of 7.6% and 13%, respectively. The Caribbean region has achieved a reasonable growth of 6.6%. We examined the reasons of this polarization of foreign direct investments to the region later in the chapter.

Whereas annual flows of FDI capture the more recent activity by foreign firms, the stock of FDI measures the value of all of the investment commitments accumulated by firms historically. Thus, this value indicates the extent of the holdings of regional assets by foreign investors in a region. In contrast to annual flows, the FDI stocks adjust to trends at a much slower pace, as they reflect not only the annual increments of investments but also decisions of multinational firms to liquidate and disinvest from their historical positions. In 2012, the stock of FDI increased at an average annual rate of 29.6% from a base of $507 billion in 2000 to a sizeable $2,310 billion in 2012. Thus, the appreciation of these stocks is comparable to that of European stocks. In Brazil, the appreciation reached a 39.6% annual average growth (UNCTAD, 2013).

An indication that traditional patterns of FDI flows are changing with the world economic realignment is the increase of foreign investment originating in Latin America. The strong long-term growth in the region since 2000 and up to the 2008 global financial crisis also generated strong national companies with increasing financial resources and liquidity to invest not only in their domestic markets but also abroad. This process of internationalization of Latin American companies has been in gestation for quite some period through exports and minor investments abroad. The surge of investment outflows from Latin America, however, can be determined by the inflection point of annual investment outflows from an average of $10 billion before 2005 to $30 billion after 2005, reaching a high level of $48 billion in 2011 (United Nations Economic Commission for Latin America [ECLAC], 2013). The largest investor abroad is Mexico, with $25.6 billion, as its corporations continue to acquire and invest in new plants throughout Latin America and also in the United States, Europe, and Asia. In fact, the value of Mexican investment outflows was larger than the FDI inflows in the same year, an indication that Mexican companies are reacting to invest in better opportunities abroad. Chilean companies are not far behind, with foreign investments of $21.9 billion in 2011 and with some of them behind the largest financial transactions, such as the merger of Chile's LAN airline with Brazil's TAM in a transaction valued at $6.5 billion. Some Brazilian companies, however, are reversing the trend by divesting from their assets abroad to fund their domestic expansion. One such example is Petrobras, which is divesting from refinery assets in the United States, Japan, and Africa to invest in the pre-salt oilfields projects in Brazil (ECLAC, 2013).

2.2   Regional Economic Polarization

The strong rebalancing of the global economy has had a differential impact on Latin America's economies. Strong demand from growing Asian economies has favored Latin American countries, which are exporters of mining and food commodities. On the other hand, countries that have mostly relied on manufacturing exports and services find themselves facing stiff Asian competition in global markets. These fundamental global economic realignments are shaping a different regional order in Latin America. The most notable differences are the competing visions and development strategies of the two regional economic powers, Brazil and Mexico. In this section we analyze the structural differences resulting from this differential realignment and identify groups that exhibit common structural economic and market conditions.

A study by Izquierdo and Talvi (2011) provides evidence of regional polarization. The authors identified a group of growing economies experiencing exchange rate appreciation and inflationary pressures, yet thriving in a surge of middle-class-driven domestic markets. Another group of economies exhibits large fiscal imbalances, loss of competitiveness to Asian competition, and dollarization. Both groups share a legacy of issues that include poor educational systems, income inequality, poor infrastructure, a large informal sector, corruption, and obsolete legal and regulatory frameworks.

Izquierdo and Talvi (2011) analyzed the structural differences of regional economies as they readjust to the new world economic order. The authors clustered 26 Latin American and Caribbean countries on the basis of (a) whether a country is a net commodity export balance (importer/exporter); (b) its share of exports to industrial countries; and (c) its share of investment in the output of its economy (investment/GDP). Izquierdo and Talvi found a two-cluster solution that discriminated well across macroeconomic indicators of aggregate demand, aggregate supply, fiscal balance, sectorial and external balances, and money demand between the groups. They concluded that the new global economic order has shaped economic structural differences in the two revealed clusters. Furthermore, they observed that these differences are increasing over time. Their analysis shows that country variance decreases within a cluster and increases between clusters over a 10-year period. They concluded that these two subregions seem to be growing apart and that clusters have become more compact over time, as evidenced by the reduction of its mean squared error over time (Izquierdo & Talvi, 2011). The two clusters are identified in the first two columns of Table 2.4 and labeled the Mexico-led cluster (1) and the Brazil-led cluster (2). The Mexican cluster includes net commodity importers and countries with a low ratio of investment to exports. The second group, labeled the Brazilian cluster, is composed of net commodity exporters with higher ratios of investments to exports to industrial countries. Izquierdo and Talvi (2011) note that Venezuela and Trinidad & Tobago, which are part of the Brazil cluster, seem to be outliers, as they do not fit clearly the profiles of either cluster. Venezuela is a net commodity exporter due to its oil exports, but other macroeconomic indicators do not fit well with the rest of the second cluster. A similar situation describes Trinidad & Tobago. These two countries join the larger Brazil-led cluster in the last step of agglomeration.

Table 2.4 Latin America Clusters

Country	Latin American Clusters	Investment to GDP % Average, 2007–2011	Exports to Advanced Economies as % of Total Exports Average, 2007–2011	Commodity Exports as % of Total Exports Average, 2007–2011
Belize	1	20.52	72.24	0.931
Guyana	1	18.522	67.9	0.659
Costa Rica	1	21.846	53.7	0.367
Honduras	1	27.916	65.32	0.31
Panama	1	26.014	51.18	0.102
Mexico	1	25.238	84.68	0.244
Dominican Republic	1	17.223	67	0.255
Suriname	1	22.415	56.44	0.11
Guatemala	1	15.756	46.46	0.552
Nicaragua	1	25.486	48.16	0.826
Bahamas	1	26.548	90.72	0.319
Barbados	1	16.416	34.74	0.55
El Salvador	1	14.526	43.48	0.266
Jamaica	1	23.668	81.64	0.866
Mean Mexico Cluster (1)		21.57	61.69	0.454
Brazil	2	19.358	42.3	0.576
Colombia	2	22.89	54.84	0.682
Argentina	2	24.188	24.2	0.647
Paraguay	2	15.336	6.86	0.591
Chile	2	22.536	48.6	0.803
Peru	2	24.332	54.34	0.676
Uruguay	2	20.042	19.04	0.731
Bolivia	2	17.252	25.22	0.895
Ecuador	2	25.614	52.66	0.908
Venezuela	2	25.598	29.48	0.944
Trinidad and Tobago	2	13.448	65.04	0.738
Mean Brazil Cluster (2)		20.96	38.41	0.74

Source: Izquierdo & Talvi (2011); and Author's elaboration.

Using the identification of the two Latin American clusters by Izquierdo and Talvi (2011), we gathered macroeconomic statistics to show the different global realignment of their economies. Table 2.5 shows the 5-year average for the investment/GDP ratio, the % of total exports to advanced economies, and the % of commodities exports of total exports for the 26 economies in the Izquierdo-Talvi study. Contrary to Izquierdo and Talvi's conclusion that the two groups differed in the gross fixed capital formation based on an earlier 2003–2006 trend, the two regional clusters showed comparable investment-to-GDP ratios. Thus, both groups show convergence on the importance of investing in future production. Where the two clusters differ significantly is the nature and destination of their exports. As we can observe from Table 2.5, the Brazil cluster exports 81% commodities (agricultural products and mining mostly), of which only 42% go to advanced markets. On the other hand, 62% of the Mexico cluster's total exports, of which only 45% are commodities, are destined for advanced economies. Mexico alone exports 84% to advanced markets—mostly the United States—and the majority are manufactured goods, with commodities representing only 24% of its exports. Brazil offers a more balanced approach with 42% of exports going to the advanced economies and 45% of these being commodity exports. A visual representation of these two clusters is offered in Figure 2.1.

Clearly, these two clusters' different strategies to integrate into the world economy may lead to substantial differences in their economic performance, which we explore in the next section.

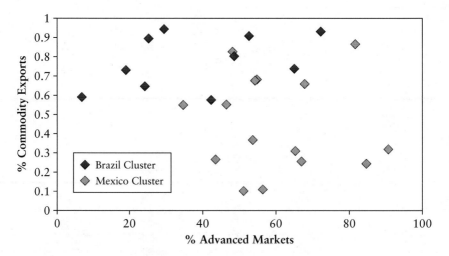

Figure 2.1 Two Latin American Clusters

Source: Authors' elaboration

Table 2.5 Macroeconomic and FDI Indicators in Two Latin American Economic Clusters

	GDP Growth Average %, 2007–2011	Inflation Average %, 2007–2011	Current Account Balance as % of GDP Average 2007–11	Primary Government Budget Balance as % of GDP Average, 2007–2011	Unemployment Average, 2007–2011	FDI flows in 2012 in millions of dollars	Annual Growth of FDI Average, 2007–2012
Belize	1.96	2.57	−4.62	−0.88	10.57	198	−7.43
Guyana	4.42	3.136	−12.78	−2.92	7.06	231	10.94
Costa Rica	3.88	7.84	−5.28	−2.38	6.58	2265	14.53
Honduras	2.94	7.84	−8.54	−3.36	5.24	1059	13.50
Panama	2.94	5.26	−8.56	−3.36	7.06	3020	37.85
Mexico	1.62	4.42	−0.8	−1.52	5.76	12659	−5.52
Dominican Republic	5.92	6.64	−7.34	−2.4	14.7	3610	37.97
Suriname	5.42	8.68	15.88	1.72	8.66	70	−140.27
Guatemala	3.38	5.88	−2.82	−2.44	3.46	1207	10.60
Nicaragua	2.94	9.5	−13.76	−0.56	8.61	810	35.20
Bahamas	−1	2.72	−12.14	−2.74	11.12	1094	3.98
Barbados	−0.26	6.5	−7.8	−5.9	9.5	356	12.89
El Salvador	1	3.06	−4.62	−2.6	6.46	516	15.15
Jamaica	−0.62	12.34	−13.38	−5.86	11.36	362	−7.43
Mexico Cluster Mean	2.46	6.17	−6.18	−2.51	8.29	1961	2.00
Brazil	4.24	5.42	−1.48	−2.18	7.6	66272	28.05
Colombia	4.24	4.46	−2.76	−3.16	11.96	15823	19.52
Argentina	6.9	8.76	1.68	−0.38	9.5	12551	28.21
Paraguay	5.06	5.5	−0.88	1.1	7.26	320	20.80
Chile	3.88	4.18	0.62	1.98	7.98	30323	18.73
Peru	7.06	3.52	−1.5	0.68	8.16	12240	11.95
Uruguay	6.14	7.82	−2.68	−1.2	7.7	2710	22.55
Bolivia	4.68	7.6	6.96	−0.18	6.84	1060	27.05
Ecuador	4.14	5.02	0.78	−1.9	7.28	587	154.77
Venezuela	2.72	27.54	6.76	−2.14	8.12	3216	−72.45
Trinidad and Tobago	0.5	8.38	21.12	0.7	5.44	2527	93.43
Brazilian Cluster Mean	4.50	8.01	2.60	−0.60	7.98	13420	32.05

Sources: United Nations Economic Commission for Latin America (2012b); United Nations Economic Commission for Latin America (2012c).

2.3   Macroeconomic Environments in Brazil- and Mexico-Led Clusters

One important aspect of global realignment is differential economic growth between the clusters and, to a certain extent, the macroeconomic environment as indicated in Table 2.5. The Brazil cluster has clearly benefited the most from the global realignment. A 5-year average (2007–2011) of GDP growth shows the Brazil-led cluster growing at 5.15% and the Mexico-led group at only 2.46%. The economies of Peru, Uruguay, and Argentina in particular have performed extremely well despite the recessionary global economy after the financial crisis of 2008.

Although a similar trend for high inflation is found in both clusters, the Brazil cluster suffers from higher inflationary pressures because of the overheating of these economies and the strong capital flows that they attract. On the other hand, inflation in the Mexico-led cluster is stickier to downturn trends.

In general, emerging economies driven by their domestic markets are gradually shifting from a position of surplus in the current account to a deficit position as industrialized economies move in the opposite direction. The Mexican cluster suffers the largest adjustment with an average of 6.18% deficit in current account in the period 2007–2011, against only 0.08% for the Brazil cluster in the same period. Fiscal balance differences between the two clusters also show how governments are adjusting to their particular economic conditions. In the Mexico cluster, countercyclical programs that stimulate and compensate for stagnant growth appear more effective. The primary public-sector average balance deficit in this cluster is 5.86%. This deficit is an indication of government efforts to stimulate their economies after the 2008 recession. The differences are clear in the Brazil-led cluster, with an average public-sector surplus of 2.18% in the period 2007–2011. With government surpluses, these economies were in a much better position to intervene and stimulate their economies, which many of them did right after the 2008 crisis, and this allowed them to bounce back from a short-term decline in their GDP growth (ECLAC 2012b; 2012c).

As for unemployment, both clusters suffered from high unemployment levels. As the Mexico cluster suffered more from the recessions in the advanced economies, these countries' average level of 11% is much higher than the 8% in the Brazil cluster.

The review of the macroeconomic performance of the two Latin American clusters shows striking differences in economic growth and in external and public balances. On the other hand, both clusters seem to converge on unemployment and inflation. Figure 2.2 provides a geometric interpretation of these results. The most drastic differences are both the current account balances and economic growth. Given that other macroeconomic conditions are comparable, foreign direct investors may focus only on these differences. To illustrate investors' response to polarization, we analyze the flows of foreign investment to these regions next.

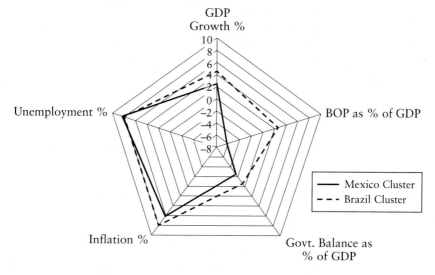

Figure 2.2 Macroeconomic Performance of Two Latin American Clusters, 2007–2011
Source: Authors' elaboration.

2.4 Polarization of Economic and Social Policies

Izquierdo and Talvi (2011) note that government macroeconomic policies should fit the structural conditions of each cluster; these differences are important components of the business context as economic agents and investors respond to these signals in different ways (Cardenas & Levy-Yeyati, 2011).

In the Brazil cluster, macroeconomic policies have been aimed mostly at maintaining inflation targets within the context of capital market openness, policy autonomy, and floating exchange rates. Inflation-targeting monetary policies have used high interest rates. Fiscal policy has been characterized as prudent, with the goal of yielding primary surpluses at all levels. The outcome of this policy combination has been currency appreciation in most of the Brazil-cluster economies. Such strong currency appreciation hurts exports and favors imports with the undesirable outcome of discouraging domestic investment in productive activities. On the other hand, high interest rates and macroeconomic stability attract short-term and foreign direct investments.

As a result, economies in the Brazil cluster have experienced a sustained period of overvalued currencies, primary fiscal surpluses, and current account surpluses. Such conditions have favored sectors of society associated with the export boom and have attracted foreign investors in the natural resources sector, as discussed earlier. On the other hand, manufacturing activity has stagnated under the pressure of low-cost imports, with pressures by local industry to introduce market-protection measures and incentives. Shrinkage of the industrial base has been compensated for by an increase in the service economy, especially related to financial services, which are less vulnerable to import competition.

With certain controls on inflation, Brazil-led cluster economies have introduced a number of policies to address social issues and provide incentives to energize their domestic markets. Policies related to the expansion of consumer and housing credit funded by public development banks, increases in the minimum wage, extension of pensions to informal-sector workers, and credit to small farmers are examples of such interventions. Further policies have targeted the issues of poverty through income-transfer programs linked to health and education conditions. The outcomes of these economic and social policies have been a reduction of poverty, creation of a solid middle-class market, a buoyant service economy, and a vibrant sector related to natural resource extraction. In Brazil alone, a middle-class market of 100 million people had an infusion of 32 million Brazilians in the period 2005–2010. This swelling of the middle class is a result of social programs such as "Bolsa Familia," a family subsidy tied to health and educational conditions, and "Minha Casa," a housing program introduced in 2002 by the Lula government (Eloy, 2010). Demographics and changing lifestyles have also shaped local demand conditions as the average number of family members decreases and the average population age increases. These market changes in Brazil have been mirrored or are even more advanced in other economies in this cluster. Chile and Uruguay have already experienced the transformation in progress in Brazil; Colombia and Peru follow closely behind. Expanding domestic markets have further attracted not only resource-seeking but also market-seeking foreign investment (Yunyun, 2010). As a result, both domestic and export markets have become engines for further growth.

Despite these successes, the Brazil-led cluster risks the hollowing out of its manufacturing industries and suffers from the so called middle-income commodity trap—the inability to sustain a period of rapid economic growth with market reforms and a shift to more value-added transformation (Inter-American Dialogue, 2012). Some experts argue that these economies should move up the development ladder through investments in innovation related to natural-resource extraction or productivity improvements in the service economies (McKinsey Global Institute, 2013). Clearly, improving competiveness in more mainstream manufacturing may not be enough to compete with the formidable Asian economies.

Until recently, the Mexican cluster countries experienced a long period of slow to negative growth, currency appreciation, reductions in manufacturing activity, sluggish private consumption, and greater dependence on short capital flows that sustained current account deficits. In Mexico alone, the US market absorbs 80% of exports. The specialization of exports in assembly operations also amplifies the impact, as these plants quickly adjust output and employment to demand contraction. About 50% of Mexican manufacturing is produced in *maquiladoras* (Schwellnus, 2011).

Against this backdrop, the Mexican cluster economies have practiced inflation targeting and flexible exchange rates. Despite the intent of monetary policies to reduce inflation, prices have remained above targets. To a great extent, the stickiness of prices has resulted from product and labor market rigidities, high inflation expectations, and, in some cases, the dollarization of these economies. Initial devaluation of currencies has also added to inflation pressures, as most of these economies also import.

Countercyclical policies have been limited to a low level of reserves and fiscal rules aimed at balancing fiscal budgets. The low level of reserves does not allow flexibility to exercise countercyclical policies to counteract the contraction in the economy. In the case of Mexico, contraction of the manufacturing sector led to a contraction of the service sector, which is closely linked to transport and wholesale trade activities. The effectiveness of further countercyclical policies may be achieved through the reduction of labor and product market rigidities, and building foreign exchanges that will help lower structural fiscal balances in periods of high commodity prices—oil in the case of Mexico.

The economies of the Mexican cluster struggle to diversify export markets. Such efforts can be attained only through productivity improvements and realignment to Asian markets and other emerging economies in sectors where these economies have comparative advantages, such as energy, mining, and services. Another effort is to lessen the dependence of the service economy on manufacturing and exports through liberalization, innovation, and incentives to create a more consumer-oriented economy.

One indication of the different conditions influencing countercyclical policies is the difference in the structural fiscal balances between clusters. The average structural balance in the Brazil cluster is 4% and in the Mexico-cluster 20% (Schwellnus, 2011).

2.5   Polarization of Foreign Direct Investments

Analysis of the sectorial destination of the foreign direct investments (FDI) flows reveals significant differences between clusters. In Table 2.5, the FDI going to the Mexico cluster economies grew at a tepid rate of 2.2% between 2007 and 2012. The decline was 5.52% for the Mexico economy alone, which received $12.6 billion in 2012, a much lower figure than the $31.3 billion FDI in 2007. This decline of interest among foreign investors was not consistent with their enthusiasm with South America as indicated by an FDI average growth of 32% for the Brazil-led cluster between 2007 and 2012. This cluster received a total of $147.6 billion in 2012. Brazil, the largest economy in this group, attracted $66.2 billion—almost twice the amount ($34.5 billion) received in 2007. In contrast, the Mexico-led group attracted $27.4 billion in 2012 (UNCTAD, 2013).

This shift in interest from investors reflects the shift in the realignment in the global economy. A study by Robles (2012) shows that in the early 2000s, investors were as enthusiastic about the Mexico-cluster economies as they are now about the Brazil cluster. In the period 2001–2005, the Mexico cluster had compound annual growth (CAGR) of FDI flows of 12.49%. These differences are found to be significant (Robles, 2012).

The Mexico cluster economies have traditionally attracted investment flows because of Mexico's proximity to the US market and its low labor costs. These comparative advantages and market-access benefits, cemented through trade agreements, have attracted foreign investors interested in setting up assembly and manufacturing facilities and in services that take advantage of tourism and English-fluency competencies. These two comparative advantages, however, have been quite vulnerable to the rise of Asian competition. With the slow-down in the US market, these countries have lost their attractiveness to foreign investors. A reduction of economic activity, especially in manufacturing, lowers foreign direct investment and leaves the Mexican-cluster economies vulnerable to short-term capital flows to sustain current account deficits. This dependence aggravates their recovery given the volatility and greater burden of external financing.

In contrast, the Brazil cluster, which attracted FDI at a mere CAGR of 2.27% between 2001 and 2005, grew at the impressive rate of 9.84% from 2006 to 2010 (Robles, 2012). The Brazil-led cluster is capitalizing on abundant natural

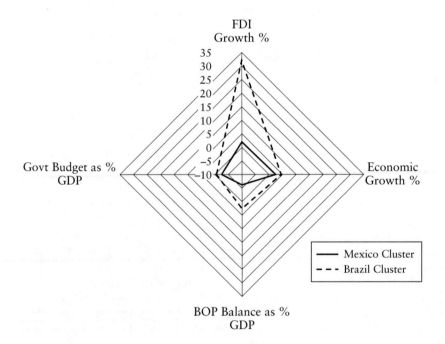

Figure 2.3 Average FDI Growth and Macroeconomic Performance by Clusters, 2007–2012

Source: Authors' elaboration.

resources to compete in world markets. FDI in this cluster is mainly invested in natural-resource extraction activities, whereas a smaller proportion of such investment is in the same activity in the Mexico cluster. In the Brazil-cluster countries, 40.7% of FDI is invested in natural-resource activities, whereas only 10.9% of such investment is in the same activity in the Mexico cluster. These countries tend to export to geographically diversified markets, as transportation costs to many destinations are equally expensive. On the other hand, their distance to world markets is a detriment to tourism flows. A relatively low level of foreign-language fluency discourages investments in the service sector.

Figure 2.3 offers a visual contrast of foreign direct investors' response to the structural and macroeconomic conditions of both clusters. As shown in this figure, there is a significant difference, illustrated by a large geometric diamond representation of the Brazil cluster and a small one for the Mexico cluster.

2.6   Strategy in a Polarized Latin America

A Contingency Approach Based on Different Policy and Market Contexts

Differential economic performance between clusters should be attributed not only to favorable or unfavorable external conditions but also to differences in public policies that steer different paths of economic and social development. These differences are important components of the business context as economic agents and investors respond to these signals in different ways.

As mentioned earlier, the favorable external market conditions and high prices for commodities have been attractive enough to incentivize export production of natural resources. In fact, Talvi and Izquierdo (2011) found that Latin American economies are characterized by a contingency based on their net commodity export position and ratio of investment-to-exports. These external contingencies shape not only the macroeconomic policies but the strategies of firms in their clusters. Thus, we posit that these contingencies lead to differential firm strategies.

In Brazil, the service sector is more diversified, with less dependence on export activities. One indication of the different conditions in which they exercise countercyclical policies is the difference in the structural fiscal balances between clusters. The average structural balance in the Brazil cluster is 4% and in the Mexico cluster 20% (Schwellnus, 2011).

In the Mexico cluster, during the global recession in 2008–2009, exports fell dramatically as a result of extreme dependence on the US and European markets. It is in this context that economies in this cluster have managed their economies with a different set of policies, summarized later. A reduction of economic activity, especially in manufacturing, lowers foreign direct investment and leaves these economies vulnerable to short-term capital flows to sustain current-account deficits. Such dependence delays their recovery given the volatility and greater burden of external financing. Similar to the Brazil-cluster economies, most of the Mexican-cluster economies have practiced inflation targeting and flexible exchange rates. Clearly the context for the Mexican cluster is one of an effort to diversify export markets and to take advantage of their incipient domestic-market growth.

The Brazil-led cluster is characterized by economic growth driven by an emerging mass middle class and global demand for commodity exports to emerging markets. As a result, the Brazil-led cluster has reoriented its productive structure to meet Asian demand. As part of this realignment, Brazil-led cluster firms have reconfigured their specific assets to make them more effective in their new markets. For instance, logistics and distribution assets that were geared toward the advanced markets of the United States and Europe (south-to-north) have to be reconfigured or developed for Asian markets (south-to-south).

It is clear that the new domestic and export market requirements for the Brazil-led cluster require a reconfiguration of strategic focus and skills. For the export market, firms invest in upgrading factory quality and productivity. They also invest in control of natural-resource expansion where nonmarket capabilities are important to secure access and rights to exploit them. Skills and resources for the domestic middle-class market require a greater presence in urban and rural sector as well as the development of basic products. When domestic- and external-market demand coexist, firms struggle with the demand for management talent.

Firms in the Mexico-led cluster face a different situation: recovering domestic markets and realignment of global markets. Multinational and local firms operating in this cluster have to align their strategies for this challenging scenario. The strategies focus on survival in depressed domestic markets and realignment of strategic-resources and skills to address the Asian markets. After a long period of building competencies for the US and European markets, firms in the Mexican clusters invest in skills needed to compete in Asian markets. A deteriorating external environment due to increased violence related to the drug traffic in Central America had dampened foreign direct investment. Firms require greater investment and focus on security and safety.

Strategy for Different Contingencies

As Latin American economies gravitate to the extreme conditions represented by the core countries in each cluster, firms must develop strategies that best fit their particular cluster-market situation. Each situation represents a particular contingency where a given strategy may result in the best strategic fit. Furthermore, contingency theory suggests that there is no one best strategy related to success (Hofer, 1975). Therefore, it is necessary first to identify these concrete extreme conditions or contingencies and second to formulate alternative firm strategies that fit each contingency.

Robles (2013) advanced a contingency approach that combines two exogenous variables: external market conditions and public policies. As proposed by

Izquierdo and Talvi (2011), the exports of Latin American economies are either commodities to emerging economies or manufactured goods to advanced economies. In terms of macroeconomic policies, we have discussed previously that these are either countercyclical in nature or aimed at prudent growth. The combination of these two variables yields a four-cell contingency, which is shown in Table 2.6. In each cell of the contingency, we identify a core of countries that follow well these external drivers. The core of countries in the Brazil cluster is found in the upper right cell in Table 2.6. The core of the Mexican cluster is found in the lower left quadrant. A few outlier countries fill the peripheral space indicated by the countries in the left upper and right bottom cells. These four different options are described in Table 2.6. Next, we discuss the firm strategies that fit each one of these four situations.

In the upper right cell, populated mostly by the Brazil cluster, success may depend on the ability of firms to secure access to natural resources and human resource talent necessary for growth and investment in strategic assets and resources attuned to exploiting opportunities in other emerging markets, particularly in Asia. Many Brazilian firms have already invested in the control of logistic and manufacturing assets in China—some with a great deal of success, others failing to accomplish their goals (Fleury & Fleury, 2010). Arbix and Caseiro (2011) argue that the ability of Brazilian firms to quickly shift their exports to capitalize on the global demand for commodities from other emerging countries has been a key factor of this country's economic growth.

Table 2.6 Strategy in Contextual Business Environments of a Polarized Latin America

	Policies	
	Countercyclical	*Prudent Growth*
Exports of Commodities to Emerging Markets and Advanced Countries and/ or Domestic Markets	Periphery of Brazil cluster Favorable export markets But stagnant domestic economy *Strategic Focus* Manage export market relationships and channels Efficiency	Brazil cluster core *Strategic Focus* Access to Natural Resources Alignment with emerging markets Manage domestic and export market growth
Exports of Manufactured Exports to Advanced Markets and/ Sluggish Domestic Markets	Mexico cluster core *Strategic Focus* Lean management Efficiency and low cost Realignment to exploit emerging market opportunities	Periphery of Mexico cluster Strong domestic economy but stagnant export markets *Strategic Focus* Alignment with emerging market opportunities

Source: Authors' elaboration.

In the lower left cell, the core of the Mexico-led cluster, a firms' future success may depend on its ability to regain competitiveness vis-à-vis Asian competitors in external and domestic markets. Nonmarket strategies aimed at securing public policies to protect the domestic market provide only a temporary solution. Selective market focus and market specialization may prove more sustainable. A more successful strategy for some firms in this cluster is to focus on an expansion to the more vibrant economies of the Brazil-led cluster. Such a strategy may require the development of firm specific advantages that are more attuned to these key markets.

The off-diagonal cells in Table 2.6 represent outlier countries that do not fit well in any of the two clusters. The upper left cell represents the outliers of the Brazil-led cluster. Izquierdo and Talvi (2011) found that Venezuela and Trinidad-Tobago do not follow the Brazil-led cluster macroeconomic policies and are primarily exporting commodities to both advanced and emerging economies. The strategy of firms in these countries is one of managing the diversified export market channels and the high-level macroeconomic uncertainty and erratic government policies in these countries. The authors' analysis also shows that the Dominican Republic and Suriname do not fit well with the rest of the Mexico cluster. The Dominican Republic in particular exports low-value-added clothing and garments, mostly to the US markets. Suriname, on the other hand, is an exporter of mining commodities mostly to the US and European markets. For companies operating in this cell, the focus is on efficiency and low cost and on preventing their buyers from switching suppliers.

Evidence of Business and Economic Polarization in Latin America

Recent empirical research provides further support for economic polarization in Latin America. We review a few of these reports in this section.

Kumar (2013) examines whether different types of capital inflows have a different impact on the total factor productivity in different economic sectors of the Mexico- and Brazil-led clusters. The sector contributions included in the analysis were agriculture, manufacturing, and services. The capital flows were those related to foreign direct investment, workers' remittances, and official development assistance. Using panel data for these variables in 20 Latin American countries, the author estimated an extended Cobb-Douglas production function for 10 countries in each cluster. The explanatory variables were introduced as shift parameters in the production function. Kumar's (2013) analysis showed polarization effects (different parameters in the estimated production function) in two sector contributions (agriculture and services), capital flows, and financial development. As expected, the Brazil-led cluster led in the agricultural-sector contribution. The Mexico service-sector contribution led the region. There were no differences between clusters on manufacturing sector contributions to total factor productivity, nor were there significant differences on the impact of official development assistance flows to total factor productivity. With respect to the impact of capital flows, FDI had greater impact in the

Mexico cluster and remittances in the Brazil cluster. The impact of the level of financial sector development was greater in the Brazil cluster. The structural differences revealed in this study may impact policies to mobilize resources to enhance the productivity of the economies in each cluster. In turn, these policies may signal changes in the business environment that lead the realignment of firms' competencies and strategies.

In another study, Marconatto, Cruz, Regoux, and Dantas (2013) investigated women's repayment of micro loans in Latin America. Using a multilevel perspective, the authors advanced a conceptual model to explain women's loan repayment performance. At the macro level, the authors included the two clusters advanced by Izquierdo and Talvi (2011). At the meso level, the model included the levels of urbanization and gender inequality. At the micro level, the authors looked into the operational efficiency of microfinance organizations in terms of loans per officer. The authors argue that economic polarization in the region has created different market environments for the microfinance industry (MFI). In the Brazil-led cluster, MFIs are larger and more efficient than those in the Mexican-led cluster. In addition, effective social programs in this cluster aimed at reducing poverty have improved the financial position of families, affecting their ability to service their loans. As a result, MFIs in this cluster tend to offer additional services such as financial counseling. The authors also observe that MFIs in the Brazil-led cluster exhibit steadier growth and lower portfolio risks than their counterparts in the Mexico-led cluster. In contrast, Mexican-led cluster MFIs face the challenge of servicing more rural populations and are less successful in attracting female clients. Using data from 407 microfinance organizations in Latin America, the authors analyzed the impact of their multilevel variables on women's loan repayment performance. The study confirmed previous findings elsewhere that female clients have superior repayment performance. The study, however, failed to determine any significant differences in such performance between clusters.

In another study, Wu and Wu (2013) looked at the impact of firm capabilities on performance across Latin America. Performance was measured by the rate of sales growth. Firm capabilities were identified in the area of operations, technology, and marketing. Using data collected by a survey of 17,916 Latin American firms by the World Bank, the author found strong evidence that the relationship between the three firm capabilities is stronger among Brazil-led cluster firms. The results led to the conclusion that the business-environment context is important in fostering such an association. The Brazil-led cluster seems to have fostered greater potential for firms to develop their operational, technological, and marketing expertise. These competencies are strongly associated with performance. In contrast, one can assume that similar efforts by firms in the Mexico-led cluster do not lead to the same result (Wu & Wu, 2013).

Akhter and Barcellos (2013) investigated the impact of Brazil's insertion into the global economy on the local competitive environment and how firms in this country have altered their strategies in response. Using the Structure-Conduct-Performance conceptual framework, they conducted in-depth interviews with officials from five large Brazilian companies. These interviews revealed that all companies found that globalization intensified competition, increased industry consolidation, and introduced greater regulatory uncertainty into their business environments. The main source of competitive threat came from Chinese firms investing in Brazil and competition in global markets. Brazilian firms have responded by improving production efficiency to compete with the Chinese low-cost threat, developing new products, and promoting a greater customer orientation and strategic marketing. The majority of these efforts led to an improvement in the Brazilian firms' performance. The Brazilian multipronged approach revealed in this study supports the conclusion advanced in Wu's paper that firms' competencies are related to performance in the Brazil-led cluster (Akhter & Barcellos, 2013).

Rodriguez, Wise, and Martinez (2013) provide a glimpse as to how Mexican exporters integrate, build, and reconfigure their competencies to address changing global-market environments. Their study focused on the important role of innovation and entrepreneurial orientation on exporters' performance. In a study of 119 Mexican exporters, the authors found that these firms must first build technology and market and social knowledge (relationship) capabilities. A proactive entrepreneurship orientation provides these exporters with market expansion and adaptation capabilities that lead to high export performance. In sum, Mexican exporters must act proactively, assume risk, and explore new avenues for growth. Their key to success is then based on their organizational learning that translates their understanding of market shifts into the ability to innovate and adapt to international demand shifts in which manufacturing flexibility is a key driver of success. Thus, the study by Rodriguez and colleagues supports Wu's findings that firm competencies are closely related to performance. The set of competencies in the Mexican-led cluster is different from those of the Brazil-led cluster (Rodriguez, Wise, & Martinez, 2013).

In sum, the articles reviewed provide further insights into regional polarization in Latin America, beyond the structural economic differences advanced by Izquierdo and Talvi (2011). The macro studies showed that polarization has impacted the agricultural and sector contributions to economic growth as well as FDI and remittance flows to the region and has created different competitive business environments in the Brazil- and Mexico-led clusters. On the other hand, these studies show uniformity in the contribution of manufacturing to growth and superior women micro-loan repayment performance across the region. The micro-level studies showed convincingly that firms must nurture different sets of competencies in the Mexican- and Brazil-led clusters. These pioneering studies reveal the importance of the environmental context on a firm's strategy.

2.7   Summary

This chapter reviewed and documented how Latin America is mirroring the change in global economic order where emerging economies are key drivers of global economic growth. The understanding of how the economies in Latin America are following two diverse paths as a result of this realignment provides the context to understand two different business environments for firms in this region. The main ideas from this review are as follows:

Two clusters of economies represent how the economies of Latin America have realigned their trade and investment orientations with the world. One group of economies is led by Brazil and composed mostly of South American countries strongly aligned with Asian economies. Another group of economies is led by Mexico and is mostly represented by Central American and Caribbean countries more aligned with the advanced economies of the United States and Europe.

The Brazil-led economies have focused on leveraging their rich natural resources to export primary commodities to Asian economies, particularly China. In contrast, the Mexico-led group has followed a strategy of exporting manufactured goods to more advanced economies.

The impact of these two strategies in the region is evident by the differential impact on the economic growth of these two clusters: a higher long-term economic-growth performance for the Brazil-led group and tepid economic growth in the Mexico-led group.

The Brazil-led group has benefited from a period of robust prices and strong demand for commodities. In addition, its sustained economic growth and social policy programs have helped create a strong middle-class domestic market in these economies.

The combined attractiveness of rich natural resources and strong domestic markets has attracted strong flows of foreign investment to the Brazil cluster. The favorable external and internal conditions have helped the economies in this cluster to recover quickly from the 2008 global financial crisis.

In terms of trade, investment, and external funding, China has played a pivotal role in Latin America. China's role has been very focused in terms of the target economies and commodities traded and invested, driving the polarization of the region even further.

China has mostly invested in importing agricultural commodities and minerals and exporting manufactured goods to the region. Similarly, China's direct investment is mostly focused on accessing natural resources. This focused investment is giving China a dominant presence in particular sectors of the target countries where it invests and trades.

The risks and challenges of polarization are also different for the two groups. The Brazil-led cluster is vulnerable to overdependence on commodity specialization and deindustrialization of their economies. The Mexico-led group is vulnerable to the sluggish growth prospects of the advanced economies in the long term and is threatened by global competitiveness superiority of the Asian economies on their manufactured-goods export industries.

In many other aspects, Latin America is not polarized. The region shares a legacy of weak global competitiveness and institutions as well as high levels of corruption. As learned in the analysis of global competitiveness, the region has poor infrastructure, education, and market efficiencies and lacks innovation capability.

The two different economic strategies of realignment in the region have produced two different macroeconomic and business environments. A Brazil-type environment is driven by economic specialization in natural-resource extraction and transformation and a higher economic integration with other emerging economies, coupled with strong domestic markets. Macroeconomic policies for this group tend to be focused on managing inflationary pressures and overvalued currency. A Mexico-type business environment is characterized by a focus on making manufacturing-based economies more globally competitive and more diversified in their market destinations.

These two external environments require strategies that fit these conditions. Firms in the Brazil-led group will need to adjust to the variability of world commodity prices if they are in extractive industries. A strong integration into global supply chains is imperative for these firms. Firms aiming at strong domestic markets in the Brazil-led group may have to develop strategies that will allow them to compete with Asian imports. For the Mexico-led cluster, firms should develop strategies that are more aligned with efforts to improve the global competitiveness of these economies, particularly in manufactured goods. Proximity to the large US market will be an advantage over Asian competition for this group.

References

Akhter, S., & Barcellos, P. (2013). Competitive threats, strategic responses and performance of Brazilian B@B firms. *Management Decision, 52*, 1628–1642.

Arbix, G., & Caseiro, L. (2011). Destination and strategy of Brazilian multinationals. *Economics, Management, and Financial Markets, 6*, 1842–3191.

Cardenas, M., & Levy-Yeyati, E. (2011). *Latin America economic perspectives.* Washington: Brookings.

ECLAC. (2012a). *See* United Nations Commission for Latin America (2012a).

ECLAC. (2012b). *See* United Nations Commission for Latin America (2012b).

ECLAC. (2012c). *See* United Nations Commission for Latin America (2012c).

ECLAC. (2013). *See* United Nations Commission for Latin America (2013).

Eloy, C. M. (2010). The revitalization of Brazil's housing finance system. *Housing Finance International, 24*, 8–21.

Fleury, A., & Fleury, M. T. (2010). *Brazilian multinationals: Competences and internationalization.* Cambridge: Cambridge Press,

Hofer, C. W. (1975). Toward a contingency theory of business strategy. *Academy of Management Journal, 18*, 784–810.

Inter-American Dialogue. (2012). *Industrial policy and innovation in Brazil: Dilma's new approach.* Retrieved from www.thedialogue.org/page.cfm?pageID=32&pubID=2796.

Izquierdo, T., & Talvi, E. (2011). *One region, two speeds? Challenges of the new global economic order for Latin America and the Caribbean.* Washington: Inter-American Development Bank.

Kumar, R. (2013). Exploring polarization and uniformity in sectors and inflows vis-à-vis growth: A study of Brazil-led and Mexico-led clusters in the region. *Management Decision, 52*, 1579–1595.

Marconatto, D., Cruz, L., Regoux, R., & Dantas, D. (2013). Microfinance in Latin America and the Caribbean: The influence of territory on female repayment performance in a polarized region. *Management Decision, 52*, 1596–1612.

McKinsey Global Institute. (2013). *Reverse the curse: Maximizing the potential of resource-driven economies.* Retrieved from www.mckinsey.com/Insights/Energy_Resources_Materials/Reverse_the_curse_Maximizing_the_potential_of_resource_driven_economies?cid=other-eml-alt-mgi-mck-oth-1312.

Robles, F. (2012, June). *Firm strategy in a polarized Latin American region.* Paper presented at the Academy of International Business Conference, Washington, DC.

Robles, F. (2013). Management in a polarized Latin American region: Special issue introduction. *Management Decision, 52*, 1565–1578.

Rodriguez, C., Wise, J., & Martinez, C. (2013). Strategic capabilities in exporting: An examination of the performance of Mexican firms. *Management Decision, 52*, 1643–1663.

Schwellnus, C. (2011). Macroeconomic and structural policies to further stabilize the Mexican economy. *OECD Economics Department Working Papers.* Retrieved from www.oecd-ilibrary.org/en/development/desa/policy/wesp/wesp_archive/2012wesp.pdf.

United Nations Conference on Trade and Development. (2013). *World investment report 2013.* Retrieved from http://unctad.org/en/pages/newsdetails.aspx?OriginalVersionID=555&Sitemap_x0020_Taxonomy=UNCTAD%20Home.

United Nations Economic Commission for Latin America. (2012a). *China and Latin America and the Caribbean building a strategic economic and trade relationship.* Retrieved from www.eclac.cl/cgi-bin/getProd.asp?xml=/publicaciones/xml/6/46566/P46566.xml&xsl=/comercio/tpl-i/p9f.xsl&base=/tpl/top-bottom.xsl.

United Nations Economic Commission for Latin America. (2012b). *Macroeconomic report for Latin America and the Caribbean.* Retrieved from www.eclac.org/publicaciones/xml/6/46986/macroeconomic-report.pdf.

United Nations Economic Commission for Latin America. (2012c). *Statistical yearbook for Latin America and the Caribbean.* Retrieved from www.eclac.org/cgi-bin/getProd.asp?xml=/publicaciones/xml/4/48864/P48864.xml&xsl=/tpl-i/p9f.xsl&base=/tpl-i/top-bottom.xslt.

United Nations Economic Commission for Latin America. (2013). *Foreign direct investment in Latin America and the Caribbean.* Retrieved from www.eclac.org/noticias/paginas/1/33941/2013-371_PPT_FDI-2013.pdf.

World Bank. (2013). *Global economic prospects.* Retrieved from http://web.worldbank.org/WBSITE/EXTERNAL/EXTDEC/EXTDECPROSPECTS/EXTGBLPROSPECTSAPRIL/0,,menuPK:659178~pagePK:64218926~piPK:64218953~theSitePK:659149,00.html.

World Trade Organization. (2012a). *World Trade Report 2012.* Retrieved from www.wto.org/english/res_e/booksp_e/anrep_e/world_trade_report12_e.pdf.

World Trade Organization. (2012b). International Trade Statistics 2012 and 2001: Trade by region. Retrieved from www.wto.org/english/res_e/statis_e/its2012_e/its12_world_trade_dev_e.htm.

World Trade Organization. (2013a). *World trade report 2012.* Retrieved from www.wto.org/english/res_e/booksp_e/anrep_e/ world_trade_ report12_e.pdf.

World Trade Organization. (2013b). *International trade statistics 2012 and 2001: Trade by region.* Retrieved from www.wto.org/english/res_e/statis_e/its2012_e/its12_world_trade_dev_e.htm.

Wu, J., & Wu, Z. (2013). Firm capabilities and the performance in regional polarization. *Management Decision, 52,* 1613–1627.

Yunyun, D. (2010). FDI in BRICS: A sector-level analysis. *International Journal of Business and Management, 5*(1), 46–52.

3 The Competitive Environment of Latin America

Introduction

The competitive landscape in Latin America has evolved significantly over the past 30 years. Formerly protected markets, which were dominated by a few large family groups and state-owned enterprises, have been replaced by open markets. Although large family-controlled domestic conglomerates still play a dominant role, there is now a stronger presence of multinational corporations from developed and emerging economies and a more vibrant small and medium-size business sector. This dynamic competitive environment will require firms doing business in Latin America to leverage the unique opportunities offered by the region's macro environment (e.g., abundant natural resources; a growing consumer market), while managing its many risks (e.g., regulatory bureaucracy). This chapter provides a better understanding of the drivers and barriers to competitiveness for firms operating in the region and of the competitive structure in Latin America.

The chapter is organized into five sections. The first section describes the factors that help explain the degree of competitiveness of firms in Latin America. The second section focuses on one of the main challenges faced by firms doing business in the region, its outdated regulatory environment, which hinders the ability of firms to grow both domestically and globally. The third section focuses attention on natural resources, an important driver of competitiveness for Latin American firms. The fourth section describes the current structure of competition in the region, highlighting the various types of organizational players and their defining characteristics. The final section summarizes our main discussion points regarding competition and competitiveness in the region.

3.1 The Global Competitiveness of Latin America

In this section we explore the various macro and micro environmental factors that help explain the degree of competitiveness of firms in Latin America. Table 3.1 summarizes the competitiveness ratings of selected Latin American

Table 3.1 2012–2013 Global Competitiveness Index of Latin American Countries

Country	Rank/144	Score (1–7)	Top Two Most Problematic Factors
Chile	33	4.65	Restrictive labor regulations; inadequately educated workforce
Panama	40	4.49	Corruption; inefficient government bureaucracy
Brazil	48	4.40	Tax regulations; inadequate supply of infrastructure
Mexico	53	4.36	Corruption; crime and theft
Costa Rica	57	4.34	Inefficient government bureaucracy; inadequate supply of infrastructure
Peru	61	4.28	Inefficient government bureaucracy; corruption
Colombia	69	4.18	Corruption; inefficient government bureaucracy
Uruguay	74	4.13	Restrictive labor regulations; inefficient government bureaucracy
Guatemala	83	4.01	Crime and theft; corruption
Ecuador	86	3.94	Corruption; restrictive labor regulations
Honduras	90	3.88	Crime and theft; corruption
Argentina	94	3.87	Inflation; policy instability
El Salvador	101	3.80	Crime and theft; access to financing
Bolivia	104	3.78	Access to financing; restrictive labor regulations
Nicaragua	108	3.73	Inefficient government bureaucracy; inadequate supply of infrastructure
Paraguay	116	3.67	Corruption; inadequately educated workforce
Venezuela	126	3.46	Foreign currency regulations; restrictive labor regulations

Source: Schwab & Sala-i-Martin (2013).

countries as determined by the Global Competitiveness Index (Schwab & Sala-i-Martin, 2013).

As a whole, the region has experienced sound macroeconomic policies and steady economic growth for several years; this has caused several countries in the region to improve their competitiveness rankings. The 2012–2013 Index reveals that the five most competitive countries in the region are Chile, Panama, Brazil, Mexico, and Costa Rica, in that order. The least competitive are Venezuela, Paraguay, Nicaragua, Bolivia, and El Salvador. The main issues hindering competitiveness are corruption, an inefficient government bureaucracy, an inadequately educated workforce, insufficient investment in R&D, a restrictive labor market, and crime. In addition to weak institutions, inadequate infrastructure is also an important challenge. In 2012, leaders from the region agreed on several mandates to help boost competitiveness over the next few years. Three of these mandates emphasize improvements to roads and transportation, electrical networks, and information technology infrastructure. Connecting the region internally and with the rest of the world will boost competitiveness by improving efficiencies in the allocation of resources and the flow of knowledge and innovation, and will reduce operational costs for companies in the region (Schwab & Sala-i-Martin, 2013).

The competitiveness of Latin American firms is influenced by macroeconomic, institutional, and market related factors. Chapters 1 and 2 provided an extensive discussion of macroeconomic factors. We focus here on five other factors: financial markets, labor markets, infrastructure, innovative capacity, and the regulatory system.

Financial Markets

A well-functioning financial market should capture the savings and investments of individuals and organizations and reallocate them to serve two economic purposes: to provide money to consumers willing to spend and to provide working capital to entrepreneurs and private-sector businesses seeking growth and expansion. "Resilient, complex, and deep (in the sense of reaching across all income levels, including the working poor) banking systems are synonymous with advanced economies, higher growth, and income equality" (Smith, Juhn, & Humphrey, 2008, p. 79). The banking system in Latin America has been notoriously exclusionary, favoring credit to large companies and affluent individuals and excluding micro and small businesses and the working poor (Smith, Juhn, & Humphrey, 2008). According to a 2010 CAF study, only 21% of the adult population use the financial system for savings, and only 12% use it for credit. Furthermore, lack of access to financing is one of the top three obstacles to growth cited by Latin American micro- and small businesses (Chironga, Dahl, Goland, Pinshow, & Sonnekus, 2012). Until recently, it also excluded middle-class consumers and medium-size businesses; however, increased access to credit cards and the entrance of foreign-owned banks to the region have improved their access to credit. Access to credit allows the middle class to start businesses and buy property. Home equity can then be leveraged to invest in education and technology, thus enhancing individual and organizational productivity (Smith, Juhn, & Humphrey, 2008). Finally, transparency and sound regulations are essential for inspiring trust in the financial market of a country (Schwab & Sala-i-Martin, 2013); both these conditions have been missing in Latin American countries. The region's sustained economic growth, adoption of technology, and more stable governments are all likely to contribute to the expansion of financial services to all sectors in the region.

Labor Markets

Two key characteristics of labor markets that impact firms' competitiveness are the size of the labor pool and the productivity of the labor pool. Productivity, in turn, is impacted by the levels of skill of the labor force and the quality of life of workers. The Global Competitiveness Index captures this factor through four of its pillars: health and primary education; higher education and training; labor market efficiency; and innovation. For instance, an unhealthy workforce will result in higher absenteeism and lower performance; access to primary education ensures that workers can perform more complicated tasks and learn and adapt to more modern production systems (Schwab & Sala-i-Martin, 2013).

There is no question that Latin America as a whole has an abundance of low-skilled labor. A closer look renders this picture less encouraging for the future. First, the size of the labor pool is matching levels of job creation, with unemployment rates registering near-record lows in 2012 and real wages increasing. Second, the jobs of the future will require middle and higher levels of skill that the regional labor force is currently unable to provide (International Monetary Fund, 2013). A World Bank Enterprises Survey showed that for the period 2002–2010, the percentage of Latin American firms that indicated skills gaps was the most important obstacle to the operation and growth of their firms ranged from 5% in Argentina, Paraguay, and Peru to 12% in Brazil and 25% in Venezuela. The low levels of skill in the region are the result of poorly funded education systems and the lack of access to education among low-income citizens. Furthermore, the meager investment in innovation and R&D by both public and private institutions compounds Latin American firms' inability to develop original innovations. Latin American governments have been working toward improving access and quality of education, including establishing educational standards and transferring more control and resources for education to the local government levels. The region has seen a steady increase in overall literacy rates and years of primary and secondary schooling, but the literacy rate still lags behind those for Asia and Eastern Europe. In terms of tertiary education, Latin America has higher rates of university enrollment than Asia, but these rates are lower than those of the United States and Western Europe. Some of the main challenges for Latin American countries in the future will be improving the quality of education, especially in the areas of math and science, and achieving equity in access to education, especially among low-income and marginalized populations (Puryear & Ortega Goodspeed, 2008).

Labor markets in the region have long been considered rigid and costly. This rigidity emanates from the laws that control employer/employee relations, which usually fall into one of three categories: laws that regulate the hiring and dismissal of employees; government-mandated employer contributions to social security, pensions, and health insurance; and collective bargaining. This complicated set of labor regulations makes it difficult for firms to allocate and reallocate human capital in a manner that is most conducive to achieving productivity and competitiveness (Sabatini, 2008; Schwab & Sala-i-Martin,

2013). In February 2013, Mexico's Grupo Elektra abandoned its investments in Argentina, citing the country's unfavorable business conditions created, among other causes, by labor regulations and unionization practices. For instance, a firm's ability to dismiss workers can be costly and litigious because of the need to provide (or pay for) advance notice before dismissal (from two weeks to three months depending on years of employment) and to provide seniority bonuses and severance payments based on wages and years of employment. The constraints imposed on firms regarding hiring and firing have led to a large number of workers employed in the informal sector—especially women and youth—where they have few legal and social protections. Some countries undertook reforms to labor regulations in the 1990s and early 2000s, primarily relating to the formal hiring of temporary workers, but the impact of these reforms was not significant enough to reduce the inflexibility of Latin American labor markets or the degree of informal employment (Universia Knowledge@Wharton, 2009; Sabatini, 2008).

The shortage of highly skilled workers is a source of competitive disadvantage for Latin American firms. This is especially challenging for firms in high-tech manufacturing and the service sector. Moreover, low wages will not be enough to compete in global markets, as cost efficiencies can be found in many locations around the world. Latin American firms' ability to recruit and retain talented workers will make the difference in developing sustainable competitive advantages in a global economy that is increasingly knowledge and technology intensive. A strong and efficient labor market will be critical if Latin America is to attract the kind of talented and innovative creative workers now in short supply.

Infrastructure

The existence of a well-developed infrastructure is critical to a country's competitiveness as it influences where economic activity is located, what type of economic activity can flourish in a region, and access to domestic and international markets. An extensive and efficient infrastructure also impacts an organization's costs associated with physical distance between markets and the ability of firms to reach rural and low-income markets, thus increasing the potential size of a market (Schwab & Sala-i-Martin, 2013). Critical to a well-developed infrastructure are high-quality and reliable systems of transportation (e.g., roads, ports), utilities (electricity and water), and telecommunications.

In general, Latin America lags behind other regions of the world in terms of infrastructure. Using a 1–7 scale, the Competitiveness Index gives the region scores of 3.30 in transport infrastructure, 4.24 in electricity supply, and 2.72 in information and communication technology (ICT) use; for comparison, the scores are 4.96, 6.13, and 5.29, respectively, for OECD countries. Water and power shortages are common across the region, with power outages and lack of access to water especially problematic in overpopulated urban centers and in low-income, rural areas. For instance, in 2011 an estimated 6% of the

Table 3.2 Infrastructure Indicators in Selected Latin American Countries

Country	Quality of Port Infrastructure 2012	Connectivity Index of Maritime Transport 2012	Paved roads/ Total roads %	Penetration of Mobile Broadband % 2013	Investment in Infrastructure as % of GDP 2011
Argentina	3.6	34.2	30.0	32	3.2
Bolivia	3.3	n/c	8.5	8	4.4
Brazil	2.6	38.5	13.5	42	2.8
Chile	5.2	33.0	23.3	35	1.7
Colombia	3.2	37.2	14.4	11	3.0
Costa Rica	2.4	14.1	26.0	28	n/a
Dominican Republic	4.7	23.7	49.4	8	n/a
Ecuador	3.9	23.1	14.8	12	5.7
El Salvador	3.9	8.8	46.9	7	n/a
Guatemala	4.0	20.1	59.1	n/a	2.2
Honduras	4.6	10.0	20.4	n/a	n/a
Mexico	4.3	38.8	36.4	24	1.7
Nicaragua	3.2	8.2	12.9	10	n/a
Panama	6.4	42.4	42.0	7	n/a
Paraguay	3.6	n/c	15.2	6	1.6
Peru	3.5	32.8	13.9	15	4.0
Uruguay	4.9	32.0	10.0	31	1.4
Venezuela	2.5	18.9	33.6	28	n/a

Notes: Quality of Port Infrastructure: Perception of executives on the quality of port facilities (1–7 scale, where 7 = well developed).Connectivity Index of Maritime Transport: Degree to which country is connected to global networks of maritime transport (Index 1–100, where 100 = well connected).

Source: CAF-Banco de Desarrollo de America Latina (2013).

region's population (30 million people) had no access to electricity; 20 million of these were low-income individuals (CAF Development Bank of Latin America, 2013). Outdated road and railway systems also make moving products costly and time consuming. Moreover, the region lags behind in connectivity, with Internet bandwidth capacity at around 20% of that of OECD countries (Schwab & Sala-i-Martin, 2013).

Investments in infrastructure development have been insufficient. In 2005, Latin American investment in infrastructure was about 2% of regional GDP (Fay and Morrison, 2005). Currently, infrastructure investments remain close to 3% of regional GDP, one-third the level of investment in China and half that in India. Between 2008 and 2011, Latin America invested US$440 billion: 48% went to transportation, 25% to energy, 20% to telecommunications, and 7% to water infrastructure projects (CAF Development Bank, 2013).

While infrastructure development has lagged behind, most countries in the region have been trying to improve their infrastructure. In terms of GDP percentages, Ecuador led infrastructure investment (6%), followed by Bolivia and Peru (4%), and Argentina, Brazil, and Colombia (3%). Infrastructure development is occurring through government-financed projects or by inviting the private sector through concessions and public-private partnerships (PPPs). Brazil and Chile, especially, have pursued PPPs for several years now, and the FIFA World Cup in 2014 and the Olympic Games in 2016 have also spurred a new wave of infrastructure development in Brazil (CAF Development Bank, 2013; Cardona, 2012). Private-sector investment seems to dominate the telecommunication sector, while public investment controls water and electricity development. Table 3.3 lists some examples of recent and current infrastructure projects. The projects in the list indicate that the priority for countries across the region is transportation-related infrastructure (land and maritime). The impact of these infrastructure improvements can be significant, as Panama's experience shows. In 2012, Panama was one of the top performers in terms of GDP growth, and the country increased its global competitiveness index ranking by nine positions (40) due to the strength of its transportation infrastructure and ports. In 2013, Panama City overtook Buenos Aires and Rio de Janeiro as the fifth best city in which to do business in Latin America. Its climb in this ranking is, in part, a result of the current expansion of the Panama Canal, which is expected to be completed in 2015. (*América Economía*, 2013f).

Table 3.3 Examples of Recent and Current Infrastructure Development Projects in Latin America

Country	Project
Argentina	Cargo Train Belgrano; Chihuido (hydroelectric power)
Brazil	High-speed train connecting Rio de Janeiro and Sao Paulo; Brasilia Cargo Airport; expansion of Guarulhos and Viracopos airports; plus stadiums, highways, underground and bus transportation systems
Colombia	Bicentennial Pipeline; Autopista de la Montaña; Bogota Metro
Ecuador	Refineria del Pacifico (refinery project); Coca Codo Sinclair hydroelectric project; Quito Metro
Guatemala	Patuca hydroelectric project; land bridge (roads, railroads, pipes)
Honduras	Hydroelectric project; interoceanic railroad
Mexico	Ethylene XXI project; trans-isthmus route (ports and railroad)
Nicaragua	Interoceanic channel (navigable channel, oil pipe, ports, and railroad)
Panama	Canal expansion; Panama metro
Peru	Metro Lima Callao; Via Longitudinal de la Sierra Project (highway); South Andean gas pipe

Source: Cardona (2012).

Innovative Capacity

"Companies achieve competitive advantage through acts of innovation" (Porter, 1990, p. 75), and thus a country's innovative capacity will either support or hinder its firms' ability to become world competitors. Innovation will become an important driver of competitiveness for Latin America in the future. The Global Competitiveness Index (GCI) framework identifies most Latin American countries' competitiveness as being efficiency driven (e.g., labor, market, financial markets); however, a few countries are transitioning to a stage of innovation-driven competitiveness. The innovation and sophistication subindex of the GCI identifies two key elements: (1) *innovation,* which is captured through measurements of private-sector spending in research and development (R&D), protection of intellectual property rights, and high-quality educational systems; and (2) *business sophistication,* which is based on the quality of business network connections in a country and the quality of individual firms' operations and strategies.

In 2012, 5 countries from the region ranked in the top 50 in the innovation and sophistication subindex: Costa Rica (35), Brazil (39), Chile (45), Panama (48), and Mexico (49). Brazil's highly sophisticated business community, bolstered by a large internal market, is breeding global industry leaders in specific subsectors and/or technologies (e.g., Embraer in aircraft manufacturing and Petrobras in deep-sea oil exploration). Costa Rica's innovation potential is grounded on its high-quality education system and investments in R&D. Mexico has sophisticated businesses, but they will need to invest more on R&D. Good rankings on these factors of innovation imply that firms in these five countries are much more sophisticated and innovative than their home countries' overall level of competitiveness would suggest, and their practices and strategies will likely have positive spillover effects on their countries' economies and other business sectors. Undeniably, the majority of Latin American countries has a long way to go in achieving the innovative capacity gains needed to sustain growth in the future. This will be an evolutionary and inevitable transition, though; as countries across the region correct and consolidate factors hindering efficiency-driven competitiveness, they will increasingly be forced to confront their weak educational systems and national research systems (Schwab & Sala-i-Martin, 2013).

The impact of the regulatory system on Latin American competitiveness is a significant source of competitive disadvantage for Latin American firms. We dedicate the next section to a more detailed discussion of the effects of the regulatory system on the region's competitiveness.

3.2   The Regulatory Environment and Ease of Doing Business

One of the main challenges Latin American firms face is their regulatory bureaucracies. Most Latin American countries are characterized by complex, outdated, and inefficient legal systems. One example is the weak level of protection of property rights in the region. In this type of environment, "an individual or a business and their assets are invisible to the law and so do not exist in a legal sense. Because they and their property have no rights under the law, they cannot be subject to binding legal contracts. This decreases the value of assets and limits the efficiency of markets" (Schaefer & Schaefer, 2008, p. 199). To better understand how the regulatory system hinders firms' competitiveness we focus here on the Ease of Doing Business indicators for selected countries in the region.

Although the rankings of some Latin American countries have improved over the past few years, much remains to be done to reduce the regulatory obstacles present in the region. The 2014 Ease of Doing Business (EDB) report analyzes the 2013 rankings for the region and the progress made over the past 12 months in all the various indicators that make up the EDB index (World Bank/International Finance Corporation, 2013).

In terms of starting a business, it takes more procedures, time, and money to start a business in Latin America than in other regions of the world (regional averages of 10 procedures, 45 days, and 35% of per capita income, respectively). Reforms implemented in 2012 to improve the process of starting a business in the region include establishing one-stop shops (Guatemala, Paraguay, and Mexico); simplifying procedures (Honduras, Brazil, and Peru); and establishing online platforms for business registration (Colombia, Panama, Mexico, and Ecuador). A second area of concern is protecting investors, with Latin America ranking lower than any other region in the world (regional average of 114, compared to 80 for South Asia, for example). Reforms in this area have focused on increasing access to information by shareholders and mandating greater disclosure requirements in annual reports. The third concern for firms doing business in Latin America regards the enforcement of contracts. In Latin America, it takes on average 778 days and 39 procedures to pursue a claim, and the cost can represent 30% of the claim.

Other areas of regulatory concern include:

Paying Taxes. The payment of taxes in the region is a problem, resulting from the number of payments required in a year; the number of hours that it takes to file and pay taxes (491); and the total tax rate as a percentage of profits (51%). The latter two are the highest in the world. Most of the significant reforms in this area made it easier for companies to file and pay taxes electronically.

Trading across Borders. Similar to the obstacles for paying taxes, time and cost are the primary challenges with regard to importing and exporting for firms doing business in the region.

Dealing with Construction Permits. Latin America's regional averages are only slightly worse than the European Union's in terms of number of procedures and days that it takes to obtain permits. Countries across the region have engaged in administrative reforms primarily aimed at streamlining and simplifying the process of obtaining permits.

Getting Electricity. The main challenge in this area is the cost (as a % of per capita income) of getting electricity. In terms of number of days and procedures, Latin America is comparable to other regions of the world.

Table 3.4 Ease of Doing Business Ranking for Selected Latin American Countries

Country	EDB Rank/ 189	EDB Rank/ LatAm	Top Two Most Problematic Regulatory Concerns
Peru	42	2	Construction permits; resolving insolvency
Colombia	43	3	Enforcing contracts; getting electricity
Mexico	53	4	Getting electricity; registering property
Guatemala	79	10	Protecting investors; trading across borders
Uruguay	88	13	Construction permits; registering property
Costa Rica	102	17	Protecting investors; enforcing contracts
Paraguay	109	20	Trading across borders; resolving insolvency
Brazil	116	22	Trading across borders; paying taxes
El Salvador	118	24	Getting electricity; paying taxes
Nicaragua	124	25	Construction permits; paying taxes
Argentina	126	26	Construction permits; trading across borders
Honduras	127	27	Enforcing contracts; starting a business
Ecuador	135	28	Getting electricity; starting a business
Bolivia	162	30	Paying taxes; starting a business
Venezuela	181	32	Paying taxes; trading across borders

Source: World Bank/International Finance Corporation (2013).

3.3   Natural Resource Competitiveness

One of the main drivers of competitiveness of Latin American countries is the abundance of natural resources in the region. As we discussed in the first two chapters of this book, a significant portion of Latin America's economic growth over the past few years has been the result of insatiable demand (and corresponding high prices) for local commodities, primarily by China but also by other Asian countries (Schwab & Sala-i-Martin, 2013). Top commodities in the region include oil and gas, minerals (e.g., copper, iron ore, silver, gold), and agricultural products (e.g., soy, sugar, cotton, lumber, coffee, meat). Over the past decade, Latin America has enjoyed the benefits of a commodity boom; even with the economic slowdown of 2008, prices and demand recovered quickly, especially for hydrocarbons and minerals. In 2008, the average contribution from natural resources to total government revenues was about 30%, with countries such as Ecuador and Venezuela registering rates as high as 45% and 50%, respectively. In the period 2000–2009, commodity exports represented 51% of total exports for the region (Sinnott, Nash, & de la Torre, 2010). The panorama for the future is changing, however, and a contraction of the region's natural-resource-based exports and a decline in commodity prices are expected. How governments and companies in the region manage these vulnerabilities will be key to whether Latin America cannot only protect its competitiveness gains of the past decade but improve upon them.

In line with our discussions on regional polarization, this commodity boom has not benefited everyone equally. Commodity-intensive economies, such as those of Brazil, Peru, Chile, and Argentina, have seen their economies strengthened from higher levels of commodity exports, while non-commodity-based sectors within these countries and less commodity-intensive countries have experienced overall losses or lower levels of growth (Haar & Price, 2008). Dependence on natural resources is also a dangerous gamble for the region. Apart from environmental degradation, commodity prices are typically volatile, improvements to productivity require hefty investments, and exploitation of natural resources can lead to internal social conflicts (Sinnot, Nash, & de la Torre, 2010).

Nowhere is the dependence on natural resources more vivid than in Peru. Peru has primarily been a mining economy dating back to colonial times, and its ability to exploit and export minerals and metals is vital to the country's overall competitiveness. In 2011, Peru's mining exports represented 59% of total exports and about 5% of its GDP. Peru was the second largest copper producer in the world after Chile. The country is also the third largest producer of silver, tin, and zinc. Mining represents about 15% of all taxes collected, 30% of all corporate income taxes paid, and 21% of all private investment. Investment in the mining sector is about 95% foreign, with China representing about 25% of the total investment and exports. A similar reliance on natural resources emerges in Chile, where 13% of its 2011 GDP was contributed by mining, and a large percentage of exports were from copper and forestry-related products (Calfucura, Martinez Ortiz, Sanborn, & Dammert, 2013).

Latin American countries are attempting to prevent the negative consequences of an overreliance on natural-resource production and exports by diversifying their economies. Resource owners in Latin America are also more competitive than in the past when it comes to relinquishing their rights to resources to the new influx of foreign investors. The higher demand and competition for access to resources have improved their options, and they are adopting local models of development and demanding not only technology transfers but more favorable overall investment conditions (Boston Consulting Group, 2008).

In summary, Latin American firms' macro source of competitive advantage is their access to abundant factors of production, specifically natural resources and unskilled labor. Our discussion points to some key areas where Latin

American firms are at a competitive disadvantage, namely access to efficient and reliable inputs and markets that are hindered by the lack of a highly skilled, productive workforce, well-established financial markets, an extensive and reliable infrastructure, and a streamlined and well-functioning regulatory system.

These macro sources of competitiveness have translated into firm-level competitive advantages for companies in the region. The competitiveness of firms in the region, especially domestic firms, is grounded on their intimate knowledge of the domestic consumer markets' needs and wants, business systems, and regulatory frameworks; on their organizational flexibility to adapt to a constantly changing external environment; and on their long-term orientation and commitment to national and regional markets. In the next section, we describe the various organizational players in the region and describe their main organizational strengths and weaknesses.

3.4   The Structure of Competition in Latin America

The competitiveness of a country's firms is intimately linked to the country's competitive environment. As Porter (1990, p. 73) states, "A nation's competitiveness depends on the capacity of its industry to innovate and upgrade. Companies gain advantage against the world's best competitors because of pressure and challenge. They benefit from having strong domestic rivals, aggressive home-based suppliers, and demanding local customers." Competition is "good" because it pressures companies into constant improvement, as no competitive advantage is enduring. A national business environment characterized by dynamic and open competition from diverse organizations is then a source of sustainable competitive advantage for firms in a country. Latin America has been notorious for the lack of competition and a tradition of tolerating monopolies. Yet, starting with the liberalization of the 1990s, attitudes toward competition have slowly changed, and Latin Americans are now more willing to embrace a vibrant competitive environment as beneficial for countries, companies, and consumers alike.

In this section, we explore the five types of organizations that shape the Latin American competitive landscape: large domestic conglomerates, multinational companies, state-owned enterprises, small and medium-size businesses, and firms in the informal sector. We describe the role each of these type of organizations plays in the region's business environment, its main organizational characteristics, strengths, and weaknesses, and its typical strategic approaches. In general, we find that the majority of companies in the region are locally owned (87%); are small to medium size (90% are SMEs, and the average firm has 47 employees); operate in the services sector (70%); are older (about 75% have been in business for more than 10 years, and the average firm age is 20 years); are held by private investors (46% have closed shareholding) and/or family owned (43%); are highly dependent on inputs from outside the region (on average, 71% import some inputs while 13% export their goods); and operate in an environment where formal and informal businesses compete side by side (Francis, Rodriguez Mesa, & Yang, 2013).

Large Domestic Conglomerates

Large domestic conglomerates (or *grandes grupos economicos* in Spanish) play a leading role in Latin America. These large domestic conglomerates are typically family owned or family controlled. Many of these conglomerates started during the 1950s and 1960s, during the period of import substitution in the region, with some dating back to the beginning of the 20th century. According to Robles, Simon, & Haar (2003), the origin of many family conglomerates centered on three strategic pillars: expansion based on the development of natural resources; growth based on diversification of an industrial base; and the acquisition of financial, construction, and service firms. The liberalization and privatization reforms of the 1990s gave rise to a second wave of formation of large domestic conglomerates that leveraged the opportunities created by the disappearance of older domestic groups, the opening of economic sectors, the influx of capital, and the overall growth of consumer markets.

The growth and stability of large conglomerates over several decades points to specific strategic capabilities of these firms. First, their horizontal and vertical diversification gives them a certain level of protection against market instability. Their broad scope and scale allow them to overcome the limitation of weak domestic capital markets by (a) generating internal revenues and profits that can be reallocated throughout the conglomerate; b) incorporating a financial services division that can provide easier access to funding; or (c) giving them the competitive standing that allows them access to global capital markets. Second, the domestic conglomerates have a deep understanding of the local markets and of nonmarket conditions, which results in organizational agility, allowing them to identify and respond quickly to new opportunities and threats. Moreover, their superior distribution networks give them wide and extensive access to markets.

A significant number of large domestic conglomerates are family owned or controlled. This ownership arrangement gives domestic conglomerates more control over resource allocation, flexibility, and the ability to make strategic decisions for the long term without having to respond to the short-term performance expectations of publicly traded companies. In general, family owners have grown up knowing the business "upside down and inside out." The conflicts of interest one usually sees between managers and owners is also minimized, as the success of the firm is tied to the reputation of the family name (Becker, 2011, pp. 122–23). Although some patriarchs have been less careful about implementing succession plans, in general, family-owned businesses are typically handed over to the next generation smoothly. This younger generation of leaders has been trained abroad and is more technologically savvy and globally minded. Thus, family groups, which tended to be more reactive and more vulnerable to changes in their external environment, are now more able to cope and to adapt to a dynamic competitive global environment. Although access to capital and technology and closed management structures can be considered strategic weaknesses, large family conglomerates will continue to dominate the competitive landscape in Latin America.

Large domestic firms enjoy additional competitive advantages. Their importance to the local economy in terms of job creation and income generation and their strong connections to the local governments yield some degree of protection from political risk and some degree of support in the face of foreign competition (although less so than was the case in the past).

The competitive advantages of large conglomerates in global markets include low-cost production, ties to existing clients, connections to cultural and country diasporas, and a diversified product portfolio. The main strategic choices for large domestic companies are:

a.   Defensive or preemptive strategies, which might include mergers and acquisitions, consolidation, and divestment of low-performing divisions in order to strengthen their competitive position.
b.   Offensive strategies, which include expanding the scope or scale of the firm through diversification, vertical or horizontal integration, and internationalization.

Over the past 20 years, many large domestic conglomerates, which were primarily national or regional champions, have looked to the rest of the world for opportunities of growth and expansion. Latin American firms that have successfully positioned themselves in global markets are known as multilatinas. An examination of the current investment trends in the region (see chapters 1 and 2) seems to point to high levels of acquisition and expansion by national champions and multilatinas, and we anticipate these firms will consolidate their role as the dominant players in the region over the coming decade. (Chapter 9 provides an in-depth discussion of strategies pursued by multilatinas and national champions.)

Table 3.5 lists some of the major domestic conglomerates in Latin America. We also describe three examples of domestic conglomerates from the region to illustrate their evolution, scope, and competitive power.

Grupo Carso (Mexico)

Grupo Carso or Grupo Sanborns SAB is a global conglomerate company with more than 78,000 employees owned by the Mexican Carlos Slim Helu. The group was founded in 1990 after the merger of Corporación Industrial Carso and Grupo Inbursa. In 2007, the conglomerate was worth more than US$6 billion and held the largest telecommunications company in Latin America (Carso Global Telecom). In 2012, the company generated revenues of more than US$5 billion and net income of US$328 million.

Table 3.5 Examples of the Largest Domestic Conglomerates in Latin America (Selected Countries)

Company	Sector
Argentina	
Techint	Metallurgy, petroleum
Grupo Arcor	Food, agro-industrial
Grupo Clarin	Media, telecommunications
Brazil	
Vale	Mining, metallurgy, energy
Odebrecht	Construction, chemicals, petrochemicals, other
CBD-Grupo Pão de Açúcar	Retailing
Gerdau	Metallurgy, financial services
Grupo Votorantim	Cellulose, paper, metallurgy, agro-industrial
Grupo Globo	Communications
Camargo Correa	Construction, cement, metallurgy
Grupo Safra	Financial services
Chile	
Empresas Copec	Energy, forestry, paper
Cencosud	Retailing
Angelini	Gas, petroleum products, energy, cellulose
Luksic/Quiñenco	Mining, forestry, beverages, telecom, financial services
Grupo Solari	Retailing, financial services
Grupo Said	Manufacturing, beverages
Grupo Matte	Paper, energy, financial services, telecommunications
Colombia	
Grupo Empresarial Antioqueño	Financial services, cement, food
Central America	
Corporacion Multi-Inversiones (Grupo Gutierrez) — Guatemala	Energy, agro-industrial, restaurants, construction, financial services
J Group — Honduras	Manufacturing, retailing
Grupo Lovable — Honduras	Manufacturing, retailing
Mexico	
Femsa	Beverages
Grupo Industrial Alfa	Petrochemicals, aluminum, electronics, telecom
Grupo Bimbo	Food
Grupo Bal	Financial services, retailing, agro-industrial, health
Grupo Mexico	Mining
Grupo Modelo	Beverages
Grupo Salinas	Financial services, retailing, telecommunications
Grupo Carso	Construction, retailing, telecommunications
Grupo Televisa	Media

(*Continued*)

Table 3.5 (Continued)

Company	Sector
Peru	
Grupo Romero	Financial services, agro-industrial, retailing
Graña y Montero	Construction, real estate
Grupo Breca	Financial services, mining, chemicals, agroindustry, health
Grupo Benavides	Mining
Venezuela	
Grupo Cisneros	Media, entertainment
Empresas Polar	Beverages, food

Note: For a complete list of domestic conglomerates/multilatinas and selected financial performance indicators, please see chapter 9.

Source: Authors' elaboration based on data from *América Economía* (2013e) and corporate websites.

Grupo Carso's divisions include subsidiaries in the construction, retail, industrial materials, and telecommunications industries. The company's products and services include shopping centers; telephone, cellular, and mobile services; steel tubes; oil-platform construction; residential, industrial, and corporate construction; and dam, aqueduct, and highway construction. The retailing side of the group includes the Sanborns department store chain, an 85% stake in Sears Roebuck de Mexico, and the troubled US computer retailer CompUSA. In 1996, Carso Global Telecom (which includes Telmex, Telcel, and America Movil) separated itself from Grupo Carso. The group also owns professional football (soccer) teams in Mexico (Club León, CF Pachuca, and Estudiantes Tecos), and in Spain (34% of Real Oviedo).

This large conglomerate is a true family business: patriarch Carlos Slim Helu has passed on the reins to his sons Carlos Slim Domit (Chairman of Telmex, Grupo Carso, and Grupo Sanborn; Co-chairman of America Movil); Patrick Slim Domit (Vice Chairman of Group Carso, Co-chairman of America Movil, CEO of Grupo Sanborn, and Chairman of Grupo Televisa), and Marco Antonio Slim Domit (Chairman and CEO of Grupo Financiero Inbursa, the financial side of group) (Grupo Carso, 2013).

Cisneros Group (Venezuela)

The Cisneros Group is a privately held global media and entertainment leader with more than 3,000 employees. The group produces and distributes some of the world's most popular Spanish-language programming, reaching more than a half-million viewers in more than 100 countries on five continents in more than 20 languages (Cisneros Group, 2013).

The group was founded in 1929, and by 1940 the firm had established itself as a solid Venezuelan brand representing international brands such as Pepsi Cola and Studebaker automobiles. In the 1960s, the group entered media and enter-tainment through the acquisition of a television channel that later became Ven-ezuela's leading TV network (Venevision). In the 1960s and 1970s the company continued to diversify across a range of consumer products, and it expanded its television business internationally. Two main additions to the group during this period include radio broadcasting and the rights to the Miss Venezuela beauty pageant. The 1980s saw Cisneros develop into a true Latin American multina-tional through multiple partnerships and acquisitions that introduced leading global brands and modern retail formats to Spanish-speaking households. The formation of Venevision International allowed the group to expand its presence to global markets through distribution, marketing, and production of popular media and entertainment content. It is today the world's largest independent producer of Spanish language television content.

Since the 1990s, Cisneros has continued its growth in Latin America while rapidly expansion abroad, especially into the US Hispanic market and into China. It has also continued to increase the scope of its media business (music, DVDs, pay TV). Over the past decade, the group has also entered the digital arena in full force with the acquisition or creation of business properties in the areas of advertising, publishing, distribution, gaming, and e-commerce (e.g., Venevision.com; it is also the exclusive representative of Yahoo! in Peru and Venezuela). Another area of horizontal expansion has been into sustainable tourism development (e.g., Tropicalia in the Dominican Republic).

As in the case of Grupo Carso, Cisneros is managed by the family of the founder, Diego Cisneros. His son Gustavo Cisneros is the current chairman of the group, and his granddaughter Adriana Cisneros (Gustavo's daughter) is the CEO and Vice Chairman. Over its more than 80 years of existence, the group's success has been driven by an emphasis on continuous innovation and value creation; growth through investments and partnerships (e.g., it brought DirectTV to the region through a partnership with Hughes Electronics Cor-poration); and a focus on the consumers and communities it serves through a strategic commitment to social leadership (primarily supporting the arts, edu-cation, and the sustainable development of local communities).

Luksic Group (Chile)

Founded in 1957, the Luksic Group is one of Chile's largest and most diversi-fied conglomerates, with more than 16,000 employees, consolidated assets of US$44 billion, total investments of US$4.5 billion, and sales exceeding US$4 billion (2013). The group, with operations focused on the South American region, has two main divisions: Antofagasta PLC (mining) and Quiñenco, S.A., which encompasses the financial, industrial, and services operations of the group. Quiñenco is 83% controlled by the Luksic group with the remaining shares listed in the Chilean stock exchange. Quiñenco's holdings include con-trolling interests in Banco de Chile, CCU (a beverage company jointly owned with the Dutch brewer Heineken), and Madeco (manufacturing of copper and aluminum based products). In 2013, the group's investments by sector were distributed as follows: financial services, 40%; energy 20%; beverages and food 10%; manufacturing, 9%; port and shipping, 8%; transport 7%; and other 6%. The group's scope of diversification ranges from metal processing and manufacturing, electric power distribution, general manufacturing, and shipping to the agriculture, fishing, food processing, and forestry sectors. The group also owns vehicle distribution, banking, telecommunications, food and beverages companies, hotels, and railways.

Its main strategic approach has been to focus on brand and consumer franchise development. The group's performance demonstrates its ability to identify business opportunities with high growth potential through its extensive business network, acquire controlling interests in each venture, and leverage acquisitions and partnerships as the base for further expansion into a sector either through infusions of capital or know-how (Quiñenco, 2013).

These three examples of large domestic conglomerates illustrate the organizational and competitive strengths of such firms. First, they are old and experienced and have endured economic and political crises successfully. This demonstrates their long-term strategic commitment to their national and regional markets and their ability to allocate and reallocate resources to adapt to cycles in the business environment. They are highly diversified, horizontally and/or vertically, and in the past few years have shown a keen eye for dying market sectors and emerging latent markets, divesting from the former and securing early-mover advantages in the latter. Finally, their ownership structures give them flexibility and agility and, with the new generations taking the helm, a more innovative and globally minded leadership with which to face their future.

Multinational Companies

The liberalization waves of the 1990s attracted many multinational companies (MNCs) to the region, motivated by a growing and more affluent consumer market, the abundance of natural resources, and the opening of opportunities in previously closed sectors. Yet, the percentage of foreign ownership in Latin America remains modest compared to that in other regions of the world (average of 9% foreign ownership stake as compared to 15% in sub-Saharan Africa and 11% in East Asia); this percentage is higher in larger firms than in SMEs (20% vs. 6%) and in the smaller Caribbean countries (11.4% vs. 5.7% for the larger countries). In addition, 87% of all firms in the region have no foreign ownership, and only 6% are fully owned by foreign investors (Francis, Rodriguez Meza, & Yang, 2013). Furthermore, in recent years multinationals have left Latin America (e.g., AT&T, Telecom Italia, Repsol) as a result of realignment of their business portfolios and to focus more on Asia. It should be noted that multilatinas have acquired many of the assets of the exiting MNCs.

The competitive advantages of MNCs over domestic firms include their abundant resources, competencies, and capabilities and their scale and scope. In addition, MNCs may be more experienced in international markets and understand the need to balance cost pressures with market needs better than a large domestic firm (except for the multilatinas). Yet, challenges remain, especially regarding MNCs' ability to adapt to local market needs, the rigid and bureaucratic legal business environment, and the political and social risks still present in the region. We discuss strategies for multinational companies operating in Latin American in chapter 8.

Table 3.6 Top Multinational Companies in Latin America in 2013

Rank 2012	Company	Country	Sector	Revenues 2012 US$ Billions	Total Assets 2012 US$ Billions
10	Wal-Mart Mexico	Mexico	Retailing	32.2	17.1
20	Bunge Alimentos	Brazil	Agroindustry	18.8	8.3
24	Volkswagen	Brazil	Automotive	16.0	n/a
26	Ambev	Brazil	Beverages	15.8	26.5
29	Carrefour	Brazil	Retailing	15.4	n/a
34	General Motors de Mexico	Mexico	Automobiles	14.0	5.5
37	Enersis	Chile	Electrical energy	13.0	788
38	Wal-Mart	Brazil	Retailing	12.7	n/a
42	Cargill	Brazil	Agroindustry	11.8	4.5
43	Fiat Automoveis	Brazil	Automotive	11.7	8.2
44	Coca Cola	Brazil	Beverages	11.7	n/a
45	Volkswagen de Mexico	Mexico	Automotive	11.6	5.4
51	Vivo	Brazil	Telecommunications	11.1	11.3
54	Ford Motor Company	Mexico	Automotive	10.2	n/a
56	Nissan Mexicana	Mexico	Automotive	10.2	n/a

* 2012 *América Economía* Ranking—500 Largest Companies in Latin America

Source: *America Economia* (2013e).

State-Owned Enterprises

State-owned enterprises (SOEs) once dominated Latin American economies, but the adoption of neoliberal policies in the early 1990s resulted in a wave of privatizations meant to improve the fiscal health of governments throughout the region. SOEs still play a role in the competitive landscape of Latin America, but their importance has diminished over the past three decades, with some notable exceptions. In Brazil, SOEs represent 12% of sales, 1.7% of profits, 51%

of assets, and 18% of market value as a percentage of gross national income. Also in line with global trends, SOEs typically dominate the natural resource extraction and energy sectors; such is the case in Latin America, where the largest SOEs are all in the oil and energy sector (Kowalski, Büge, Sztajerowska, & Egeland, 2013).

The rounds of privatization of SOEs that characterized the 1990s had mixed results, with privatizations being more successful in countries such as Chile and Colombia and less so in Argentina and Mexico. In many cases, failures were caused by governments' unwillingness to give up a "cash cow," by a strong sense of nationalism, or by the SOEs not being financially attractive to private investors (Robles, Simon, & Haar, 2003). In line with SOE trends for the rest of the world, many SOEs from Latin America have entered international markets and are competing with companies in the for-profit sector. This has also required that they adopt more professional management and operational processes. Two successful examples of this trend are Petrobras and Embraer. In the following paragraphs, we profile three SOEs in the region, Petrobras, Pemex, and PDVSA.

Petróleo Brasileiro (Petrobras)

Petrobras is the largest state-owned enterprise in Latin America—and the largest company in the region overall. This 60-year-old SOE has more than 82,000 employees and in 2012 registered revenues of US$138 billion, net profits of US$10.4 billion, and total assets of US$332 billion (*América Economía*, 2013e). The company has been on the list of Boston Consulting Group's global

Table 3.7 Top 10 State-Owned Enterprises in Latin America, 2013

Rank 2012*	Company	Country	Sector	Revenues 2012 US$ Billions	Total Assets 2012 US$ Billions
1	Petrobras	Brasil	Oil & Gas	137.7	331.6
2	Pemex	Mexico	Oil & Gas	126.7	155.5
3	PDVSA	Venezuela	Oil & Gas	124.5	218.5
6	Petrobras Distribuidora	Brasil	Oil & Gas	39.2	9.0
7	Ecopetrol	Colombia	Oil & Gas	37.7	56.8
15	Comision Federal de Electricidad	Mexico	Electricity	23.9	76.0
18	Eletrobras	Brasil	Electricity	19.3	84.3
25	Codelco	Chile	Mining	15.9	31.6
27	Petroecuador	Ecuador	Oil & Gas	15.6	9.5
35	YPF	Argentina	Oil & Gas	13.6	16.2

* 2012 *América Economía* Ranking—500 Largest Companies in Latin America

Source: *América Economía* (2013e).

challengers since 2008, and it ranks 25th in *Fortune*'s Global 500 list (Bhat-tacharya et al., 2013; *Fortune*, 2013). The current CEO, Maria das Graças Silva Foster (considered the most powerful woman in Latin America), is committed to turning Petrobras into a modern, global energy conglomerate that includes well-developed businesses in natural gas and oil and significant investments in alternative energies. Its oil and gas operations include exploration, extraction, refining, purchasing, and transportation of oil, gas, and petrochemicals. Petrobras is the global leader in offshore, deep-oil exploration. The company controls the Brazilian energy market in both production and distribution. Its subsidiary Petrobras Distribuidora—the largest petrochemical retailer in Brazil—ranks as the fourth largest SOE and the sixth largest company in the region, with revenues of US$39 billion in 2012. Petrobras began its internationalization in the early 1970s to minimize its vulnerability to oil crises. Its international activities, both upstream (exploration, production) and downstream (refining, commercialization), are managed by Braspetro. In 2011, the company operated in 27 countries in North America, the Middle East, Latin America, Asia, and Africa, which generated 12% of its total revenues (Fleury & Fleury, 2011). Since the mid-1990s, Petrobras has expanded the scope of its operations into renewable energy sources, focusing primarily on gas and biofuels (ethanol) and, more recently, electricity generation. In 2011, investments in renewable energy were estimated at US$1.3 billion (Fleury & Fleury, 2011).

The main competitive strengths of Petrobras lie in its commitment to innovation, social and environmental leadership, vertical integration, and horizontal diversification. Over the years, Petrobras has acquired competencies in operational efficiency, innovation and technological development, and marketing (Fleury & Fleury, 2011). Recently discovered deep oil reserves offshore will also support the company's continued dominance in oil production. It is estimated that Petrobras's inflation-adjusted investments in these new oil discoveries exceed what NASA invested in the 1960s to put a man on the moon (Romero, 2012). In addition, Petrobras's mixed ownership (although majority owned by the Brazilian government, it has traded on the NYSE since 2000) has forced the company to adopt a more transparent corporate governance system and allows it to seek capital and contracts in the global market (Fleury & Fleury, 2011). The main challenge Petrobras will face in the future is meeting its self-imposed goal of raising production to 4.5 million barrels a day (Romero, 2012).

Petróleos Mexicanos (PEMEX)

Petróleos Mexicanos is the second largest SOE and the second largest company in the region, with revenues of US$126.5 billion and total assets of US$155 billion in 2012 (*América Economía*, 2013e). It ranks 36th in the *Fortune* Global 500 (*Fortune*, 2013). Yet, the company saw net losses of US$29 billion in 2012, which reflect the operational and financial performance problems the company has been facing for several years. PEMEX has a monopoly on extraction, production, and commercialization of oil and gas in Mexico, and this gives it a unique competitive advantage in the domestic market. However, PEMEX also faces significant challenges to growth and expansion both domestically and internationally. First, Mexico's once-massive oil reserves are basically gone, and the reserves of shale oil and gas and deep-water oil in the Gulf of Mexico will cost money to develop. Second, PEMEX's position as a primary cash cow for the Mexican government (34% of total government revenues in 2011) has left the company with little money to invest in updated production facilities and technology. Finally, a constitutional ban had precluded PEMEX from raising capital in the open market. In 2013, and in spite of fierce opposition, President Peña Nieto succeeded in pushing forth a constitutional reform that will allow foreign investors to partner with PEMEX through production-sharing contracts or licenses. This private investment is expected to unleash new exploration and to increase oil production and exports (Wade, 2013; Williams, Martin and Cattan, 2013).

PDVSA

Petróleos de Venezuela, S.A. (PDVSA), is the third largest state-owned enterprise and the third largest overall in the region, with revenues of US$124.5 billion and net profits of US$4.2 billion in 2012 (*América Economía,* 2013e). It ranks 38th in the *Fortune* Global 500 (*Fortune,* 2013). The company was founded in 1975 and has some of the largest oil reserves in the world. PDVSA's exploration and extraction activities are based in Venezuela, but the company has refining and commercialization subsidiaries in Europe, China, the United States, and the Caribbean (Citgo is its marketing arm in the United States and the Caribbean). In addition to oil and natural gas, PDVSA also has a strong position in the production of finished petrochemical products, including lubricants, additives, asphalts, solvents, and specialty products for the industrial, automotive, aviation, and marine sectors. The company is currently investing heavily to increase production, primarily to raise revenues greatly needed to finance the needs of the Venezuelan state. Most of this investment will go to adopting more modern extraction technologies that can be applied to PDVSA's mature oil fields and deteriorating facilities. PDVSA—lacking capital, sufficient management talent, and updated technology—will need significant assistance to undertake this proposed increase in production. Yet, attracting private investment, domestic or foreign, will be difficult given the Venezuelan government's strong hold on the company (O'Donnell, 2013; PDVSA, 2013).

As these cases show, state-owned enterprises that adopt more hybrid models of ownership and management and long-term growth and expansion strategies, and that invest in innovation and social and environmentally responsible initiatives are likely to perform well in both national and global markets.

Small and Medium-Size Businesses

Small and medium-size businesses (SMEs), those with fewer than 100 employees, range from 89% to 94% of private-sector activity and employment in the region (Francis, Rodriguez Meza, & Yang, 2013). Most SMEs (referred to as PyMES in Spanish) are focused on the domestic market and are particularly involved in small-scale agriculture and services. The main challenges faced by SMEs are their limited access to financing and technology and their overreliance on the intuition and experience of a manager or founder for most decision making. Some SMEs may also lack well-structured organizational procedures and processes. Faced with increasing competition, SMEs have strategic choices to make to stay relevant in the competitive landscape; they may specialize in a niche market through a customized product offering or insert themselves into an MNC's or large domestic firm's value chain, serving as suppliers of inputs or services.

The value of SMEs for the continued development of the region is evident by the various stimulus measures and programs directed at enhancing the growth and competitiveness of SMEs. For instance, in November 2013, Argentina's government announced a program to subsidize small natural gas producers in exchange for their meeting production goals. The program will benefit around 50 SMEs in the sector and will be effective through 2017 (*América Economía*, 2013a). In the same month, the Inter-American Development Bank announced a US$900,000 program to support Peruvian women-owned SMEs. In Peru, a country that ranks second as the most entrepreneurial in the region, 17% of SMEs are managed by a woman. The program, FINPYME Mujer Empresaria, aims to increase the competitiveness of these SMEs. Probide (Association for Development and Well-Being) and the University of San Ignacio de Loyola will be in charge of selecting 50 SMEs to participate in the program. This will require assessing their strengths and weaknesses, helping them identify financing sources, and providing technical development. The SMEs that are eligible to apply to the program are from a variety of sectors, including education, financial services, tourism and hospitality, and food services, and they must have been in business at least three years and have a minimum of US$350,000 in annual sales and 11 employees (*América Economía*, 2013b). Recognizing that the inefficient regulatory system is one of the main obstacles for SMEs in the region, the Brazilian Ministry for Micro and Small Enterprises is working toward reducing the number of days it takes to open or close a small business in the country from 180 to 5 days. This measure, which aims to stimulate the growth of SMEs, was to be implemented gradually through 2014 and is part of a larger program call "To Think Simple" (Pensar Simples). Other components of the program include creating an electronic portal for SMEs and a one-stop shop where SMEs can take care of all their regulatory needs without having to go to several offices to take care of permits and other paperwork (*America Economia*, 2013c). Finally, a US$5 million, five-year program (2009–2013) from the European Union helped internationalize 1,200 SMEs in Guatemala. These SMEs belong to sectors that include artisanal crafts, agro-products, home decoration and gifts, energy, the environment, infrastructure, and information technology (*América Economía*, 2013d).

The Informal Sector

Estimating the size of the informal sector in Latin America can be difficult. The informal sector can be defined as businesses that are not legally registered at inception, become informal over time (e.g., by not renewing registrations or paying taxes), or are legally registered but engage in informal practices. A recent report by the World Bank showed that among the firms surveyed, 64% indicated having to compete with firms in the informal sector; this applied to firms of all sizes. Although only 10% of all firms seem to start as and remain informal (i.e., not registered legally), a larger percentage reportedly engage in informal business practices (e.g., selling without receipts, hiring unreported workers), with about half the firms surveyed indicating they compete with firms that are engaged in these informal practices. This was especially the case for SMEs in the larger and medium-size countries in the region (Francis, Rodriguez Meza, & Yang, 2013). By other accounts, the size of the informal sector can be as large as 30–40% of a total country's economy, as is the case for Mexico and Brazil.

Operating in the informal sector also has some negative implications for firms. First, micro and small businesses in the informal sector lack legal identity and legal protections, which raises their business risk and operational costs. It also limits their ability to grow because they lack access to financing sources in the formal sector.

3.5   Summary

In this chapter we described macro and micro environmental factors that drive and hinder competitiveness in Latin America and identified the competitive structure and dynamics in the region. The main drivers of competitiveness are availability of natural resources, primarily land and minerals, and an abundant unskilled labor force. Internal sources of competitive advantage for the region's firms include their intimate knowledge of domestic consumer markets needs and wants, business systems, and regulatory frameworks; their ability to adapt to a constantly changing external environment; and their long-term orientation and commitment to domestic markets. Latin American firms' main competitive challenges include the region's weak infrastructure; an insufficient supply of highly skilled labor and management; and an inefficient and corrupt regulatory system.

The competitive landscape in Latin America is composed of large domestic conglomerates, multinational companies, state-owned enterprises, small and medium-size businesses, and the informal sector. Large domestic conglomerates' main strengths lie in their deep knowledge of domestic markets, their widely diversified portfolios, and their family-run management. State-owned enterprises continue to struggle to meet acceptable levels of operational efficiency and financial performance, while small and medium-size businesses face regulatory challenges, a high cost of doing business, and lack of access to financial resources. Part II of the book is dedicated to exploring strategic options for firms from within and outside the region, with a focus on entrepreneurs, MNCs, and global Latinas.

References

América Economía. (2013a). Argentina lanza estímulos para PyMES petroleras. November 29. Retrieved from www.americaeconomia.com/node/105983.

América Economía. (2013b). BID capacitará a mujeres de PyMES Peruanas. November 12. Retrieved from www.americaeconomia.com/node/104797.

America Economía. (2013c). Ministro apuesta por reducir de 180 a 5 días la apertura de PyMES en Brasil. October 25. Retrieved from www.americaeconomia.com/node/103705.

América Economía. (2013d). UE contribuyó a internacionalización de 1200 PyMES de Guatemala. September 13. Retrieved from www.americaeconomia.com/node/100932.

América Economía. (2013e). Las 500 mayores empresas de América Latina 2013. Retrieved from http://rankings.americaeconomia.com/2013.

América Economía. (2013f). Las mejores ciudades para hacer negocios de América Latina. Retrieved from www.americaeconomia.com/negocios-industrias/ranking-2013-las-mejores-ciudades-para-hacer-negocios-de-america-latina.

Becker, T. H. (2011). *Doing business in the New Latin America*. 2nd ed. Santa Barbara, California: Praeger.

Bhattacharya, A., Bradtke, T., Ermias, T., Haring-Smith, W., Lee, D., Leon, E., Meyer, M., Michael, D., Tratz, A., Ukon, M., & Waltermann, B. (2013). *Introducing the 2013 BCG Global Challengers*. Retrieved from www.bcgperspectives.com.

Boston Consulting Group & Knowledge@Wharton. (2008). *Special report: The new competition for global resources*. Retrieved from http://knowledge.wharton.upenn.edu/special-report/the-new-competition-for-global-resources.

CAF Development Bank of Latin America. (2013). *La infraestructura en el desarrollo integral de America Latina*. Retrieved from http://publicaciones.caf.com/publicaciones.

Calfucura, E., Martinez Ortiz, A., Sanborn, C., & Dammert, J. L. (2013). Natural resource extraction: The good, the bad, and the ugly. *Americas Quarterly*, 7(1), 62–79. Retrieved from http://americasquarterly.org/charticles/natural-resource-extraction-chile-peru-colombia/pdf/AQ-Natural-Resource-Extraction.pdf.

Cardona, M. (2012). TalkingPoint: Infrastructure investment in Latin America. *Financier Worldwide* (September). Retrieved from www.financierworldwide.com/article.php?id=9776.

Chironga, M., Dahl, J., Goland, P., Pinshow, G., & Sonnekus, M. (2012). *Micro-, small, and medium-size enterprises in emerging economies: How banks can grasp a $350 billion opportunity*. McKinsey Company.

Cisneros Group. (2013). Retrieved from www.cisneros.com/about-us/history.

Fay, M., & Morrison, M. (2005). Infrastructure in Latin America and the Caribbean: Recent developments and key challenges. *The World Bank, Report #32640-LCR*. Retrieved from http://siteresources.worldbank.org/INTLAC/Resources/LAC_Infrastructure_complete.pdf.

Fleury, A., & Fleury, M.T.L. (2011). *Brazilian multinationals: Competences for internationalization*. Cambridge: Cambridge University Press.

Fortune. (2013). Retrieved from http://money.cnn.com/magazines/fortune/global500/.

Francis, D.C., Rodriguez Meza, J. L., & Yang, J. (2013). Mapping enterprises in Latin America and the Caribbean. *The World Bank Group, Latin America and the Caribbean Series, Note No.1.* Retrieved from www.enterprisesurvey.org.

Grupo Carso. (2013). Retrieved from www.carso.com.mx/EN/Investor_relations/Documents/2012.pdf.

Haar, J., & Price, J. (Eds.). (2008). *Can Latin America compete? Confronting the challenges of globalization.* New York: Palgrave Macmillan.

International Monetary Fund. (2013). *Regional economic outlook: Western Hemisphere.* Washington, DC: International Monetary Fund.

Kowalski, P., Büge, M., Sztajerowska, M., & Egeland, M. (2013). State-owned enterprises: Trade effects and policy implications. *OECD Trade Policy Papers, No. 147.* Retrieved from http://dx.doi.org/10.1787/5k4869ckqk71-en.

O'Donnell, T. (2013). The PDVSA post-Chávez: Will partnerships with the private sector and Chinese experts boost oil production? *Americas Quarterly* (August 29). Retrieved from www.americasquarterly.org/content/pdvsa-post-chavez-will-partnerships-boost-oil-production.

PDVSA. (2013). La nueva PDVSA. Retrieved from www.pdvsa.com.

Porter, M. E. (1990). The competitive advantage of nations. *Harvard Business Review* (March–April), 73–91.

Puryear, J. M., & Ortega Goodspeed, T. (2008). Coveting human capital: Is Latin American education competitive? In J. Haar and J. Price (Eds.), *Can Latin America compete? Confronting the challenges of globalization*, pp. 45–62. New York: Palgrave Macmillan.

Quiñenco, S.A. (2013). Estrategia corporativa. Retrieved from www.quinenco.cl/esp/estrategia_corporativa.html.

Robles, F., Simon, F., & Haar, J. (2003). *Winning strategies for the new Latin markets.* Upper Saddle River, NJ: Financial Times Prentice Hall.

Romero, S. (2012). Brazil, where oil and women mix powerfully. *The New York Times* (April 10). Retrieved from www.nytimes.com/2012/04/11/business/energy-environment/women-take-the-reins-of-power.

Sabatini, C. (2008). Labor reform: Undercompetitive economies and unprotected workforce. In J. Haar and J. Price (Eds.), *Can Latin America compete? Confronting the challenges of globalization.* New York: Palgrave Macmillan.

Schaefer, P. F., & Schaefer, P. C. (2008). Property, the rule of law, and development in the Americas. In J. Haar and J. Price (Eds.), *Can Latin America compete? Confronting the challenges of globalization.* New York: Palgrave Macmillan.

Schwab, K., & Sala-i-Martin, X. (Eds.). (2013). The global competitiveness report 2012–2013. *World Economic Forum.* Retrieved from www3.weforum.org/docs/WEF_GlobalCompetitivenessReport_2012-13.pdf.

Sinnott, E., Nash, J., & de la Torre, A. (2010). *Natural resources in Latin America and the Caribbean: Beyond booms and busts?* Washington, DC: The World Bank.

Smith, J., Juhn, T., & Humphrey, C. (2008). Consumer and small business credit: Building blocks of the middle class. In J. Haar and J. Price (Eds.), *Can Latin America compete? Confronting the challenges of globalization.* New York: Palgrave Macmillan.

Universia Knowledge@Wharton. (2009). *Brazil's dilemma: How to make its labor market more flexible.* Retrieved from www.wharton.universia.net/index.cfm?fa=printArticle&ID=1349&language=English.

Wade, L. (2013). The easy energy is gone: Will Mexico amend its constitution to drill for oil? *Slate.com*. Retrieved from www.slate.com/articles/health_and_science/energy_around_the_world/2013/11/mexico_constitution_and_oil_drilling_will_pemex_be_privatized.html.

Williams, A., Martin, E., & Cattan, A. (2013). Mexico passes oil bill seen luring $20 billion a year. *Bloomberg.com* (December 13). Retrieved from www.bloomberg.com/news/2013-12-12/mexico-lower-house-passes-oil-overhaul-to-break-state-monopoly.html.

World Bank/International Finance Corporation. (2013). *Doing business 2014: Latin America*. Washington, DC: The World Bank.

4   The Latin American Consumer Market

Introduction

Wander around on any major Latin American city and you are likely to see throngs of consumers shopping to their heart's content. Many will be on their smartphones while browsing brand-name clothing or shoes. Today's Latin American consumers look very much like any other consumers in developed countries. The Latin American consumer market has grown in size and purchasing power; it has also become increasingly segmented and sophisticated, while remaining distinct from other markets around the world. This chapter provides an overview of the size and growth of Latin American consumer markets and their current and evolving consumption patterns. Competing for this growing and increasingly affluent market will demand that firms from inside and outside the region develop a deep understanding of consumers' characteristics and expectations.

At the end of this chapter, the reader will be able to (a) identify the economic, geographic, sociocultural, and technological factors that drive the growth of Latin American consumer markets and (b) understand the size, characteristics, and consumption patterns of consumer markets in the region.

This chapter is composed of five sections. The first section describes the size and main demographic characteristics of the Latin American consumer market, providing detailed data on country and regional consumer markets. The second section provides a comprehensive overview of the economic, geographic, sociocultural, and technological factors that have driven the growth of Latin American consumers' purchasing power. The next section assesses the role of connectivity in the growth and sophistication of consumer markets in Latin America and its implications for accessing these consumers. The fourth section presents a profile of the typical Latin American consumer and the evolving and contradictory nature of the values that guide consumer behavior. This section also highlights some differences in consumption patterns among three country markets. The concluding section summarizes key concepts and introduces the reader to the implications for marketing strategy to be discussed in the next chapter.

4.1   Size of the Latin American Market

Over the past decade, the Latin American consumer market has grown in size and sophistication. Across the region, the size of the middle class has increased and poverty has decreased. The liberalization and global insertion of the Latin American economies, increased urbanization, and growing connectivity have also resulted in consumer markets that are increasingly cosmopolitan and demanding. Differences in race, ethnicity, social class, and geography still exist, however, and this landscape points to a consumer market that is rich in opportunity but is also complex to navigate.

Market Size and Growth

The total Latin American population is estimated at 581 million (World Bank, 2013b), representing about 8% of the world's population (Population Reference Bureau [PRB], 2013). Individual country markets range in size from large ones like Brazil (196 million) to small ones like Panama (4 million). The rate of population growth has been declining slowly in the past few years, primarily due to lower birth rates in Brazil and Mexico (1.8 and 2.2 percent, respectively). Yet, the population will continue to grow at a 1.1% average rate for the region and will reach 640 million by 2020 and 780 million by 2050 (Corpart, 2012; PRB, 2013). The population in the region is mostly urban (79%), and density is high for the countries in Central America and the Andean region. Average household size is five, especially for low-income households (PRB, 2013; TNS Discover, 2010; World Bank, 2013b).

Measured in terms of income, Latin America is a large and increasingly affluent market. The region's total GDP in 2012 was US$5.34 trillion (World Bank, 2013b), representing 7% of total world GDP, with a gross national income (GNI) per capita of US$9,000 for the region (World Bank, 2013b). Brazil is by far the largest and most important economy. Argentina, Colombia, Chile, Mexico, Peru, and Venezuela are the next most important markets in terms of GDP contribution and per capita income (World Bank, 2013a). Table 4.1 summarizes key population and GDP data for selected countries in the region.

According to Global Information, by 2025 the Latin American market will reach 661 million people with a GDP of US$15 trillion (Global Information, 2012), thus opening significant opportunities for consumer products and services directed at all income levels. The size and growth of the Latin American economy translates into US$3.7 trillion in purchasing power[1] for the region. Consumption per person in 2012 was US$6,360, and it is expected to reach US$11,100 by 2020 (Corpart, 2012). Brazil and Mexico are the two largest markets, accounting for about 40% and 23% of the region's total purchasing power, respectively (Cambridge Insight, 2013).

Brazil is by far the largest and most important economy in the region, with a 2012 GDP of US$2.5 trillion. In fact, Brazil's share of Latin America's GDP is

Table 4.1   Market Size for Selected Latin American Countries

Country	Population 2012 (Millions)	GDP 2012 (US$ Billions)	GDP Growth Rate % (2012)	Income per capita US$	Household Income US$
Mexico	120	1,200	3.9	9,800	28,000
South America					
Argentina	41	471	7.3	11,500	26,000
Bolivia	10.5	27	5.2	2,600	
Brazil	200	2,300	0.9	11,400	24,500
Chile	17.5	270	5.6	15,400	32,000
Colombia	48	400	4.0	7,800	22,000
Ecuador	15.5	84	5.1	5,400	
Paraguay	6.7	26	−1.2	3,800	
Peru	30	197	6.3	6,600	
Uruguay	3.4	49	3.9	14,500	
Venezuela	30	381	5.6	12,700	
Central America	44				
Costa Rica	4.8	45.5	5.1	9,400	
El Salvador	6.3	24	1.9	3,800	
Guatemala	15	50.5	3.0	3,400	
Honduras	8	18.5	3.9	2,300	
Nicaragua	6	10.5	5.2	1,800	
Panama	3.8	36	10.8	9,500	

* Figures are rounded up

Sources: United Nations Economic Commission for Latin America and the Caribbean [ECLAC] (2013); Long (2013); Ogier (2013); World Bank (2013a, 2013b).

equivalent to that of Mexico, Argentina, Chile, Colombia, and Venezuela combined (Ogier, 2013). Brazil has now bypassed the United Kingdom as the sixth largest economy in the world (Powdrill & Hughes, 2012), and the Economist Intelligence Unit estimates that by 2016, Brazil could overtake France as the fifth largest world economy in the world (Ogier, 2013). Economic growth has been especially strong in the northeast, north, and central west regions of the country (Ogier, 2012). Mexico is the second largest economy in the region with a GDP of US$1.2 trillion. Mexico's economy is equivalent to those of Argentina, Colombia, Chile, and Peru combined (Ernst & Young, 2013); it is expected to become the 10th largest economy in the world by 2020 (Powdrill & Hughes, 2012).

The Emerging Middle Class

The region has also seen the emergence of a larger middle class and a decrease in poverty and income inequality. Although there are various definitions of what constitutes the middle class, we rely on the latest World Bank report on Latin

America's middle class (Ferreira, Messina, Rigolini, Lopez-Calva, Lugo, & Vakis, 2013). Using 2009 data, this report defines the middle class as those with a per capita, per-day household income of between US$10 and US$50 at purchasing power parity. On this basis, a family of four with an annual household income of between US$14,600 and US$73,000 would be considered middle class (about US$3,650 per person, per year). This places the lower income boundary for the middle class at the 68th percentile, resulting in a middle class amounting to 30% of the total population.[2] In addition, the study identifies a moderately poor segment, which is between the very poor (those with per capita income of under US$4) and the middle class as just identified. This "vulnerable segment" earns household income between US$4 and US$10 per day. If we add this segment to the middle class as described, we find that 68% of the total population in Latin America now lives above the poverty line.

The middle classes now make up the majority of the population in Chile, Brazil, Mexico, Uruguay, Costa Rica, and Colombia. It is estimated that by 2020, the middle class will represent the majority of consumers across the entire region (Corpart, 2012). According to Ferreira et al. (2013, p. 11), the emerging middle class in Latin America is "urban, better educated, and largely privately employed, and with beliefs and opinions broadly in line with those of their poorer and less-educated fellow citizens." Although we find income differences across countries, the study found that middle-class families across the region are primarily urban, have heads of households with higher levels of education, are more likely to be employed in the private sector, and have female members of the household participating in the labor force. In spite of demographic similarities, the values and beliefs held by people in Latin America are still largely determined by nationality. As such, a middle-class person in Colombia is more likely to share values and beliefs with a lower-income Colombian than with another middle-class person from Mexico, for example.

As middle-class families' incomes continue to grow, these families will be able to spend more on discretionary purchases and higher-quality products. The sectors likely to benefit the most will be electronics, telecommunication services and devices, financial services, retailing, health care, consumer durables, and entertainment.

The Base of the Pyramid

In spite of the significant economic gains the region has experienced over the past decade and the reduction in poverty across the region, significant income inequalities remain. The total population under the poverty level (earning less than US$4 per day) amounts to about a third of the region's population, about 165 to 170 million people; 68 million of them are considered extremely poor (United Nations Economic Commission for Latin America and the Caribbean [ECLAC], 2013; Ferreira et al., 2013). These percentages vary widely among countries in the region. In Central America it ranges from 20% in Costa Rica to 62% in Honduras, while in South America it ranges from 14% in Chile to 51% in Bolivia.

It reaches 51% in Mexico (World Bank, 2013b). If we add to this figure the vulnerable segment mentioned earlier (US$4–US$10 per day), we have a market of low- and moderate-income individuals (those living on annual per capita income below US$3,650) of 400 million people with a purchasing power of more than US$600 billion, a considerable market in and of itself (TNS Discover, 2010; Inter-American Development Bank [IADB] 2013a).

It is important to highlight some key facts about the Base of the Pyramid (BoP) market that point to some of its consumer preferences and market potential. TNS Discover (2010) and World Resources Institute data (2006) show that BoP consumers are very family oriented, with love and belongingness being very important to them; they are focused on the present but are optimistic about the future. Research reveals that BoP consumers are sophisticated and discriminating, are reasonably well connected, and adapt easily to technology. Also, they are willing to pay higher prices for goods and services they perceive as delivering greater consumer value (Subrahmanyan & Gomez-Arias, 2008). In terms of their purchasing habits, 70% of low-income consumers buy leader brands for specific product categories because of the brand's reputation and reliability. Maintaining social status and keeping face are important to them; thus, BoP consumers do not want to feel excluded or be reminded that they are poor through their purchases (Antúñez de Mayolo, 2011; TNS Discover, 2010). Furthermore, BoP consumers are dependable borrowers as demonstrated by the high repayment rates of microfinance organizations and their low default rates on credit card debt.

Approximately half of the BoP's spending goes to food, energy, housing, and transportation, in that order; the rest is spent on health, telecommunications, water, and other products such as clothing, education, and entertainment (e.g., 9 out of 10 consumers own a color TV and listen to the radio) (Dansk Industry, 2007; TNS Discover, 2010). Housing, education, and banking, increasingly through mobile technology, are three of the fastest-growing sectors at the base of the pyramid. Colombia leads the way in Latin America with an active private sector serving BoP markets through innovative credit systems. Low-income Colombians with no access to formal banking are buying homes and appliances on credit. Collaborative partnerships such as Credifamilia, for instance, have allowed low-income Colombians to obtain mortgages for new, affordable homes. In Brazil, preschools are rare in low-income neighborhoods; PUPA is a company in Brazil that offers an installment delivery and payment plan for educational toys and books specifically targeted to developing young children and caregivers without much education (IADB, 2013b). Furthermore, the deficient public health systems and risks associated with being in poor health have moved Latin Americans to be concerned about their lifestyles. Not only will demand for health services increase but so will demand for products and services that help low-income consumers (and middle-class consumers, for that matter) maintain a healthy lifestyle.

The BoP market in Latin America offers substantial profitability potential. The market is large in size and purchasing power and is continuing to grow.

Its increased urbanization and connectivity have also reduced communication and distribution obstacles. Finally, the market is underserved, and the lack of competition opens opportunities for companies willing to adopt innovative business models that satisfy BoP consumers' needs.

4.2   Drivers of Purchasing Power in Latin American Markets

This section provides a comprehensive overview of the economic, political, technological, and sociocultural factors that have driven the growth of Latin American consumers' purchasing power in the past decade or so. Strong economic growth, easier access to credit, and improved living conditions have given rise to a more socially mobile consumer who is well informed and well connected and who has adopted more individualistic behaviors while continuing to value cultural traditions.

Economic Drivers

Economic Growth and Stability

As discussed in previous chapters, the past decade has been marked by favorable external conditions and rising domestic opportunities for many Latin American economies. This growth is expected to continue; by 2020, the region's economy will reach US$10.7 trillion, equivalent of 9% of the global GDP (Corpart, 2012).

Job creation and real income gains during the past decade have spurred consumer spending—Latin America is now a region with a purchasing power of almost US$4 trillion. This economic boom has also boosted consumer confidence and optimism vis-à-vis the future, a key element for consumers who are considering purchasing high-ticket items such as housing and cars.

Economic globalization will continue to be a primary driver of consumption. The shift in economic realignment discussed in chapter 2 has also increased awareness and exposure to other emerging economies and cultures and their products. For instance, penetration of Asian products has intensified, and Latin American consumers are becoming more familiar with Asian brands and cultures. In some countries, the increased Asian presence is evident not only in consumer electronics, appliances, and automobiles but also in retail and food establishments, which Latin Americans are embracing. Furthermore, increased purchasing power has impacted not only consumption of products but also an interest in travel within and outside their countries. With a strong currency, Brazilians are traveling abroad in hordes, combining shopping and tourism.

Poverty Reduction and Social Mobility

Sustained economic growth has had a direct impact on upward social mobility, pushing thousands of people in the region into higher income brackets. This is most evident in the emergence of a larger middle class and a decrease in poverty and income inequality. In the period 2004–2011, GNI increased from 2% in Mexico to 8% in Argentina (ECLAC, 2013), and 70 million people were lifted out of poverty between 2003 and 2011 (World Bank, 2013a). A 2013 report by the IDB/World Bank indicates that the size of the middle class in Latin America and the Caribbean expanded by 50% from 2003 to 2009, to 152 million people. In Brazil alone, more than 60 million people have joined the middle class since 2005; that is equivalent to the population of Italy (Ogier, 2012). Although a large percentage of the population still lives on under $2.00 a day, this percentage has dropped consistently over the past 10 years (25% in 2012 versus 30% in 2009 and 44% in 2003). Thus, by 2009, both the emerging middle class and low-income individuals represented about a third of the region's total population. By 2012, these figures had improved even further, and for the first time the number of people in the middle class exceeded the number living in poverty (Ferreira et al., 2013; TNS Discover, 2010). The region's middle class will continue to grow in size and purchasing power thanks to sustained economic growth and improved social conditions.

Access to Credit

Access to credit has been one of the major drivers of consumer growth, allowing consumers to buy high-ticket items they would not be able to afford otherwise. In spite of high interest rates (ranging from 30% to 230%), the availability of store credit and the use of credit cards has exploded throughout the region, both in urban and rural areas (Latin Business Chronicle, 2012; Price, 2013). In 1990, only 3% of Latin American households had a credit card; that figure is expected to grow to 25% by 2020. In Brazil, for instance, the number of credit cards issued between 2002 and 2006 grew 91% to 79 million; mortgage lending rose 26.5% between 2005 and 2007, and consumer loans expanded by 800% from 2002 to 2012 (Chester, Fox, Gervaz, Reise, & Valls, 2010; Price, 2013). The use of credit card partnerships among financial institutions and merchants (e.g., airlines, car manufacturers, mobile operators, and retailers) has also increased, and some merchants now generate a significant percentage of their domestic profits from financial services (60% in Brazil; 15%–25% in Chile) (Bartolumeu Días, Gonçalves, Ibáñez, Massunaga, & Sawaya, 2011).

A recent report by the International Monetary Fund shows that real credit in the region has experienced rapid growth since 2004. In the period 2004–2007, the average growth rate was 12.4% per year, and although this growth slowed down in 2008–2009, real credit growth recovered in the period 2010–2011, registering an average of 10.3% for the region. This growth has not been evenly distributed across the region, with countries such as Bolivia, Guatemala, Honduras, and Uruguay not experiencing much growth (less than 6%) and others, like Brazil, Paraguay, and Peru, growing steadily even through the 2008–2009 crisis period. Furthermore, mortgages and consumption credit have grown faster than corporate credit throughout the period 2005–2011. Mortgage credit is especially robust in Brazil (31% growth rate), while consumption credit is most significant in Argentina (22% growth rate) (Harbo Hansen & Sulla, 2013).

Sociodemographic Drivers

Dual-Income Households

Dual-income households have greatly contributed to the increase in household purchasing power[3] throughout the region, ranging from US$1.4 trillion in Brazil to US$176 billion in Chile. The increasing presence of women in the workforce—53% of working age women in 2008—has resulted in a series of social and demographic changes (United Nations Development Program/International Labor Organization [UNDP/ILO], 2009). Women's insertion into the workforce has resulted in increased financial independence, and women are now able to make more purchasing decisions on their own for themselves and for their households. Yet, women still carry the burden of family obligations, thus resulting in high levels of stress and time constraints. Women in Argentina, for instance, report always lacking time, being in a hurry, and needing to multitask (TNS Discover, 2010). Products and services that streamline family living will be in great demand; examples include smartphones, Internet services, packaged and frozen foods, child care, and automobiles. One-stop retailers are also likely to see increased traffic from women working outside the home.

Other important sociodemographic changes include a slight but continued increase in the divorce rate in the region since 1980 (Kenny, 2013; National Healthy Marriage Resource Center, 2013) and growth in the number of single-parent families and in the number of couples without children or with fewer children (TNS Discover, 2010). The new types of family structures now evident in Latin America will mean increasing demand for products and services that meet the specific needs of these households. These may include time-saving or low-price products of reasonable quality for lower-income, single-parent households or entertainment and travel services for middle-income couples without children.

Young Consumers

Latin America is a relatively young market where 28% of the population is between 0 and 14 years of age. Those ages 0–24 are expected to reach 255 million by 2020, equivalent to 40% of the region's total population. Furthermore, two-thirds of the population is between 15 and 64 years of age (400 million), and Latin America's working-age population is expected to reach about 470 million by 2040. This net increase of 85 million from 2007 is equivalent to about two-thirds of today's labor force in the United States or Western Europe (Corpart, 2012; Cadena, Remes, & Restrepo, 2011). This large working-age population will not only help sustain economic growth in years to come but also likely result in a robust and dynamic domestic market.

In addition, children in Latin America are increasingly informed and sophisticated consumers, and their voices and tech savvy have become part of the family dynamics (TNS Discover, 2010). Not only are they important influencers of family purchases, but also they have more income of their own with which to engage in direct consumption. This young market will represent a competitive advantage for the region vis-à-vis more developed but aging countries such as those in Europe, Japan, the United States, and even China (Powdrill & Hughes, 2012).

An Aging Population

In spite of its young population, Latin America has not escaped the global trend of an increasingly aging population. Latin America's seniors (65 years or above) currently account for 40 million (7%) of the total population and will grow to about 83 million in 2020 (Corpart, 2012; PRB, 2013). Because of the lack of pension and retirement funds and weak public social systems, it is likely that people will work longer. This will likely be accompanied by rising demand for financial and health-care services to meet the needs of this age demographic.

Connectivity

Related to globalization is the increased penetration of smart telecommunication technologies and devices in the region. These technologies have intensified the strength and frequency of communications among family and social networks, as is the case elsewhere in the world. With a culture based on strong relationships and family orientation and an economic context in which an increasing number of members of a household work outside the home, telecommunication services have found a thriving market in Latin America.

In 2012, Latin America was expected to surpass the rest of the world in information technology (IT) spending by 1.8 times. This represented an IT market of US$97 billion (including hardware, software, and IT services) and a growth rate in IT spending of 12.2%. Latin America's telecommunications services sector was expected to grow even more impressively—at 2.8 times the average global growth rate (Molinski, 2012).

These new technologies have made it cheaper and easier for consumers to access information about trends, product and service options, promotions and prices, and online purchases. Today, Latin American consumers are more informed and better equipped and thus more demanding and sophisticated. We discuss connectivity in Latin America in greater detail later in this chapter.

Changing Social Norms and Values

Latin Americans are still considered relatively traditional and conservative. Latin Americans' strong religious beliefs and sense of family duty shape their social norms and individual behaviors. In addition, people in the region have a high level of respect for hierarchy and authority and favor clearly defined gender roles.

Yet, these traditional values now coexist with a mix of more "modern" values, especially individualism, social tolerance, and a greater concern for environmental sustainability. The growth of individualism in the region has led to a greater need for personalization and customization of purchases and has increased demand for purchases that satisfy consumers' needs for self-esteem and self-realization. Latin Americans are focusing on self-improvement, education, and skill building to realize their own potential as individuals. In countries such as Mexico and Argentina, this need is being driven by fears about the future; self-improvement acts as a type of insurance against potential reversals of good fortune and economic slowdowns. In Colombia and Brazil, on the other hand, a growing sense of stability and optimism about the future are providing the motivation for self-improvement (Galgey, 2011).

Social tolerance is also on the rise. Several countries in the region, for instance, have passed progressive legislation to protect the rights of lesbian, gay, bisexual, and transsexual (LGBT) individuals. Argentina became the first Latin American country to legalize same-sex marriage in 2010. Mexico City passed a law in 2009 allowing gay and lesbian couples to marry and to adopt children. Other countries, such as Colombia, Ecuador, and Brazil, have recognized domestic partnerships for same-sex couples (Huffington Post, 2013). A more tolerant and inclusive society will have an impact on consumers' values and will open up market opportunities in niche segments. Furthermore, changes in social norms are resulting in smaller households, which will increase demand for housing and housing-related products and services (Cadena, Remes, & Restrepo, 2011).

Social awareness and expectations regarding the need for environmental sustainability are also evident throughout the region. As major Latin American economies have relied on intense exploitation of natural resources for their economic growth, Latin Americans are becoming worried about the degradation of the region's pristine and rich natural resources. For instance, the massive Belo Monte hydroelectric project under construction in the Xingu River in northeast Brazil, which generates energy to support the intense iron-ore extraction in the Amazon and the aluminum and metallurgic industries in northern Brazil, has generated substantial opposition and protests in Brazil and the world (Amazon Watch, 2013). Moreover, more than 75% of consumers in Mexico, Argentina, Colombia, and Brazil, for instance, indicated that making the world a better place was important in their lives. More than 75% of consumers surveyed in Argentina, Brazil, Colombia, and Mexico also believe their individual actions can be part of the solution through their individual choices (Galgey, 2011).

Geographic Drivers

Geographic Fragmentation

Gallup, Gaviria, and Lora (2003, p. 11) define geographical fragmentation as "the probability that two individuals taken at random do not live in similar ecozones." On the basis of this definition, they found that Latin America was more fragmented than any other region in the world, particularly Ecuador,

Colombia, and Peru. They identified seven geographical zones, including tropical highlands, lowland Pacific coast, lowland Atlantic coast, Amazon, temperate Southern Cone, Mexican-US border, and highland and dry Southern Cone. This geographic fragmentation lends further support to our discussion of economic fragmentation in chapter 2.

Latin America's high level of geographic fragmentation has a direct impact on the growth and composition of consumer markets in the region. Geography impacts climate and health, agricultural yields, labor productivity, exposure to natural disasters, and access to markets. These geographic differences point to different patterns of development across the region, with coastal cities, for example, registering significant economic growth, including an influx of foreign direct investment. The disparities in economic vitality among regions will be reflected in the size and purchasing power of consumer markets and will shape the expectations and buying behaviors of consumers.

Urbanization

Eighty percent of the region's population is urban (TNS Discover, 2010), making Latin America the most urban region in the developing world. Latin America's largest cities—those with 200,000 inhabitants or more—number almost 200 and contribute more than 60% of the region's GDP. The 10 largest cities alone—including Mexico City (20.5m), Sao Paulo (19.9m), Buenos Aires (13.5m), Rio de Janeiro (12m), and Lima (9.1m)—account for 50% of GDP. This is comparable to the level of economic activity concentrated in cities that one is likely to find in the United States and Western Europe (Cadena, Remes, & Restrepo, 2011; PRB, 2013). The most significant growth in the years to come will happen in middle-size cities, those between 200,000 and 10 million people. A study by McKinsey shows that most of the growth in Latin America will be experienced in urban areas. For example, by 2025, the 200 largest cities will generate GDP growth of about US$3.8 trillion, and their per capita GDP will reach $23,000 (McKinsey Global Institute, 2011).

The benefits of urbanization are related to the agglomeration effects associated with urban centers. The larger markets and higher population density of primary and secondary cities will appeal to producers who can benefit from economies of scale, enhanced productivity, and more efficient distribution. As these metropolitan areas exceed their capacity, demand from city, state, and national governments for construction, transportation, and public services will increase.

Increased urbanization and decaying cities' infrastructures in Latin America are also shaping consumer values in the region. The growth of cities and megacities means traffic congestion, longer commutes, and lack of protection against urban violence. Such a hostile environment for shopping increases demand for convenient and time-saving products and services and fosters a reliance on neighborhood stores and services. Convenience and home delivery services

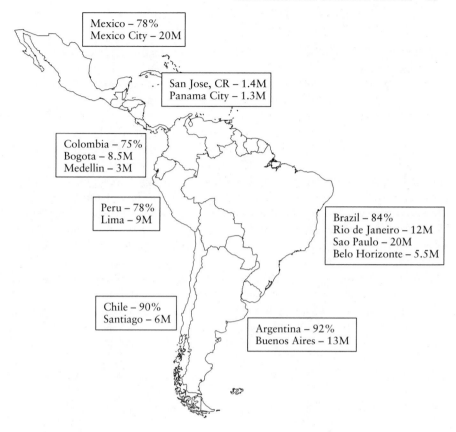

Figure 4.1 Urbanization in Latin America

Note: % indicates the percentage of urban population in the country.

Source: Authors' elaboration, based on data from Dobbs et al. (2011) and the World Bank (2013b).

have evolved to supply families and individuals with almost anything imaginable. Time and simplicity of consumption have also emerged as top priorities (Corpart, 2012).

Urban centers across the region also differ in terms of economic and social performance. Monterrey, Mexico, for example, is home to a strong technology cluster and has the lowest share of people living in poverty in the region. Other cities are implementing innovative sustainable living solutions (e.g., Curitiba, Brazil; Medellin, Colombia; Panama City; and Viña del Mar, Chile), and some, like Buenos Aires and Bogota, excel in terms of health-care coverage for their citizens (Cadena, Remes, & Restrepo, 2011). These regional differences will impact consumers' value perceptions and their demand for specific products and services.

4.3   Connectivity in Latin America

Connectivity is a major driver of Latin American consumer purchasing power, and telecommunications is a high-growth sector. In this section, we describe the growth of various telecommunication-related products and services and assess the impact of this growth on the purchasing patterns of consumer markets in the region.

Wireless telephony (devices and service) has experienced a boom in Latin America. The Mexican leader America Movil has more than 200 million customers in 16 countries (Molinski, 2012). Cell phone penetration is high and growing, and penetration of smartphones was expected to grow to 33% by 2014 (Powdrill & Hughes, 2012). Mobile subscriptions have already surpassed 100% penetration in the region. According to Business Monitor International (2012), in 2011, Panama and El Salvador had the highest mobile penetration in the region, 196% and 154%, respectively. Nine other countries in the region, among them Argentina, Brazil, Colombia, Chile, Guatemala, and Honduras, had penetration rates above 100%, indicating that people own more than one mobile line. Most of the growth in the region is coming from low-income segments, who prefer prepaid services; these accounted for more than 80% of the mobile market in 2011(Williams & Wing, 2011). Although voice communication is still the primary service, nonvoice communication and data-based services are growing at a fast pace (e.g., instant messaging, e-mail access, ring tones, and social media).

Internet penetration is moderate at about 50% for the region as a whole, with Internet users in Latin America representing about 8% of the world's users (Powdrill & Hughes, 2012). Brazil and Mexico account for half of the Internet users in the region, with Brazil being the largest market (79 million users). Estimates of Internet penetration in the region range from 24% in Paraguay to 67% in Argentina. Internet penetration is higher among younger consumers and the more affluent class, which are most likely also the first segments to adopt new technologies and set trends. Mobile broadband access is already preferred over fixed broadband access. Mobile broadband subscriptions increased 127% per year between 2007–2011, and are expected to grow 50% annually between 2012–2017. In addition, the use of Internet cafés remains popular, especially among lower-income consumers. Visiting social networking sites and downloading music and videos are the two most common activities, with the time spent on social networking sites, such as Facebook, Hi5, and Sonico, growing three times faster than Internet use overall. In 2011, it was estimated that about 115 million people (96% of the online population) visited a social networking site (Powdrill & Hughes, 2012; TNS Discover, 2010).

According to research conducted by TNS Discover (2010), Latin American consumers have an intimate relationship with their mobile devices, which have allowed them access to the internet at more affordable rates than ever before. Their research also shows that Latin American consumers' needs with respect to functionality and brand perceptions have evolved significantly over the past few years, with the region's consumers preferring strong brands that can provide

Table 4.2 Connectivity in Latin America

Country	Mobile Subscriptions % Penetration 2011/2016*	Broadband Internet % Penetration 2011/2016*	Internet Usage % of Population 2012
Argentina	137	14	67
Bolivia			20
Brazil	116	8.8	39
Chile	132	14	59
Colombia	101	12.6	56
Costa Rica	68 / 114	5.6 / 8.4	43
Ecuador			27
El Salvador	154 / 150	3.3 / 4.9	24
Guatemala	123 / 137	2.0 / 2.7	16
Honduras	116 / 135	0.2 / 0.7	16
Mexico	83	13	37
Nicaragua	68 / 100	1.0 / 1.3	14
Panama	196 / 200	7.4 / 9.0	43
Paraguay			24
Peru	88	4.8	34
Uruguay			56
Venezuela	102	9.8	40
Central America - Avg.	118	50	
South America - Avg.	123		

* Forecast

Sources: Authors' elaboration based on data from Business Monitor International (2012); PRNewswire (2013).

multiple telecommunication resources on a single platform. The low cost of messaging technology (MIM) has been especially relevant in Latin American markets, where 9 out of 10 messages are now sent through mobile devices.

Business users constitute a large market segment. A recent survey by Four Points by Sheraton showed that 45% of Brazilian travelers carry three to four tech devices when traveling, with smartphones and tablets being the most popular devices. While this percentage is lower than that for other countries surveyed (e.g., the United States, Germany, China), it represents a significant market for telecommunication devices. A similar trend is observed in Argentina, Chile, Mexico, and Peru (Chesnut, 2013).

Use of mobile commerce is also growing, at rates ranging from 21% in Argentina to 31% in Mexico and Chile. Mobile banking is by far the largest M-commerce sector, with mobile shopping being a close second (Ericsson, 2013). Sixty-one percent of the population in Latin America is unbanked, and cash is still the primary means of payment. Ability to access formal financial services and improved personal safety are two key benefits of mobile banking, especially for those living in rural areas or zones of high crime incidence. The convenience offered also appeals to younger, more tech-savvy urban consumers who can now handle their regular banking transactions from their smartphones or tablets. Issues related to e-commerce are explored in greater depth in chapter 5.

4.4   Consumption Patterns in Latin American Markets

In this section, we focus on specific consumption patterns of Latin American consumers. We start by providing a profile of Latin American consumers while exploring the current consumer contradictions and value conflicts that are shaping consumers' purchasing preferences and behaviors. We then highlight differences among three country markets: Brazil, Mexico, and Chile.

A Profile of the Latin American Consumer

The typical Latin American consumer is young, urban, family centered, warm, affectionate, traditional, conservative, and religious. Although our earlier discussion identifies a "typical" Latin American consumer on the basis of the convergence of contextual variables in the region, geographic, economic, and cultural differences also indicate we can no longer assume a stereotypical Latin consumer identity, as differences exist between and within regions (Latin Business Chronicle, 2012). For instance, the younger and older generations have diverged in terms of values such as individualism and cultural tolerance. Although Spanish is spoken throughout most of Latin America, the largest market in the region—Brazil—is Portuguese speaking, and indigenous languages are common throughout the region (Mexico has 68; Colombia has 60). Moreover, the region is quite diverse in terms of ethnic and racial composition. For example, Colombia and Brazil have significant population segments of African descent; Brazil (largest outside Japan) and Peru have large populations of Japanese ancestry (Powdrill & Hughes, 2013). Since there is no one single Latin American market, understanding current trends and perceptions of value in Latin American consumer markets will be critical to firms doing business in the region.

Consumer Contradictions and Value Conflicts

Latin American consumers may have changed their lifestyles and consumption in response to the drivers already discussed, but they remain loyal to their traditions and customs. A new set of consumer priorities arises to resolve the potential contradictions between old and new. In this section we identify these contradictions and point to the new values that may emerge.

Individualism and Community Contradictions

Latin American consumers face the dilemma of adopting more individualistic values and keeping some of the traditional ones. This contradiction pits the traditional community-oriented Latin American values of strong relationships (family, neighborhood, and friends) lending support and stability against the individualistic values of self-reliance and empowerment. Family is still at the heart of Latin American culture. Research by TNS Discover (2010) shows that on a scale of 1–10, family is rated at 9, as the most important value in their lives. Latin American consumers are also collectivist oriented (we will discuss cultural values in more detail in chapter 6), which has a direct impact on how consumers make purchasing decisions and shop. For instance, Latin Americans rely heavily on family input and tend to shop as a family unit, more so than people from other cultures. Furthermore, Latin Americans value tradition and are more worried about the loss of their cultural identity than other consumers around the world (60% vs. 56%) (Powdrill & Hughes, 2012).

Yet, Latin Americans are increasingly seeking to express their individuality through customized or personalized products and services—66% of Latin American consumers express this need against 50% globally (Powdrill & Hughes, 2012). More revealingly, the number of persons per household in the region is projected to decline by 18 percent in 2020 (Latin American Herald Tribune, 2013). In Brazil, with economic growth and good job prospects, Brazilians are postponing marriage and household formation. In large urban cities, these single professionals prefer to live alone. These households drive an increase in consumption of ready-to-eat meals and frozen meals, which reached a level of $1.2 billion in 2012 (*Economist,* 2012). This trend is just one indication of the abandonment of the traditional multigenerational family household of the past for the more modern single-household lifestyle. The challenge for firms is to offer more individual-size products that fit the small consumption footprint and preferences of Latin American consumers living alone. As in many other large world cities, neighborhood stores in Latin American cities stay open late to serve these single household customers returning from work or evening school, or typically through small windows to protect them against crime and violence.

Skepticism and Trust Contradictions

Another reality facing Latin American consumers is that they live in an environment characterized by crime, corruption, lack of transparency, and distrust of institutions, including business firms. As mentioned in previous chapters, these conditions have not changed much despite the efforts of certain governments to eradicate corruption and reduce violence. According to Latinobarometro, an opinion poll center for Latin American issues, street violence is the number one concern for Latin Americans. The level of violence is perceived at its highest in Guatemala, El Salvador, Brazil, Mexico, Honduras, Bolivia, Colombia, and Argentina (Latinobarometro, 2012). In addition, Latin American consumers are naturally risk averse and dislike uncertainty. For instance, they are less likely to adopt innovative products with which they are unfamiliar or that they see as unreliable (Ericcson 2013; Latin Business Chronicle, 2012)). Given the widespread distrust of nearly everything, whom do Latin Americans trust? For instance, taxi services are widely used in Latin America, as not everyone owns a car. Safer-Taxi services are on the rise because many Latin Americans have been robbed when they have used a public taxi hailed on the street. Safer-Taxi services offer mobile applications that provide not only the number to call but also the profile of the taxi, a description of the car, and customer opinions of the service (Canigueral, 2012). In the case of advertising claims, Nielsen offers some insight into this challenging question, for when asked to state whom they trusted, both personal sources and commercial information, 92% of Latin Americans placed their trust in people they know. The second most trusted source, branded websites, received 73% support. Other sources ranked lower than 60%, with the least trust placed in ads on social networks (35% of those surveyed) (Nielsen, 2013). It is clear that Latin Americans place greater trust in information coming from family and close friends. This represents a real challenge to business firms, as they have to gain the trust of the group, not just the individual consumer. A further challenge is that this trust and message have to be relevant to group members when they are searching for information—thus the importance of consumer opinions and ratings on public social networks. Clearly, Latin American consumers searching for true and genuine answers rely on their social networks and opinion leaders for advice. TV broadcasts are still an important medium for Latin Americans, for whom the opinion leaders tend to be the entertainment celebrities and/or political commentators. The topic of television advertising will be discussed further in chapter 5.

Fast and Easy or Slow and Complex

The days of slow pace and long lunch breaks are gone in Latin America. The fast pace of modern life places a demand on time and efficiency. With such a hurried and stressful lifestyle, Latin Americans believe it is important to pause and take a deep breath before moving on to the next task. In Latin America, finding the time to slow down and take a pause seems to be a stress reliever. The Latin American culture thrives on socialization and breaking up the day with long meals with families and friends. A casual walk in any of the large Latin American cities reveals cafes and restaurants full of customers in lively conversations at all hours of the day and well into the late evening. The slow pace of the break generates the energy to move to the next task, whether it is shopping or returning to work or home. As noted before, congestion and traffic complicate these short interruptions. In this environment, Latin American consumers are concerned with time saving and shopping efficiency. To compensate for time lost for the break, Latin Americans save time in other, less important transactions such as banking, government services, and home chores. Thus, these transactions are delegated to others, friends and family, or done online so that they can be done outside work hours. Finding an equilibrium between a hurried life and leisure, especially among working women, is key to managing the complex requirements of modern life in urban Latin America (TNS Discover, 2010).

Moreover, urban consumers with long commutes and hectic schedules will seek out convenience and time savings. Mobile banking, for example, appeals to urban, connected professionals who may want to avoid long lines at a bank or handling too much cash. As access to credit, security of online purchases, and penetration of Internet services improve, the convenience of online purchases will appeal more and more to consumers throughout the region.

Passivism versus Activism

With individualism on the increase, incremental prosperity, and the empowerment of new communications technologies, Latin Americans realize that they have the power to make things happen and take control of their lifestyle. These empowered consumers can make a difference in terms of their daily responsible consumption. A number of Latin American cities and local entrepreneurs have introduced responsible collaborative use of services such as public bicycling systems and car sharing. Smart technology and mobile phone penetration enables Latin American consumers to use these services. For instance, a number of carpooling services are very popular in the region, using a variety of names such as Vayamos Juntos in Argentina, En Camino in Chile, Caronetas in Brazil, Pico y Placa in Colombia, Aventones in Mexico, and Voy Contigo in Uruguay (Canigueral, 2012). Whether it is green consumption or sharing rather than owning, Latin American consumers are gradually being converted to the idea that they can have an impact and improve their natural environment and quality of life. This empowerment impact goes beyond consumption to other larger issues such as corruption, unethical behavior, and environmental and social issues. In past decades, such activism was oriented toward issues of abuse of power and absence of democracy. Although the issues have changed, the form and strategies for protest remain very powerful, as demonstrated by Brazilians taking to the streets in 2013 to protest corruption, poor infrastructure, and the high cost of living in their country (Economist, 2013).

In chapter 5 we translate these trends and value contradictions into a set of core and peripheral values that guide consumer purchasing behaviors in the region; we then propose a model for building brands that satisfy those values.

Differences in Consumption Patterns

In this section we highlight differences in consumption patterns by discussing specific consumer behaviors in Brazil, Chile, and Mexico.

Brazil's Consumer Market

Brazil, with a population of 198 million and a 2012 GDP of US$2.5 trillion, is the largest economy in the region. Household consumption in Brazil is estimated to reach R$3.53 trillion in 2020 (about US$1.6 trillion), up by 50% from 2011 (Powdrill & Hughes, 2012). President Rousseff's policies to sustain economic growth will continue to drive strong domestic demand. Brazilians have long been considered the most optimistic consumers and the most active shoppers in Latin America. They also display the strongest need for novelty and new experiences in the region and are much less concerned than other consumers in the region about losing their own values and traditions.

Brazilian consumer purchases of tech devices (e.g., smartphones, tablets) have been on the rise. Brazil is the world's third largest market for computers and the fourth largest for cars. Brazilians are also frequent visitors of shopping malls and are active tourism spenders (e.g., ocean cruises). The more affluent families buy clothes in Miami and take their children to Disneyland on a regular basis. The emerging middle class shows great potential in the area of consumer goods. It is the largest market for Carrefour outside France and the second largest for Nestle (Ogier, 2012). Other sectors that are likely to experience growth include financial services, pharmaceuticals, retailing, housing, construction, and infrastructure.

A 2010 report on Brazilian consumers points out that companies targeting Brazilian middle-class consumers often treat them as poorer versions of more affluent market segments. Middle-class consumers differ from consumers in Classes A and B in many more ways than income levels (Chester, Fox, Gervaz, Reise, & Valls, 2010). As an example, companies found that middle-class consumers can be even more brand loyal than would be expected and that quality is of utmost importance as it is a way to maximize consumers' limited income. Consumers prefer to buy the higher-priced product from a set of comparable products and products that enhance the user's sense of self-esteem and social standing. As such, a "cheap" product is not likely to be successful; instead, adapting a quality product by offering a smaller or simplified version may be a better strategy.

Chile's Consumer Market

Chile has 17 million people and per capita household income of more than US$30,000, the highest in the region. Domestic demand is strong, and continued growth will be supported by investments in mining, energy, and infrastructure. Chile is also the most economically and politically stable country in the region.

Chileans are known for being efficient and hardworking but also conservative and highly risk averse. Chile's private savings rate is 21%; Chileans prefer to save and spend wisely rather than overleverage themselves with mortgages and credit card debt (Kientz, 2011). They also have become more demanding citizens, expecting better governance from the government and showing more concern for the environment and other social issues. The market for organic products, for example, is small, but demand is growing 20% annually, despite the fact that organic products can be 25% more expensive than non-organic products (Herrera, 2010).

Mexico's Consumer Market

Mexico is the second largest market in Latin America, with 120 million people and US$1.2 trillion in GDP in 2012. Mexico's consumer market is less optimistic about the future than Brazil's, but it has been experiencing an enhanced sense of optimism thanks to healthy economic growth. As a result of the country's close geographic and trade links with the United States, Mexican consumers have been more exposed to foreign brands than consumers in other countries in the region, and they tend to be very brand loyal. They consistently rate brand name as more important than price and in times of economic hardship are more likely to cut back on overall spending than to switch to cheaper brands. Mexicans are also very concerned with preserving their own traditions and cultural identity and are likely to respond to products and services that they perceive as culturally appropriate and locally responsive (Powdrill & Hughes, 2013).

4.5 Summary

Latin America has strong economic fundamentals and demographics, with younger populations that are actively expanding their income levels. Social mobility has led to the emergence of a larger middle class and a reduction in poverty across the region. The middle class—which is mostly urban, well educated, and formally employed—will continue to generate domestic market demand and discretionary spending. Consumers are increasingly connected, socially and environmentally aware, and ready to express their values, beliefs, and personalities through their purchases. The sectors poised for the most significant growth include telecommunications, energy, health care, housing, and financial services.

Notes

1. We define purchasing power as net disposable income (i.e., the personal income, after taxes, that an individual has to spend on goods and services).
2. Upper-income or high-net-worth individuals, those with a household per capita income above US$50 per day, represent 2% of the total population.
3. Household purchasing power is defined as the total disposable income for a household (i.e., the net income of all individuals living in a household, after taxes, that is available for purchasing goods and services).

References

Amazon Watch. (2013). *Groups protest World Bank support for destructive dams and fossil fuels.* Retrieved from http://amazonwatch.org/news/2013/1012-groups-protest-world-bank-support-for-destructive-dams-and-fossil-fuels.

Antúñez De Mayolo, C. (2011). *How to formulate value propositions to overlooked low income consumers? Some Latin American experiences.* PAD, Universidad de Piura. Retrieved from http://ink.library.smu.edu.sg/cgi/viewcontent.cgi?article=1009&context=sgbed2011.

Bartolumeu Días, Y., Gonçalves, L., Ibáñez, D., Massunaga, S., & Sawaya, A. (2011). *Creating value through credit card partnerships in Latin America.* McKinsey on Payments.

Business Monitor International. (2012). *Central America telecommunications report Q2 2012. London.* Retrieved from www.businessmonitor.com.

Cadena, A., Remes, J., & Restrepo, A. (2011). Fulfilling the promise of Latin America's cities. *McKinsey Quarterly* (August). Retrieved from www.mckinsey.com.

Cambridge Insight. (2012). *The Latin America consumer market.* Retrieved from www.cambridgeinsight.com/pdf/2013_Latin_America_Consumer_Summary.pdf.

Canigueral, A. (2012). *Collaborative consumption exploding in Latin America*. Retrieved from http://ouishare.net/2012/08/collaborative-economy-explosion-latin-america/.

Chesnut, M. (2013). Road warriors gird up with gadgets. *Latin Trade*. Retrieved from http://latintrade.com/2013/04/road-warriors-gird-up-with-gadgets.

Chester, F., Fox, Z., Gervaz, J., Reise, N., & Valls, A. (2010). The Brazilian consumer: Opportunities and challenges. In *First-hand perspectives on the global economy*, 37–41. Retrieved from http://knowledge.wharton.upenn.edu/special-report/first-hand-perspectives-on-the-global-economy/.

Corpart, G. (2012). The Latin American consumer of 2020. *Americas Market Intelligence*. Retrieved from http://americasmi.com/archivos/pdf/Article_-_LatAm_consumer_2020_-_20120904.pdf.

Dansk Industry. (2007). *Working with the bottom of the pyramid: Success in low-income markets*. Retrieved from www.eclac.cl/publicaciones/xml/4/50844/2013-598_PII-BOOK-WEB.pdf.

Dobbs, R., Smit, S., Remes, J., Manyika, J., Roxburgh, C., & Restrepo, A. (2011), *Urban world: Mapping the economic power of cities*. Retrieved from www.mckinsey.com/mgi

Economist. (2012). The attraction of solitude. Retrieved from www.economist.com/node/21560844.

Economist. (2013). Bubbling anger about high prices, corruption, and poor public services boils over. Retrieved from www.economist.com/news/americas/21579857-bubbling-anger-about-high-prices-corruption-and-poor-public-services-boils-over.

Ericsson Consumer Lab. (2013, June). *M-commerce in Latin America: An Ericsson consumer insight summary report*. Retrieved from www.ericsson.com/res/docs/2013/consumerlab/m-commerce-in-latam.pdf.

Ernst & Young. (2013). *Time to tune in: Latin American companies turn up the volume on global growth*. Retrieved from www.ey.com/latinoamerica.

Ferreira, F.H.G., Messina, J., Rigolini, J., Lopez-Calva, L-F, Lugo, M.A., & Vakis, R. (2013). *Economic mobility and the rise of the Latin American middle class*. Washington, DC: IBRD/The World Bank. Retrieved from www-wds.worldbank.org/external/default/WDSContentServer/WDSP/IB/2012/11/22/000333038_20121122050119/Rendered/PDF/NonAsciiFileName0.pdf.

Galgey, W. (2011, March 1). The Latin American consumer: New opportunities, new challenges. *The Futures Company*. Retrieved from www.wpp.com/~/media/sharedwpp/about%20wpp/what%20we%20do/the%20store/thestore_latamretailforum_the futurescompany_mar11.pdf

Gallup, J. L., Gaviria, A., & Lora, E. (2003). *Is geography destiny? Lessons from Latin America*. Washington, DC: Stanford University Press/The World Bank.

Global Information. (2012). *Mega trends in Latin America*. Retrieved from www.giiresearch.com/report/fs257433-mega-trends-latin-america-html.

Harbo Hansen, N-J., & Sulla, O. (2013). Credit growth in Latin America: Financial development or credit boom? *International Monetary Fund Working Paper*. Retrieved from www.imf.org/external/pubs/ft/wp/2013/wp13106.pdf.

Herrera, M. J. (2010). Chile-Organic products report. *GAIN Report*. Washington, DC: US Department of Agriculture Foreign Agricultural Service.

Huffington Post. (2013). *6 most LGBT-friendly countries in Latin America*. Retrieved from www.huffingtonpost.com/2013/06/03/lgbt-friendly-latin-america_n_3378373.html.

Inter-American Development Bank [IADB]. (2013a). *IDB promotes socially inclusive businesses*. Retrieved from www.iadb.org/en/news/news-releases/2013–06–06/latin-americas-base-of-the-pyramid-market.10474.html.

Inter-American Development Bank. (2013b). *What are the most promising base of the pyramid business models in Latin America?* Retrieved from www.nextbillion.net.

Kenny, C. (2013). Divorce's rise in emerging economies helps women get ahead. *Business Week.* Retrieved from www.businessweek.com/articles/2013-09-05/divorces-rise-in-emerging-economies-helps-women-get-ahead.

Kientz, R. (2011). *Looking for an emerging market? Try Chile on for size.* Retrieved from http://seekingalpha.com/article/297986-looking-for-an-emerging-market-try-chile-on-for-size.

Latin American Herald Tribune (2013). Trend toward smaller families in Latin America. Retrieved from www.laht.com/article.asp?ArticleId=347561&CategoryId=12394.

Latin Business Chronicle. (2012). *LatAm consumers: No easy answers.* Retrieved from http://latinbusinesschronicle.com/app/windows_various/print_news/print_display. aspx?article.

Latinobarometro. (2012). *La seguridad ciudadana, el problema principal de América Latina.* Retrieved from www.latinobarometro.org/latino/LATContenidos.jsp.

Long, G. (2013, April 4). Edging towards developed status. *Latin Trade.* Retrieved from http://latintrade.com/2013/04/edging-towards-developed-status.

McKinsey Global Institute. (2011). *Building globally competitive cities: The key to Latin American growth.* Retrieved from www.mckinsey.com.

Molinski, M. (2012). Tech in Latin America: A consumer-driven market. *Market Watch—The Wall Street Journal.* Retrieved from www.marketwatch.com/story/tech-in-latin-america-a-consumer-driven-market-2012.

National Healthy Marriage Resource Center. (2013). *Marriage trends in Latin America: A fact sheet.* Retrieved from www.healthymarriageinfo.org.

Nielsen. (2013). Global ad spend: 1H global ad spend increases 2.8%, led by Latin America and Asia Pacific. Retrieved from www.nielsen.com/us/en/newswire/2013/global-ad-spend-1H-global-ad-spend-increases-2-8-led-by-latin-am.html.

Ogier, T. (2012). Brazil: Consumer fever and some headache. *Latin Trade.* Retrieved from http://latintrade.com/2012/05/brazil-consumer-fever-and-some-headache.

Ogier, T. (2013). Brazil: Roaring again. *Latin Trade.* Retrieved from http://latintrade. com/2013/05/country-report-brazil.

Population Reference Bureau [PRB]. (2013). *2013 world population data sheet.* Retrieved from www.prb.org/pdf13/2013-population-data-sheet_eng.pdf.

Powdrill, G., & Hughes, C. (2012). The coming decade for Latin America: Belleza del sur. *The Futures Company.* Retrieved from www.wpp.com/~/media/sharedwpp/readingroom/ consumer%20insights/the_futures_company_coming_decade_latin_america_ dec12.pdf.

Price, J. (2013). Credit is king. *Latin Trade.* Retrieved from http://latintrade.com/2013/02/ credit-is-king.

PRNewswire. (2013). *Latin America mobile data, voice, and forecast.* Retrieved from www.prnewswire.com/news-releases/latin-america—mobile-voice-data-and-fore casts-211241761.html.

Subrahmanyan, S., & Gomez-Arias, J. T. (2008). Integrated approach to understanding consumer behavior at bottom of pyramid. *Journal of Consumer Marketing, 25*(7), 402–412.

TNS Discover. (2010). *Changing consumers in Latin America.* Retrieved from http://twit ter.tns-gallup.com.ar/TNS_Discover_LatAm_Book.pdf.

United Nations Development Program & International Labor Organization [UNDP/ILO]. (2009). *Work and family: Towards new forms of reconciliation with social co-responsibility.*

Retrieved from www.ilo.org/wcmsp5/groups/public/@dgreports/@gender/documents/publication/wcms_111375.pdf.

United Nations Economic Commission for Latin America and the Caribbean [ECLAC]. (2013). *Latin America and the Caribbean in the world economy.* Briefing paper. United Nations-ECLAC. Retrieved from www.eclac.cl/publicaciones/xml/4/50844/2013-598_PII-BOOKWEB.pdf.

Vakis, R. (2013). *Economic mobility and the rise of the Latin American middle class.* Washington, DC: International Bank for Reconstruction and Development/The World Bank.

Williams, A., & Wing, L. K. (2011). Latin America's wireless boom. *Latin Trade, 19*(3), 34–39.

World Bank. (2013a). *Latin American and Caribbean overview.* Retrieved from www.worldbank.org/en/region/lac/overview.

World Bank. (2013b). *Latin America and Caribbean.* Retrieved from http://data.worldbank.org/region/latin-america-and-caribbean.

World Resources Institute. (2006). *The market of the majority.* Retrieved from www.wri.org/publication/market-majority.

5 Reaching Latin American Consumers

Introduction

The Latin American consumer in the second decade of the 21st century has moved far from the traditional pattern, becoming more sophisticated, discerning and less frugal. This evolution is the result of increased consumer confidence in the economies of the region and of individual progress. Consumers at the bottom of the pyramid have been lifted economically by social programs and interventions, which have made basic necessities such as education, health, and housing accessible and affordable. Consumers at the top of the pyramid have experienced increased affluence and gains from long periods of economic stability and from the expanding business opportunities of the past decade.

The consumer values that characterized consumers at the end of the 20th century have remained engrained in a generation old enough to remember the economic and political crises of the time (Robles, Haar, & Simon, 2002). These memories, however, are not shared by a generation of younger Latin Americans who came of age in the better economic times of the past decade. As younger generations are typically market trendsetters, new and more optimistic consumer values characterize consumers today and will shape the future of Latin markets. In addition, increased real discretionary income and increased job security make conspicuous consumption the norm. The memories of past crisis, particularly inflation, cast an environment of caution and restraint on spending.

In this chapter we discuss how firms should develop propositions that meet these values and build brands that resonate with these values. We also discuss how firms should position their brands in the marketplace to target particular market segments. Next, we discuss the importance of media in reaching these consumers. We end the chapter with a discussion of two particular channels to reach these markets: grocery retailing and fast-food franchising. We conclude the chapter with a summary of the key concepts.

5.1 Consumer Values in Emerging Latin America

Latin American Consumer Priorities and Values

As Latin American consumers resolve their contradictions and obtain a balance between the old culture and the new, consumer priorities and values emerge.

The new Latin American consumer is more individualistic, better informed, and cautious with money; he or she possesses higher expectations and is concerned with issues such as nutrition, health, social responsibility, and personal safety and security. Some of these issues and values are more important than others, which suggests that Latin American consumers will prioritize and attempt not to compromise on important values. Other values are peripheral, and consumers may be more flexible in finding a consumption solution. We identify the core values next.

Core Values

Emerging "Me" Identity. Individualism, empowerment, and modernism create pressure to seek a strong identity. Because consumers are embedded in their local national milieu, Latin American consumer individualism has generated a variety of local identities that are characterized by the most immediate environment first (the city), country second, and passion for a local activity (soccer, music, or food) third. Thus, we can examine the archetypal Buenos Aires *porteño,* who is a mix of a strong self-image, Argentine pride, fierce loyalties to a favorite soccer team, and a passion for beef or tango. The Rio de Janeiro *carioca* is casual and relaxed, with high priority placed on an aesthetic lifestyle that reflects the beauty of the city and its inhabitants. *Cariocas* are passionate about soccer, music, food, and physical fitness. The *chilango* is the name used for the Mexico City resident who celebrates the cachet of being at the center of the country's political power and cultural dynamism. The *chilango* culture is manifested in a particular style of speech (jargon), trendy fashion style, food consumption, and music and vivid entertainment, such as the masked *luchadores* (wrestlers).

In these examples, Latin Americans find their identity in the context of their national society and search for their identities as individuals, which often involves layers—family and friends, neighborhood, city, and country. These layers can be visualized as concentric circles of varying degrees of influence, with the most immediate at the center. It is difficult to generalize about the identity of the Latin American consumers; thus, a deeper understanding of their local environment is necessary.

Affordability and Liquidity. After suffering the impact of several economic recessions and the slowdown of economic growth after the 2008 global financial crisis, Latin American consumers are concerned with the use of their money. Although such concerns have been omnipresent in Latin America, a more optimistic view of the future in terms of employment and real income gains creates a different approach. With larger incomes and better information, Latin American consumers are looking beyond the basics. Latin American consumers are searching for more value-added choices and more product categories and are very informed and sensitive to the cost-benefits of alternative options. As a result, the traditional assertion of strong loyalty to brands based on familiarity and emotional attachments is vanishing (Balvé, 2012). Increased importance of control over spending is another manifestation of how Latin American consumers are coping with money problems. Careful budgeting and recordkeeping are necessary not only to control expenditures but also to avoid future problems, particularly with transactions with banks and utilities. Having access to money deposits also provides a sense of control. With a lack of trust in financial institutions, Latin American consumers prefer cash transactions to credit. In fact, in many places cash is the only acceptable method of payment and receives a discount.

Easy, Convenient, and Fast. Latin American urban consumers are attaching greater value to time and simplicity as they cope with the demands of busy lifestyles. With these constraints, they are concerned about wasting time and are demanding faster and simple solutions. For instance, payment with cash is simple and transparent and yields savings in terms of discounts from the full price because vendors prefer cash. Payment with credit cards also gives a sense of control but carries the risk of overspending. As such, it is limited to more affluent consumers. Electronic payments and use of smartphone technologies to finalize transactions are still in their infancy but offer a great promise to meet the pressures of Latin American consumers (Ericsson, 2013). A related aspect of this value is time convenience. Consumer time pressures, the urgency of needing to meet deadlines, and the low cost of labor and transportation have created a delivery economy where almost everything can be delivered to where the customer is, whether at home, at work, or even in transit from one place to another.

Honesty, Trust, and Authenticity. Latin American consumers have reached their limit of tolerance for corruption, dishonest behavior, or lack of truth. They can easily distinguish the fake or pirated products from the authentic products. They are demanding greater transparency in transactions and search for genuine products.

Health, Safety, and Security. Concern with personal health has moved Latin American consumers to become more aware of the quality of what they eat and consume. For instance, obesity is on the rise, primarily because of the proliferation of fast-food restaurants and prepackaged foods. In order to combat obesity, Latin Americans are likely to turn to healthier living, which will impact the demand for gym memberships, diet products, and health supplements (Corpart, 2012). Consumers are also dealing with more stress and seek to release this stress by engaging in consumption behaviors that increase their well-being (e.g., spa treatments, yoga). Within a climate of violence, safety and security concerns are becoming important considerations in shopping behavior. Latin American consumers have adapted their strategies to shop for goods and services on the basis of their perception of the safety and security of the retail environment. Well-lit areas and the presence of security guards provide some halo of security. As mentioned, delivery services allow consumers to avoid the risk of going to the vendor as the products are delivered to the home of the consumer. In sum, this priority suggests that Latin American consumers are very cautious and avoid unnecessary personal risks for them and their immediate social network.

Empowerment. Consumer empowerment and the realization that their consumption practices can make a difference and help them to change the world have given Latin American consumers a sense of mission. In the 2012 Global Consumer Monitor poll, Argentina, Brazil, Colombia, and Mexico ranked as the top four countries whose citizens agreed with the statement that one can make a difference to the world through the choices and actions one makes. Furthermore, these four countries ranked higher than world averages on the importance of one's personal life in making the world a better place (Calgey, 2011). Energy and activism have become another important value for Latin American consumers. The promise of more responsible and collaborative consumption emerging from this priority is a positive sign for the region.

Social Connectivity. Latin Americans are extremely social in nature. Large families and a variety of social-group affiliations require good connectivity and nurturing. Digital technology and social media have allowed Latin Americans to keep these large webs of connections. As an example, a study of social media use worldwide reports that 5 Latin American countries are in the top 10 countries in number of hours per month on social networks: Brazil, Argentina, Peru, Mexico, and Chile. Brazilians were at the top of the list, with 13.8 hours, significantly more than the world average of 5.8 hours (Comscore, 2013). These trends will continue to increase in intensity.

Peripheral Consumer Values

Other consumer values are relevant to the consumer in Latin America but are not as influential in consumption preferences as those reviewed in the preceding section. Among these values are quality, prestige, uniqueness, novelty, consumption experience, and globalism.

Some of these consumer values and priorities may become important for particular market segments or unique consumption situations. For instance, it is clear that quality, prestige, and uniqueness will be important for affluent consumers in the same way that globalism may not be relevant to consumers at the base of the pyramid. Another layer of variation is regional differences within a country. For instance, northeastern Brazilians have a different lifestyle from southern Brazilians. The same is true in Mexico, where a northern culture is more attuned with the United States than with the central region.

5.2   Building a Relevant Brand in Latin America

Building a strong brand is the principal challenge for any business strategy anywhere. Brands are valuable assets, and firms invest in building their reputation and maintaining it once they are established in the marketplace. The challenge for firms is to build brands that resonate with Latin Americans' values and help consumers achieve their personal goals. Furthermore, in this period of optimism and confidence, brands should celebrate a Latin American country's developmental progress. The brand message should also reassure Latin American consumers of the firm's commitment and compromise to serve their needs in the long term. These general brand-building principles are difficult to implement in practice. A good start, however, is to build a brand strategy that integrates some if not all of the consumer priorities that we have reviewed and that meets the particular consumer needs in the market category in which the brand participates. To summarize, these values are:

1.   Strong identity, optimism, and confidence
2.   Trust, transparency, honesty, and authenticity
3.   Easy, convenient, and fast
4.   Value-to-price and liquidity
5.   Safety and security
6.   Empowerment to tackle the large social issues
7.   Connectivity

It is a challenge for any brand today to address all of these issues and to claim market superiority on the delivery of the brand. In addition, finding the architecture to deliver promises is the role of many parts of any organization. For instance, organizational credibility may be responsible for addressing the values of consumer trust, honesty, and transparency, whereas a product strategy provides reassurance of claims of authenticity.

A Brand Architecture for Latin America

A systematic brand strategy is therefore a carefully orchestrated effort to develop a brand architecture that supports the goal of creating economic value, and relevance and that resonates with the Latin American consumer. This architecture is deconstructed into several brand-building block efforts in Figure 5.1.

The first building block is the brand salience. This effort establishes the brand identity and initiates engagement with the Latin American consumer. A well-orchestrated communications strategy is the approach to reach this goal. The second building block is brand meaning. The effort here is to establish credibility and to showcase the benefits of the marketing offer in the Latin American marketplace. One part of this effort appeals to the rational side of the Latin American consumer. For consumer goods, communicating and demonstrating the product benefits in many different ways are at the center of this effort. In addition, the benefit-to-cost argument is essential way to address the fourth consumer priority, value-to-price. A second component of the second building block is to create a brand personality that appeals to the emotional side of the Latin American consumer. The effort here is to bring out the heritage, history, and character of the brand and/or the firm to showcase the warmth and feelings intrinsic to the

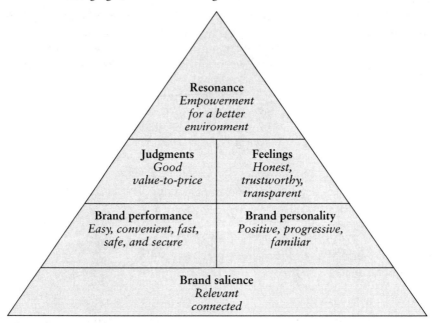

Figure 5.1 Latin America Brand Architecture

Source: Adapted from Keller (2012).

brand experience. For instance, the Coca-Cola slogan "Open Happiness" after the 2008 global financial crises resonated very well with the optimism and consumer confidence in Latin America (*Wall Street Journal,* 2009).

The third building block moves the consumer to make the brand the preferred choice. This is accomplished through brand comparisons with alternative choices that demonstrate the superiority of the brand's functional performance and relevance to important consumer priorities, as well as clearly demonstrating the price-to-value ratio. This part of the strategy communicates the firm's capabilities and competencies that support the brand's performance. A second component of this building block is the effort to seek an emotional response and connection with the Latin American consumer. Here, the firm seeks a positive emotional response and positive feelings that lead to brand loyalty and alignment with the personal lifestyle of the Latin American consumer.

The final building block is brand resonance. Here, the effort is to address the more altruistic aspirations and the larger social and environmental concerns of Latin American consumers. This effort particularly addresses the second priority, Latin American consumers' lack of trust due to endemic corruption and opacity and also their concerns about the environment and social issues. Such effort requires corporate commitment to undertake credible actions that regain consumer trust and addresses the environmental concerns.

Establishing an integrated brand strategy in Latin America is a challenge. For non-Latin American multinationals, the Latin American brand strategy is an extension of their global brand strategy that is localized to the region and country while keeping some of the integrity of the global platform. For companies from the region, the brand strategy can extend beyond the country of origin of the corporation without a loss of national identity. For instance, the LAN airline brand is recognized and established throughout Latin America, but travelers associate the brand with its Chilean roots. Strong Latin American national brands, on the other hand, focus exclusively on gaining the trust of consumers within their country.

The brand strategies that resonate most with Latin American consumers become icons in their marketplaces as consumers show their admiration and appreciation in many different ways. Havas, one of the world's largest communications corporations, based in Paris, performed a global survey of the 20 most meaningful brands in Latin America. The results are shown in Table 5.1 (HavasMedia, 2013).

It is interesting to note that most of the brands are from the consumer-food categories, suggesting how important food consumption is in Latin America. Among this list, the French multinational Danone registers 4 of the top 20 entries. Danone as a group and brand is recognized as the most meaningful

Table 5.1 Top Meaningful Brands in Latin America

Rank	Brand	Sector	Country
1	Colun	Energy	Chile
2	Danone	Consumer Foods	Brazil
3	Tetra Pak	Packaging	Mexico
4	Bimbo	Confectionery	Mexico
5	Carozzi	Confectionery	Chile
6	Nestle	Consumer Foods	Chile
7	Iansa	Sugar	Chile
8	Soprole	Dairy Products	Chile
9	Coca-Cola	Beverages	Brazil
10	Jumex	Fruit juices	Mexico
11	Nike	Sporting goods	Mexico
12	La Costena	Consumer foods	Mexico
13	Del Valle	Fruit juices	Brazil
14	Danone	Consumer Foods	Mexico
15	Petrobras	Oil	Brazil
16	La Serenisima	Dairy products	Argentina
17	Nestle	Consumer Foods	Mexico
18	Coca-Cola	Beverages	Chile
19	Natura	Cosmetics	Brazil
20	Bonafont	Water	Mexico

Source: HavasMedia (2013).

brand in Brazil and the sixth most important in Mexico. In addition, Danone's Bonafont water brand is also recognized in Mexico. Furthermore, Danone shares consumer appreciation with its joint venture with La Serenisima in Argentina. For this reason, we analyze the brand strategy architecture of Danone Brazil, with a special emphasis on its successful water brand, Bonafont.

A Case Study of Building a Brand: Bonafont

Danone Brazil. Brazil is a key country market for the French corporation and accounts for a quarter of the group's global revenues. With a long presence in Brazil since 1970, Bonafont produces dairy products under the Actimel, Activia, Densia, Paulista, Danito, and Danone brand names, water under the Bonafont brand name, infant nutrition under the Aptamil brand name, and general nutrition products under the Nutricia brand name. The company has established a strong corporate presence and in 2012 gained a respectable 38% market share in the fresh-dairy-products market and 39% of the nutrition-market segment (Danone, 2012).

One reason for Danone's success in Brazil is its emphasis on developing new products that appeal to the Brazilian consumer. In 2012, Danone introduced 18 new Activia flavors that Brazilians appreciate, such as passion fruit and morango (strawberries).

The children's market is another important segment where Danone offers a number of options under the Danoninho brand name. Beyond product consumption, Danone also focuses on infant nutrition and celebrates the triumphs of disadvantaged children. For instance, Danone tells a story ("Danone conta uma historia"), recounting tales of hospitalized infant patients and their happy moments in their delicate situation.

To keep prices attractive, Danone puts a lot of emphasis on productivity increases. The company reported an increase of 50% in productivity in the Activia line in Brazil in 2008. To make this product affordable, Activia is available in at least three different size formats, from individual to family servings.

A global study by Havas of top meaningful brands identified Danone as the top brand in Brazil. A meaningful brand was defined as one that makes a difference in consumers' lives. The study revealed that 76% of Brazilians agree that brands play an important role in their quality of life and well-being. The study also found that 6% of Brazilians consider the impact of a brand on the environment when they decide to buy. About 45% of Brazilians also think that brands communicate honestly about their commitments and promises, and 50% trust their brands. In contrast, only 36% of average Latin Americans trusted their brands (HavasMedia, 2013).

In this environment of trust and environmental concern, how does Danone score at the top of meaningful brands among Brazilians? The Danone-Bonafont bottled-water brand in Brazil tells the story of well-orchestrated brand architecture.

Bonafont Bottled Water. The Bonafont case is particularly important as it is an example of a regional brand owned by a global multinational. The brand was first introduced in Mexico in 1992 by Mexican private investors with major market success. Danone acquired the brand in 1996 and kept the brand slogan of "agua ligera," or light water. The brand icon is a stylized figure of a slender and fit person. In Mexico, Bonafont is available in three formulations. Under the Bonafont brand name, Danone offers natural water and carbonated water. Under the Levité brand name, the company offers a variety of naturally flavored bottled water. Natural water comes in two options: individual clear plastic bottles and a large water jug for home consumption, which is distributed directly to homes and small vendors.

In 2008, Danone introduced the brand in Brazil, replicating the Mexico marketing strategy and slogan: "agua leve," or light water. The Brazilian water market offers great market potential, as water consumption is low, 52 liters per capita per year, compared to 145 in Mexico.

A commodity market with very low participation in the general Brazilian beverages market, which is dominated by carbonated soft drinks, this category received little attention in terms of investment in advertising and store shelf space. With the state of Sao Paulo accounting for 40% of market, Danone launched a replication of the Mexican market approach of offering both individual bottles of water and residential delivery of water in large jugs. The market performance has been extremely successful, with a 55% CAGR from 2008 to 2012 (Danone, 2013).

Bonafont Brand Architecture in Brazil. The target segment for Bonafont is the very active, pressured, and multitasking Brazilian woman between 28 and 34 years old who does not have much time to take care of herself. As a result, this target group faces a conflict between the need to show professional success by being fit and well presented and the lack of time required to achieve a balanced life. The outcome of this conflict for Brazilian women is on the one hand the awareness that long days of work are taxing their health through the accumulation of toxins and on the other hand the emotional demand that they be at their best in front of family, friends, and coworkers. Thus, Bonafont's basic argument is that water is a purifier of toxins as a cleanser of the internal body system. Since the quality and safety of public water systems are suspect, purified water such as Bonafont provides the appeal of purity and convenience. In particular, Bonafont argues that its water is light on other components such as minerals or additives. In addition, a water break is perceived to be like a pause in a busy day of activities and may relieve stress. With these two arguments, Bonafont addresses the second brand building block, the rational benefit of elimination of toxins and the emotional one of regaining control of a stressful day and feeling well.

The third building block is about gaining preference and relating to the human side of the consumer. Facing a commodity market in Brazil where water is frequently not branded, Bonafont has the advantage of the name, the

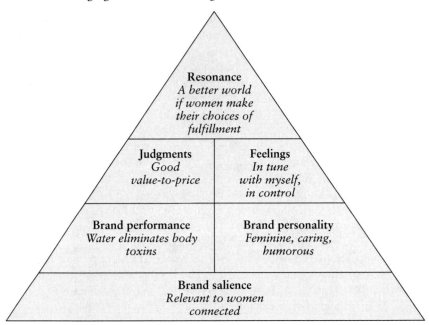

Figure 5.2 Bonafont Bottled Water—Brazilian Brand Architecture
Source: Authors' elaboration.

association with Danone, and a clear, distinctive package. In addition, its home delivery system offers the convenience of having water at home and in a personal package. The personality side of the brand is accomplished by appealing to the feminine values of intuition and concern for external beauty and health among Brazilian women. In addition, Bonafont promotes a brand that is positive and energetic.

The last building block appeals to the most altruistic values of consumers. In this case, Bonafont makes it clear that one is at her best when she is honest and confronts the dilemmas in life and appreciates the value of a water break during the day to reflect on larger problems. To capture this moment, Bonafont concludes its advertising with a statement that the world could be better if women could make independent decisions to feel fulfilled and free of social pressures.

5.3 Latin American Media Patterns

Media Penetration

Old media have achieved a high level of penetration in Latin America. As Table 5.2 shows, free TV, out-of-home (media such as outdoor advertising that reaches consumers while in transit or waiting), and radio are the key universal

Table 5.2 Media Use and Penetration in Latin America (% of households)

Country	Free TV	Pay TV	Time of TV Watching Per Day*	Radio	Newspapers	Magazines	Out-of-Home	Internet	Time Spent Online (hours/month)**	Time Spent in Social Media (hours/month)**	Total Broadband (Mobile & Fixed)	Social Media % of Population**
Argentina	95	71	6 hs	68	43	21	91	54	24.1	10.2	16	41.7
Brazil	97	35	2 hs 51 min	76	34	40	86	44	35.6	13.8	14	37.7
Chile	99	60	3 hs 51 min	73	48	35	90	64	19.5	7.2	17	
Colombia	94	78	4 hs	68	39	32	91	63	26.7		8	
Costa Rica	97	58		77	81	13	94	41	18.9			
Ecuador	98	24		86	65	41	99	55			7	
Mexico	97	36	2 hs 33 min	54	27	27	98	48	18.8	7.3	15	34.1
Panama	94	50		62	69	12	70	51				
Peru	98	64	3 hs 20 min	84	69	23	100	60	21.5	8.3	4	
LatAm									26.1			33.3

Sources: * Latin Link (2013); ** Comscore (2013).

media channels. These old media channels have always been popular ways to reach Latin American consumers. Watching TV stills attracts the Latin American household, as the number of hours in front of the large screen indicates. Argentines watch 6 hours of TV every day, which is significantly more than the world average of 3 hours and 12 minutes (Latin Link, 2013). Colombians, Chileans, and Peruvians are not far behind with 3 to 4 hours of daily watching. Pay TV is still limited by affordability but reaches 78% of Colombian households and 71% of Argentine households. Radio is also important, particularly for Latin Americans on the go during the day; they listen to radio stations for the latest news and music entertainment. Print is less preferred but is still a strong medium, as newspapers in the region remain economically viable and have experienced modest increases in circulation of 1.8% in Brazil in 2012 and about 10% in Peru (US Media Consulting, 2013). Peru represents the average growth between 2007 and 2012.

New media penetration is growing steady and surpassing some of the traditional media levels. The Internet has reached more than 50% of the population in Latin America, with Chile and Colombia leading the pack. Latin Americans seem to be quite engaged with the Internet with the number of hours per month spent online ranging from 18.7 hours in Peru to 26.7 hours in Colombia and Mexico; the average for the region was 24 hours.

As we discussed in chapter 4, connectivity in the region is on the rise. Mobile subscriptions have already surpassed the 100% penetration mark in most countries, with the 2012 average for the region at 112%. Mobile penetration is particularly strong in Argentina, Brazil, Chile, Uruguay, El Salvador, and Panama (PRNewswire, 2013). The penetration of smartphones, although relatively small at this time, is showing the way of the future. In Mexico, 20% of all mobile devices are smartphones; in Colombia 22% are. Broadband connections are another indicator that homes will be increasingly wired and have access to rich media content such as movies and games. Chile, Mexico, and Brazil lead the region with 17%, 15%, and 14% broadband penetration, respectively.

Following worldwide trends, social media participation is on the increase in the region. Latin Americans spent 28% of their total time online on social media sites (US Media Consulting, 2013). Argentina leads the way with the highest rate of usage among Internet users, with 41.7% of Internet users in social media sites and 15% of the population active on Twitter. Brazil and Mexico followed with 37.7% and 34.1%, respectively (eMarketer, 2012). In 2013, Facebook was the number one destination for social media in the region, with a total of 179 million accounts, and it is estimated that it would have a penetration of 70% among all Internet users in 2014. Of these, 60 million accounts were in Brazil, which makes this country the second largest Facebook population in the world. Other Latin American countries are also among the largest Facebook user populations in the world: 32.7 million in Mexico and 16.3 million in Argentina (eMarketer, 2012).

Social media are an important influence on purchase decisions in Latin America. As one report mentions, 62% of users indicate that comments on social media influence their shopping decisions, 59% use social media to find product information, and 37% follow brands on these sites (US Media Consulting, 2013).

Reaching Latin American consumers, whether through old or new media, requires a financial commitment and investment by firms. Next, we analyze the patterns of advertising expenditures on the different media channels and by country to observe how firms make their media mix decisions.

Advertising Expenditures

At a time when the rest of the world is experiencing modest growth in advertising expenditures due to slow economic growth and budget crises, Latin America is the number one region in increase in advertising expenditures. In the first half of 2013, advertising expenditures in the region grew by 13.1% over the same period the previous year to reach $13.5 billion, a contrast to the 3.5% growth worldwide. In 2012, advertising expenditures grew at the rate of 19.6% after a record growth of 31.6% in 2011 (Nielsen, 2013). In the same year, 2012, advertising expenditures in Brazil grew 10.7% and were expected to easily reach $22.2 billion in 2014, making this country the fifth largest media market worldwide (US Media Consulting, 2013). In general, the region has been experiencing strong growth in media expenditures.

The breakdown of these expenditures by media reveals how companies in Latin America split their communications investments across media channels. Table 5.3 shows the statistics for a selected group of countries. TV advertising receives the bulk of media expenditures in the region, with close to 50% of the total media budget. Pay TV is receiving increasing attention, but its potential will be realized as more homes subscribe to this media channel in the region. Currently, pay TV reaches about 50% of all homes in Latin America. In some markets, such as Brazil, pay TV is expected to reach 90% of homes in 2018 (US Media Consulting, 2013).

Table 5.3 Allocation of Advertising Expenditures by Media Channels in Latin America

Country	Free TV	Pay TV	Newspapers	Magazines	Radio	Out-of-Home	Cinema	Internet	Other
Argentina	37.4	9.4	35	4.8	3.2	5.0	1.3	6.1	
Brazil	63	4.0	11.8	7.1	3.0	3.0	0.3	5.1	1.1
Chile	44.9	4.6	26.6	1.9	6.8	8.6	0.3	6.2	
Mexico	56	6.0	7.0		8.0	8.0	48	8.0	
Peru	49.7		16.5		12.1			3.5	
Venezuela	26.9	5.6	23.5	5.6	10.2	8.5		6.0	14.3

Source: US Media Consulting (2013).

Print is the second media channel of importance in Latin America and remains a viable channel of engagement with Latin American consumers. As mentioned before, newspaper circulation is increasing, and advertising expenditures in this media channel reflect the importance of this source of information for Latin Americans. According to World Press Trends, newspaper circulation in Latin America grew 9.1% and advertising expenditures by 37.6% from 2008 to 2012. This growth is in contrast to a contraction in newspaper circulation of 13% in North America and a corresponding decrease of 23.3% in advertising expenditures (World Press Trends, 2013).

The Internet is clearly the media channel with the most potential. As Table 5.3 indicates, companies in Latin American are allocating between 3% and 8% of their media budgets to the Internet and are expected to increase this to 15% by 2016 (eMarketer, 2013a). With an estimated audience of 255 million and reaching 48.2% of Latin America's population in 2012, firms cannot ignore this significant audience (Internet World Stats, 2013). As mentioned before, Latin Americans also trust this source and especially social media, which is another reason to expect increasing expenditures for this media channel in the future. The majority of the Internet advertising budget is for display advertising, as indicated in Table 5.4. This form of textual online advertising is as high as 70% of total online advertising expenditures in Colombia and 61% in Mexico. Search advertising is important in Brazil and Peru. As Internet use of rich media increases with broadband penetration, one would expect greater expenditures on mobile, video, and social media. In fact, Argentina is already there. In a survey of online video viewing worldwide, Argentina ranks as the number one country with 95.6% video reach among its internet users (eMarketer, 2012). Chile was not far behind with the third largest penetration (91.4%), and Brazil numbered eighth with 87.8%. Similarly, increased penetration of smartphones in the region will drive more expenditure in mobile advertising. In 2013, mobile advertising accounted for only 3.7% of all Internet advertising in Latin America, with Mexico leading the region with 10.3%. About 67% of those ads were delivered to smartphones in the region and 74% in Mexico (eMarketer, 2013b). Thus, Latin America is not far behind advanced countries when it comes to digital advertising.

Table 5.4 Allocation of Online Advertising by Type (%)

Country	Display	Search	Classified	Social Media	Video	Mobile	E-mail	Other
Brazil	42	55		5				
Chile	51	49						
Colombia	70	17		8	2.5	1.16	1.07	
Mexico	61	28	12					
Peru	53	47						
Uruguay	36	35.6				3	3	24

Source: US Media Consulting (2013).

In sum, communicating with Latin American consumers is based on a mix of old and new media approaches. The use of old media channels such as TV and print advertising is still very important; new media and particularly digital are growing in use and importance. After establishing brand salience, firms turn to deliver the product through a mix of retail channels, including e-commerce. Next, we analyze the retailing structure of Latin America.

5.4 Retailing in Latin America

Retailing provides the platform where Latin American consumers fulfill their needs and exercise their values. The current retail platforms in the region are a mix of traditional and modern and are continuously evolving and expanding to match the evolving lifestyles, values and pressures of Latin American consumers. New retail technology has also opened up alternative channels not only to shop but also to engage customers before, during and after their shopping visit. As the region is largely urbanized, most of the modern retail expansion has taken place in the largest metropolitan areas but they are not gradually reaching the secondary and tertiary cities in most countries in the region. In the midst of these changes, traditional places such as small convenience stores close to home in neighborhoods and fresh open markets are still vibrant and viable.

Latin American Retail Market Attractiveness

The Latin American region has become one of the most attractive retail markets in the world because of a combination of factors that propel an expansion of retail investments and growth. Among the favorable factors, one can mention a large concentration of urban middle-class markets, increasing real disposable income, expansion of consumer credit, improved consumer confidence, and large untapped markets in secondary cities. Latin America is the most urbanized region in the world, with more than 80% of the population living in cities (UN Habitat, 2012). According to McKinsey's Global Institute, the region has 198 large cities with populations of 200,000 or more, which account for 60% of the region's GDP. Furthermore, the 10 largest cities in this group account for 50% of the output (McKinsey Global Institute, 2011). Take, for instance, one of the largest metropolises in the region: Mexico City, which has a massive concentrated market of 22 million people, including 2 million households with an annual income of $100,000 or more. Mexico City is a market magnet for all type of retailing, but future growth potential lies in the 25 Mexican cities with populations of 500, 000 people or more (Business Monitor International, 2013a).

A. T. Kearney ranks the top retail world markets and produces a Global Retail Development Index (GRDI) that is based on retail market attractiveness and other factors such as market saturation and investment risks. In 2013, 7 out of 30 top global retail development markets were in Latin America (see Table 5.5). According to the GRDI, Brazil, Chile, and Uruguay were ranked the number

Table 5.5 Top Latin American Attractive Retail Markets

Country	Global Rank	GRDI Score	Market Attractiveness	Market Saturation	Urgency To Enter	Retail Investment Risk
Brazil	1	69.5	100	45.3	48.3	86.2
Chile	2	67.1	95.6	18.7	54.3	100
Uruguay	3	66.5	92	63.5	36.5	73.9
Peru	12	56.5	52.9	63.4	49.3	60.4
Colombia	18	52.1	59.2	43	32.4	73.6
Mexico	21	49.2	79	12.1	30.6	75
Panama	22	48.7	49.7	37.2	37.2	70.8

Source: A. T. Kearney (2013).

one, two, and three most attractive retail markets in the world (A. T. Kearney, 2013). The second tier of Latin American retail markets includes Peru (12), Mexico (21), and Panama (22). According to this report, Mexico is the most mature retail market in the region, where consumer spending has expanded significantly and competition is more sophisticated. Brazil is peaking in retail development, and consumers are seeking modern retail formats and greater connection with global consumer trends. Peru is starting its peak period; the middle class is expanding and exploring more modern retail formats. With such a number of attractive retail markets, the retail industry is not only expanding in reach and number of outlets but also going experiencing consolidation and innovation. Thus, Latin American consumers are enjoying greater attention and improved offerings and retail services. It is in this context that consumers have to align their consumer and shopping values. The shopping trade-offs of this balancing result in a preferred retail brand and format options. We explore the shopping values of Latin American consumers next.

Latin American Consumer Shopping Values

Early in the chapter, we identified seven consumer priorities or values. These priorities translate into shopping values and expectations. Table 5.6 shows the translation and provides a short explanation of shopping values. The search for strong identity and confidence opens a realm of purchasing possibilities and expectations. With more discretionary income and confidence, Latin American consumers expect to have a good and satisfactory purchase experience. They seem to be entitled to have access to any option to buy from any vendor. This gained confidence translates into expectations of respect, attention, assistance with the purchase, and some degree of buying comfort, rather than being pressured. Latin American shoppers pay attention to cues such as the store ambiance and location and the staff to determine whether there is an affiliation with their status. The second value, trust, transparency, honesty and authenticity

Table 5.6 From Consumer to Shopping Values

Purchasing Proximity	Consumer Values	Shopping Values	Value Description	Expected Shopping Benefits
Emotional Proximity	Identity, Optimism, and Confidence (Social Inclusion)	Purchase experience: Do I belong here?	You deserve a good experience and to be treated well.	Respect, attention, assistance, buying comfort; store ambiance Affiliation with staff and shopping customers
	Trust, Transparency, Honesty, and Authenticity	Vendor trust	Do I trust this retailer?	Satisfactory history of purchasing experiences Credibility of promotions and prices
	Empowerment	Make a difference	Live a better life	Environmentally friendly product choices Recycling options Store support of neighborhood
Rational Proximity	Value-to-Price and Liquidity	Affordability	Can I afford to buy this item? Do not make a buying mistake.	Product quality Credit availability Purchase plans tailored to income possibilities Price discounts with cash purchases
	Safety and Security	Protect yourself and assets	Do not be exposed to personal risks.	Product quality Store location Store cleanliness and hygiene Use of security guards Delivery services
Transaction Proximity	Simple, Convenient, Fast	Practicality and efficiency	Use my shopping time efficiently.	Familiarity with store layout or services Assortment and product mix Store location and proximity to other stores and public transportation Store hours Delivery services
	Connectivity	Engaged at all stages	Be informed and leverage your technology	Take control and plan your purchases

Source: Authors' elaboration.

can easily translate into vendor trust. A history of satisfactory experiences will gain trust, as will credible promotions and prices that seem to be fair. The third consumer value, simplicity, convenience, and speed, translates into a shopping strategy that favors practicality and efficiency. Location, store hours, and proximity to public transportation and delivery services are important considerations. The consumer priority of value and liquidity correlates with affordability and buying risk. As discussed before, affordability and buying restraint are still dominant values, and consumers tend to spend within the confines of their budget and their liquidity in terms of cash or credit on hand. The majority of Latin American consumers spread their purchases over payment installments that match their cash flows and cycles of wage income. For these reasons, Latin American consumers consider store-based customer credit and payment flexibility even for the most common purchases. Having liquidity and cash on hand can also bring price discounts from retailers that wish to reduce their credit financing costs. Safety and security are very important shopping considerations. The store location is a key factor. The degree of personal security and cleanliness of the store are personal safety cues, as is the presence of private security guards at the entrance. The consumer value of empowerment relates to the shift of control over how the shopper may exercise his or her buying power to contribute to society and at the same time observe the retailer's practices and commitment to this end. Retail practices that encourage sustainable consumption such as returnable bottles or reduced packaging, the availability of environmentally friendly products, and the support of small producers are all indications that reassure consumers. Finally, technology has made an impact on both retailers and consumers. Modern retailers in Latin America in particular are investing in technology to offer a better experience, lower costs, and attract shoppers. Retail credit cards, store loyalty programs, and scanning technology are giving Latin American retailers a wealth of information about their customers. In turn, with large penetration of mobile phones, customers are using this technology to their advantage and accessing better promotions and sophisticated information about new product introductions and exclusive promotions.

Retail Strategies and Formats in Latin America

A retail strategy in Latin America needs to address the shopping values explained earlier. For such a strategy, retailers may start with a value proposition that captures their positioning, targeting, and differentiation strategy to attract desirable customers to their store. This value proposition allows the retailer to close the gaps in what the customer expects from their shopping experience. In Table 5.7, we cluster the Latin American shopper expectations in three dimensions of distance between the retailers and the customer: rational, emotional, and transactional proximities. Using their expertise, technology, and resources, organized retailers will identify how many and which of these proximity gaps they would like to close and how (format strategy). For instance, Walmart in Latin America has been successful in closing the rational and proximity gaps with a replication of its global value proposition of "save money, live better" with its traditional large discount-store formats. Walmart in Latin America also tries to get closer to the customer through its small neighborhood and express store formats, using the Aurrera Express name in Mexico. Walmart is also enhancing the transaction proximity with a push to expand its global e-commerce Latin America unit with a strong presence in Argentina, Mexico, and Chile (Internet Retailer, 2013).

The more strategic components of a Latin American retail strategy include decisions with respect to retail format, service level and store ambiance, product mix, store size, retail credit, locations, and use of retail technology, among others that are identified in Table 5.7. Some of them are easy to implement and have become almost universal features among retailers in Latin America, such as home delivery services. Differentiation based on delivery service is not possible as Latin American customers expect to receive this benefit for free.

As part of their strategy, Latin American retailers need to choose between targeted strategies and more mass-market approaches. A targeted strategy is more effective as retailers may develop a more focused strategy and offer benefits that their target segments value the most. At the core of this targeted strategy is the way consumers develop their shopping priorities as they have to make trade-offs among the diverse benefits they expect from their shopping experience and leverage their buying power. These trade-offs depend on the purchase category and urgency, as well as the type of customer. For instance, Latin American consumers prefer to purchase food in small quantities and from small vendors where they can choose the product for freshness and even bargain over the price. This shopping strategy favors the small independent neighborhood store. For more durable and hard goods, they prefer a more organized retailer among the variety of modern retail formats. On the other hand, affluent Latin American consumers are more likely to patronize stores on the basis of location, perception of quality of the products and services, and store ambiance. Low-income consumers may look at affordability, credit availability, and payment flexibility. For instance, two retailers that have focused on the low-income shopper with success are Casas Bahia in Brazil and Elektra in Mexico. Both retailers focus on a narrow category of home appliances at low cost. As appliances are high-ticket items for low-income consumers, these retailers offer retail credit that allows low payments over a long period of time and a sound collection system that resolves payment issues to enable customers to meet their payment obligations (Booz & Co., 2006). Walmart is also developing a special format for the low-income segment in Argentina. Under the Chango Mas name, Walmart is focusing on the low-income suburban areas of Buenos Aires and the interior and building stores that offer groceries at very affordable prices, even lower than those at their hypermarkets (Euromonitor, 2013).

Next we turn our attention to the structure of retail in Latin America. As there are many types of retailers, we focus on the category of mass grocery retailing. Latin Americans expend about 50% of household income on food,

Table 5.7 Retail Strategy for Latin America

Purchasing Proximity	Shopping Values	Customer Shopping Benefits	Retail Strategy	Strategic components
Emotional Proximity	Purchase experience	Respect, attention, assistance, buying comfort; store ambiance. Affiliation with staff and shopping customers	Service level and shopping climate	Store value image: Nice and trendy. Ambiance comfort. Staff attitude. Staff profile recruited from same social experience or neighborhood
	Vendor trust	Satisfactory history of purchasing experiences. Credibility of promotions and prices	Value proposition	Experience guarantees. Extended warranties. Return policies
	Make a difference	Environmentally friendly product choices. Recycling options. Store support of neighborhood	Social and environmental policies and practices	Community involvement. Environmental practices
Rational Proximity	Affordability	Product quality. Credit availability. Purchase plans tailored to income possibilities. Price discounts with cash purchases	Retail format and value positioning	Product mix and assortment. Store size. Price and quality positioning. Private-labels offerings. Promotion and cash discounts. Retail credit availability. Loyalty and rewards programs

Purchase protection: Yourself and assets	Product quality Store location Store cleanliness and hygiene Use of security guards Delivery services	Cleanliness and customer safety	Product handling and display Extended warranties Returns policies Use of security guards
Transaction Proximity Practicality and efficiency	Familiarity with store layout or services Assortment and product mix Store location and proximity to other stores and public transportation Store hours Delivery services	Convenience: Bring the store to the customer	Location Extended hours Shopping services Ordering and delivery services Self-service and payment
Engaged at all stages	Take control and plan your purchases	Use of tetail IT	Engagement strategy before, during, and after shopping Online shopping Shopping assistance Services connectivity

Source: Authors' elaboration.

and this category is the most important in terms of revenues and number of retail outlets.

Retail Structure and Competition

The Latin American retail market recovered quickly after the 2008 global financial crisis, and a number of countries outside the Mexico cluster experienced double-digit growth rates. In recent years, the retail markets have been growing at more moderate growth rates of 2% to 6%, reaching the level of $1.3 trillion in 2013 (Latin American Retail Connection [Laretco], 2013; Standard & Poors, 2013). The exception to this trend is Chile, which grew at 10.2% in the first quarter of 2013.

Four countries in Latin America accounted for 74% of total retail sales in 2013: Brazil, Venezuela, Mexico, and Colombia (see Table 5.8). Brazil is by far the largest retail market in the region, with 34% of the region's total. Other countries, however, exhibit higher levels of retail penetration of the total economy and retail sales per capita. The retail sector in Colombia, Peru, and Chile represents the largest share of GDP, an indication of how important this sector is for their economies. In retail sales per capita, Venezuela is the number one market, with $5,793 in 2013, followed by Chile with $3,264 and Colombia with $2,924. It is interesting to note that on per capita basis, Argentina is very far from the rest of the other countries, as seen in Table 5.8. With Argentina the third largest economy in the region, the retail sector seems to offer room to increase in potential.

Latin Americans expend a great deal of money on food, and the retail sector is a reflection of this pattern. About 50% of total retail sales are accounted by organized food retailers (Canadian International Markets Bureau, 2012).We

Table 5.8 Latin American Retail Sales (US$ Billions)

Country	2010	2011	2012	2013	Annual Growth 2012/ 2013	% of Regional Sales	Retail Sales as % of GDP	Retail Sales per capita
Argentina	19.6	21.2	22.9	24.5	7	2.1	2.7	591
Brazil	354.0	407.4	443.0	493.5	11.4	43	19.1	2,467
Chile	49.7	51.8	53.4	54.7	2.4	4.8	21.5	3,264
Colombia	108.1	122.1	130.6	139.9	7.2	12.2	39.8	2,924
Mexico	185.8	200.2	194.1	214.6	10.5	18.7	15.8	1,827
Peru	35.6	39.0	42.1	45.5	8.1	4.0	23.6	1,527
Venezuela	91.0	117.4	141.1	175.8	24.5	15.2	18.1	5,793
Total	844.1	959.1	1,027.3	1,114.6	8.4	100		
Regional Annual Growth Rate	6.3	13.6	7.1	8.4				

Source: Business Monitor International (2013).

Table 5.9 Latin American Mass Grocery Retail Sales by Channel (US$ Billions)

Retail Format	Brazil		Colombia		Mexico		Venezuela	
	Sales	% of Total	Sales	% of Total	Sales	% of Total	Sales	% of Total
Supermarket	56.6	63.3	7.3	49	15.7	19.5	2.4	70
Hypermarket	15.3	17	7.3	48	44.1	54.7	0.9	25
Discount	12.3	13.7	n.a.		12.8	16	n.a.	
Convenience	5.3	6.0	0.4	3	7.9	9.8	0.2	5
Total	89.5	100	15	100	80.5		3.5	105

Source: Business Monitor International (2013).

focus on this segment to analyze the penetration of different formats. Table 5.9 shows the total revenues of mass grocery retailers in four Latin American countries. Supermarkets are the predominant format for grocery retail sales in Brazil, Colombia, and Venezuela. Hypermarkets, a more mature retail format, is the preferred format in Mexico and the second most important in Colombia. Discount stores have made inroads in Brazil and Mexico and are in early stages in the other countries. Convenience stores represent the smallest share of total revenues, but, as mentioned before, this format fulfills an important role in large metropolitan areas in the region.

E-commerce in Latin America

Online buying is a small but growing avenue for Latin American shoppers. The region is the fourth largest market in value in e-commerce behind the United States, Europe, and Asia. Brazil is the largest market in Latin America with sales of $13 billion, which pales in comparison with the US market with $187 billion in sales and Chinese market, with $75.3 billion.

Latin America is, however, the second fast-growing market after Asia (Pulso Social, 2013). In 2013, the fastest-growing regional market was Asia, with 34% average annual growth, followed by Latin America at 21% (Cushman & Wakefield, 2013). The fastest-growing market in the region was Mexico, which recorded 43.2% growth in 2013, followed by Colombia with 41.9%, which made these two regional markets the fourth and fifth fastest-growing markets in the world in 2013 (US Media Consulting, 2013). In contrast, a mature market such as the United States grew at 13% in the same year.

E-commerce in the region accounts for a small percentage of total retail sales, ranging from a low of 1.4% in Peru to a high of 5.6% in Colombia. In mature markets such as the United States, the penetration is also low at 6.5% (Cushman & Wakefield, 2013). Higher penetration of e-commerce will depend on higher Internet penetration, debit or credit card penetration, and reliable delivery and low-cost transportation. On these facilitating factors, Latin American does not score well. The top countries in the region on these factors ranked 26th (Chile) and 27th (Brazil). Furthermore, the lack of consumer trust in credit and debit

Table 5.10 E-commerce in Latin America

	Sales 2012 US$ Billions*	% of Total Retail Sales*	2007–2012 Average Annual Growth*	Internet Penetration**	Use of E-commerce %***	Cards per Capita
Argentina	3.3	2.4	32	66.4	21	
Brazil	13	3.4	20	45.6	30	4.6
Chile	1.7	2.2	14	58.6	31	2.5
Colombia	2.1	5.6	41.9	59.5	28	
Mexico	6.2	1.4	43.2	36.5	31	
Peru	0.8	0.5	22.3	36.5		
China	75.3	4.1	101	40.1		
US	231	8	11.2	72.3		6.2

Sources: * Cushman & Wakefield, Global Perspectives on Retail, 2013; ** Internet World Stats (2013); *** Ericcson (2013).

cards may be another impediment. Despite these challenges, many companies in Latin America have their e-commerce platforms ready and are betting that they will bring increasing revenues in the future. For instance, Walmart e-commerce revenues in the region were $383 million in 2012, which is a small share of the $27.2 billion the retail giant grossed in Latin America. Another online retailer, Amazon, also reports similar level of revenues for the region—$320 million in 2012 (Internet Retailer, 2013). The real promise for e-commerce in the region is mobile e-commerce. With already good penetration of smartphones, m-commerce already accounts for about one-third of total e-commerce sales.

5.5   Summary

Latin American consumers in the past decade have become confident and pleased with their lifestyles and consequently more discerning and demanding. Their rational side makes them more focused on value, convenience, and time saving, seeking an efficient shopping experience. On the emotional side, Latin American consumers look for, honesty, transparency, and relevance in terms of making a contribution to the environment and society.

   In reaching Latin American consumers, firms need to develop brands that resonate well with their values and priorities. In this chapter, we advanced the concept of building a brand platform that creates salience using a mix of the old and new media and celebrates optimism and confidence at the same time that it delivers realistic benefits. Brands should also be perceived to be affordable and within reach of the Latin American budget. Furthermore, brands should build trust and be perceived as honest, transparent, and authentic. Finally, brands should indicate how they help the consumer and society achieve the larger aspirations of a better world in the immediate consumer space (family, neighborhood, country, and the world).

We also reviewed the important role of retailing in the region. Retailers need to build their own brand platforms on the pillars of the product brands and the shopping values of Latin American consumers. In building their brands, retailers in Latin American need to reach rational, emotional, and transactional proximity to consumers. Latin American consumers perceive a good shopping experience by being treated with respect, attention, and assistance. They are also practical and want to buy well without making mistakes while staying within their budgets. Latin American consumers want to take control of their shopping and are empowered by access to credit and new technologies to do so. Although in its early stages, e-commerce has a bright future in the region, and recent growth rates are an indication of this promise.

References

A. T. Kearney. (2013). *The Global Retail Development Index*. Retrieved from www.atkearney. com/consumer-products-retail/global-retail-development-index.

Balvé, M. (2012). *Breaking through the boundaries*. Retrieved from http://rwconnect.esomar. org/breaking-through-the-boundaries/.

Booz & Co. (2006). *Successful retail innovation in emerging markets: Latin American companies translate smart ideas into profitable businesses*. Retrieved from www.booz.com/ media/file/SuccessfulRetailInnovationinEmergingMarkets.pdf.

Business Monitor International. (2013). *Latin American retail trends and country reports for Argentina, Brazil, Chile, Colombia, Mexico, Peru and Venezuela*. Private paid report can be accessed at www.businessmonitor.com.

Calguey, W. (2011). *The Latin American Consumer of 2020*. Retrieved from www.wpp. com/~/media/SharedWPP/About%20WPP/What%20we%20do/The%20Store/ thestore_latamretailforum_thefuturescompany_mar11.pdf.

Canadian International Markets Bureau. (2012). *Top grocery retailers in Latin America*. Retrieved from www.ats-sea.agr.gc.ca/lat/6240-eng.htm.

Comscore. (2013). *Futuro digital Latinoamerica*. Retrieved from www.comscore.com/ Insights/Blog/2013_Digital_Future_in_Focus_Series.

Corpart, G. (2012). *The Latin American Consumer of 2020*. Retrieved from www.americasmi. com/en_US/expertise/articles-trends/page/the-latin-american-consumer-of-2020.

Cushman & Wakefield. (2013). *Global perspective on online retailing 2013*. Retrieved from www.cushmanwakefield.com/en/research-and-insight/2013/global-perspectives-on-retail/.

Danone. (2012). *Investor Relations Seminar, St. Petersburg, FL*. Retrieved from http:// media.corporate-ir.net/media_files/IROL/13/131801/presentations/16-NOV-12_ M._LOZANO_E.__GIACOMINI,_M._CAMARA_&_M._BORGES_-_Danone_ Brazil.pdf.

Danone. (2013). *A Danone for every taste in Brazil*. Retrieved from www.danone.com/ en/en-images/en-images.html?archiveItem=3&oldCat=2.

eMarketer. (2012). *Social networks reach 3 in 10 Latin Americans*. Retrieved from www. emarketer.com/Article/Social-Networks-Reach-Three-10-Latin-Americans/1009291.

eMarketer. (2013a). *Latin America—New media trend watch regions*. Retrieved from www.newmediatrendwatch.com/regional-overview/104-latin-america.

eMarketer. (2013b). *Mobile ad market in Mexico leads Latin America.* Retrieved from www.emarketer.com/Article/Mobile-Ad-Market-Mexico-Leads-Latin-America/1010169.

Ericcson. (2013). *M-commerce in Latin America.* Retrieved from www.ericsson.com/res/docs/2013/consumerlab/m-commerce-in-latam.pdf.

Euromonitor. (2013). *Wal-Mart Argentina S.A.* Private paid report. The report is accessed from www.euromonitor.com/retailing-in-argentina/report.

HavasMedia. (2013). *Meaningful global brands infographics.* Retrieved from file:///Users/fernandorobles/Desktop/LATAM%20BOOK%20v2/Chapter %205-Marketing/Readings %20Ch%205/Branding/Havas%20Meaningful%20Global%20Brands%20Global%20Infographic.webarchive.

Internet Retailer. *WalMart Latin America hires new CEO.* Retrieved from www.internetretailer.com/2013/01/11/walmart-latin-america-hires-new-ceo.

Internet World Stats. (2013). Retrieved from www.internetworldstats.com/stats2.htm.

Keller, K. (2012). *Strategic brand management: Building, measuring, and managing brand equity.* 4th ed. Upper Saddle River, NJ: Prentice Hall.

Latin American Retail Connection. (2013). *Latin American retail market.* Retrieved from http://laretco.com/.

Latin Link. (2013). *The latest media consumption in Latin America.* Retrieved from http://latinlink.usmediaconsulting.com/2012/01/the-latest-on-social-media-in-latin-america/.

McKinsey Global Institute. (2011). *Urban world: Mapping the economic power of cities.* Retrieved from www.mckinsey.com/insights/urbanization/urban_world.

Nielsen. (2013). *Global ad spend: 1H Global ad spend increases 2.8%, led by Latin America and Asia Pacific.* Retrieved from www.nielsen.com/us/en/newswire/2013/global-ad-spend-1H-global-ad-spend-increases-2–8-led-by-latin-am.html.

PRNewswire. (2013). Latin America mobile data, voice, and forecast. Retrieved from www.prnewswire.com/news-releases/latin-america—mobile-voice-data-and-forecasts-211241761.html.

Pulso Social. (2013). *It is not just Brazil, online retail sales accelerate in Argentina, Colombia and Mexico.* Retrieved from http://pulsosocial.com/en/2013/08/13/its-not-just-brazil-online-retail-sales-accelerate-in-argentina-colombia-and-mexico/.

Robles, F., Haar, J., & Simon, F. (2003). *Winning strategies for the new Latin markets.* Upper Saddle River, NJ: Financial Times-Prentice Hall.

Standard and Poors. (2013). *Industry report card: Latin American retailers' performance continues to benefit from solid consumer availability.* Retrieved from www.standardandpoors.com/ratings/articles/es/us/?articleType=HTML&assetID=1245354807469.

UN Habitat. (2012). Retrieved from www.unhabitat.org/pmss/listItemDetails.aspx?publicationID=3387.

US Media Consulting. (2013). *Latin America's media market 2013.* Retrieved from http://usmediaconsulting.com/img/uploads/pdf/Latam-and-Brazil-Media-Market-2013.pdf.

Wall Street Journal (2009). Coca-Cola to uncap "open happiness" campaign. Retrieved from http://online.wsj.com/news/articles/SB123189331806379409.

World Press Trends. (2013). *Global newspaper circulation and advertising trends in 2012.* Retrieved from www.marketingcharts.com/wp/print/global-ewspaper-circulation-and-advertising-trends-in-2012-30062/.

Part II

Culture and Managerial Styles in Latin America

6 Latin American Business Culture

Introduction

This chapter provides an overview of Latin American business culture and its influence on managerial behavior. Latin American business culture is rooted in its European colonial heritage. This legacy has created organizational and decision-making styles characterized by the concentration of power, multilevel hierarchical structures, and strong networks of relationships and paternalism. After economic reforms in the 1990s ushered in a long period of economic stability and insertion into a globalized world, Latin American firms have adopted efficient and effective managerial systems. The business culture in the region is not homogeneous, and substantial differences exist across different countries.

The chapter starts with a brief snapshot of Latin American cultural values based on historical roots and traditions. The next section introduces key organizational cultural frameworks based on the values that influence business organizations and managerial styles in Latin America. With a good understanding of the frameworks, in the next section we contrast Latin American business culture with that of other world regions. The following section explores whether Latin America is a monolithic cultural bloc or a collection of individual national business cultures. In particular, we explore business culture differences between the Brazil-led and the Mexican-led economic clusters. The concluding section summarizes the key ideas in the chapter, which build the foundation for the managerial topics discussed in chapter 7.

6.1 Introduction to Latin American Culture

Culture is a fundamental aspect of society that shapes a range of individual, group, and organizational behaviors. Culture itself is developed over time and through social interactions with members of a referent group. Social anthropologists such as Mead, Levi-Straus, and, more recently, Schein (Mead, 1964; Levi-Strauss, 1963; Schein, 1992) posit that individuals within a culture share assumptions, meanings, and resolutions to common problems that shape their behavior within the group. Some of these cultural codes are explicit and reflected in religion or tradition. Others are subconscious and nonverbal and thus difficult to detect by individuals from other cultures.

Latin Americans as a group share a common set of cultural values derived from common historical roots and similar development efforts. Latin Americans value personal relationships because these relationships traditionally have been important for advancement in life. Once established, these relationships are maintained and never placed in conflict or in question. Thus, the value that emerges is one that is referred to as *simpatia*—kindness or empathy toward others. Showing empathy toward others is manifested in an effort to understand the individual and the context surrounding the individual. Understanding of others is facilitated if the two individuals also share the same context, which could be economic, social, or political or simply family links. The latter interpretation has also been identified as the tendency for classism or *familism* in Latin American culture (Osland, De Franco, & Osland, 2007).

Relationships are based on *confianza,* or trust. One characteristic of *confianza* is the initial effort to gather information on other people to establish common bases of group membership and evaluate indicators of trust and loyalty in business situations. Latin Americans are more likely to place greater trust in members of the same group or class than in those who are not. Outsiders are thus at a disadvantage in gaining the level of trust necessary to conduct business transactions (Osland et al., 2007). An emphasis on group welfare is one of the core traits of the collectivistic business culture of Latin America, which is discussed later in the chapter. The intrinsic advantage of trust in and loyalty to the group is the expectation that other members will eventually reciprocate. Emphasis on the advancement of the group can clearly lead to nepotism, which is frequently observed in business organizations in Latin America.

The outcome of collectivism, classism, and trust is referred to as *personalismo,* or particularism: the expectation that one will be treated differently and receive individualized attention. In some circumstances, Latin Americans expect to be the exception rather than the rule. Such expectations and behaviors are often effective in an effort to manage highly bureaucratic business systems and organizations in Latin America, particularly the public bureaucracy (Osland et al., 2007). This is particularly illustrated by the Brazilian way of seeking alternative channels to find solutions, the so-called *jeitinho* (Barbosa & Da Matta, 2006).

Paternalism and *power* are two related values commonly associated with Latin American culture. The roots of paternalism are grounded in the colonial heritage, in which members of society expected rulers or patrons to take care of them. Paternalism in modern Latin American societies and business is exercised at all levels, from family to organizations where managers and supervisors concentrate and exercise power in decisions. As a result, little input or information is shared or incorporated from others outside the closed social or business group. Because they lack influence on important decisions, subordinates in Latin America perceive that they should therefore not be held accountable for their performance. Mistakes or failures are to be shared with those who have power or control. Hence, a culture of low accountability permeates Latin American culture (Osland et al., 2007).

A legacy of colonialism and the influence of Catholicism—where individuals had little control over the affairs of the state, the economy, or external events—have resulted in a sense of *fatalism,* or resignation and acceptance of faith and destiny. Fatalism makes Latin Americans less confident that they can guide their professional future and development purely through individual efforts and education. This situation reinforces the lack of accountability mentioned before and increases the perception of uncertainty in general, particularly the outcome of future events that will be determined by destiny (Osland et al., 2007).

A few other values that characterize Latin American culture related to business are *respeto* (respect), honor, and courage. These other cultural values have their roots in a colonial system that valued and rewarded these traits.

6.2   Latin American Culture under Four Cultural Frameworks

As a whole, Latin American culture is distinct from the cultural patterns of other regions with different historical and social development patterns. In this section, we analyze Latin American culture from the perspectives of four well-known frameworks.

Four organizational cultural frameworks are relevant to contrast Latin American business culture with that of other regions: Hall, GLOBE, Hofstede and Trompenaars (Hall, 1959; House, Hanges, Mansour, Dorfman, & Gupta, 2004; Hofstede, 1980; Trompenaars, 1994). Hall's central focus is to understand the communication aspects of cultures. Hofstede's framework focuses on the characteristics of organizational cultures, that is, how organizations such as firms or governments function within a given culture. Trompenaars explores the individual within a culture across a number of behaviors, decision-making styles, motivations, and aspirations.

Latin American Business Culture According to Hall

Hall focuses on understanding how individuals within a culture communicate and participate in social interactions. Hall places particular attention on the influence of the context in which the communication takes place. Thus, he describes cultures in terms of the degree of openness to others (individual distance), their idea of compromise and styles of negotiation, and their concept of time (strict or flexible), among others. On the basis of his study of socialization within cultures, Hall identifies *low- and high-context* cultures (Hall, 1959).

Low-context cultures are more explicit and direct. Individuals in these cultures express their intentions clearly, and such understanding does not change with the social context. Low-context cultures tend to use explicit rules and norms to guide their behaviors. Written forms of rules and norms avoid misinterpretations or capricious interpretations by individuals. Low-context cultures are monochronistic and adhere to plans, meeting deadlines and punctuality. Anglo-Saxon and Germanic cultures are considered low context.

In high-context cultures, the behavior and communication styles of individuals are largely influenced by the specific situation and by relationships with others. Thus, individuals adapt their behavior and intentions to the situation. Take, for instance, the concept of agreement. Individuals may be influenced to agree with others on the basis of the strength of their personal relationships rather than the expectations of the agreement per se. Agreement may be communicated in forms that are understood only by members of the group—such as a handshake or a particular nod of the head. These nonverbal behaviors can be an important part of intragroup communication. Individuals who are not members of the group may miss or misinterpret these signs.

Hall identifies Latin America countries as having high-context societies. In such cultures, business communications are shaped by some of the cultural values that were discussed in the first section, particularly familism, personalism, respect, and paternalism. Latin Americans are often not direct in their communications with others. They aim to be polite and friendly, avoiding confrontation. Courtesy and goodwill gestures preface introductions in the search for relationships and trust. Another feature of business communications in Latin America is formality and the use of professional titles as indicators of power relations and the need to confer respect. Communications also emphasize the avoidance of conflict or stress in relationships by offering indirect and implicit messages that are not confrontational or negative and that allow for face-saving outcomes. Time perception in Latin American cultures is flexible, as people tend to be polychronistic (Wardrope, 2005).

Latin America Business Culture According to Hofstede

Hofstede's cultural framework describes organizational cultures in different countries across five dimensions: power distance, individualism, masculine or feminine dominant values, uncertainty avoidance, and long-term orientation (Hofstede, 1980).

The first dimension in Hofstede's framework is the level of power sharing in organizations. The lower the distance, the lower the level of participation. In cultures with low power distance, individuals at lower levels are empowered to make decisions by themselves. As mentioned in the first section, Latin America is characterized by the concentration of power at the top of the organization, and input from subordinates is largely ignored. Table 8.1 supports this observation. Latin America has an average score of 67.8, which indicates high power distance, a result that is similar to Japan (average of 54) but not as high as China (average of 80). Power sharing is more prevalent in the United States, with a score of 40.

The second dimension describes the level of individualism or collectivism in a society. In more individualistic societies, organizational decisions are made mostly on the basis of the interests of the individual (personal benefit). In collectivistic societies the individual makes decisions of greater benefit to the community, even if they may be detrimental to his or her own welfare. Latin

Table 6.1 Hofstede's Values for Selected Latin American Countries

	Power (PDI)	Individualism (IDV)	Masculinity (MAS)	Uncertainty Avoidance (UAI)	Long-Term Orientation (LTO)
Argentina	49	46	56	86	
Brazil	69	38	49	76	65
Chile	63	23	28	86	
Colombia	67	13	64	80	
Costa Rica	35	15	21	86	
Ecuador	78	8	63	67	
El Salvador	66	19	40	94	
Guatemala	95	6	37	101	
Jamaica	45	39	68	13	
Mexico	81	30	69	82	
Panama	95	11	44	86	
Peru	64	16	42	87	
Uruguay	61	36	38	100	
Venezuela	81	12	73	76	
Latin American Average	67.8	22.3	49.4	80	
US	40	91	62	46	29
China	80	20	66	30	118
Japan	54	46	95	92	80

Source: Geert Hofstede—http://geert-hofstede.com.

America is a collectivistic society, as indicated by a low average score of 22.3, similar to that of China, which scores 20. Japan is also collectivistic but not as much as Latin America (average score of 54). The United States is a highly individualistic society with a score of 91. As noted in chapters 4 and 5, the level of individualism is on the rise in Latin America, but this increase builds on a low individualistic base.

The third dimension in Hofstede's framework defines whether the predominant values in organizations are masculine or feminine driven. A masculine society is distinguished by a culture driven by competition, achievement, or success, which are predominant masculine values (a high score on this dimension). On the other hand, feminine societies are more caring for others, and the desire not to stand out from the crowd drives decisions (a low score on this dimension). With an average score of 49.4, Latin America seems to balance both masculine and feminine values. In recent years, Latin America has elected more female presidents that any other world region (Calvano & Marcus-Delgado, 2013). Greater gender equality in politics has not, however, been paralleled in business, although recent studies suggest that this asymmetry is changing and that women in Latin America are gaining influence in business (Martinez-Nadal, 2013). Japan, China, and the United States score higher than Latin America in masculine values (see Table 6.1). In fact, Japan shows a very high score on masculinity, one of the highest in the countries analyzed by Hofstede.

A fourth dimension of Hofstede's framework is uncertainty avoidance. This dimension describes how individuals behave under situations of ambiguity and poor information. In cultures with low tolerance, individuals' decision making aims to minimize uncertainty, and these cultures tend to be risk averse. In cultures with high tolerance for ambiguity, individuals behave in a way that reflects a rational evaluation of alternative options in an uncertain situation. The Latin American cultural value of fatalism may factor into the results for this region. On the average, Latin American countries score high in uncertainty avoidance. Individuals in organizations do not cope well with ambiguity and make decisions on the basis of intuition and emotions rather than after a careful evaluation of their options. Like Latin America, Japan also scores high on this dimension, with an average of 92. In contrast to Latin American culture, however, the Japanese culture supports efforts to eliminate emotions from decision making. Instead, Japanese people are overcautious and make an inordinate effort to increase the predictability of their actions and minimize any potential risks before making any business decisions. In contrast, individuals in China and in the United States are more entrepreneurial and risk takers. In these countries, change and innovation are encouraged as ways to reduce business uncertainty.

The fifth dimension of Hofstede's framework is long-term orientation. In the United States, individuals and organizations tend to favor behaviors and decisions that produce immediate results, thus exhibiting a short-term orientation. In contrast, Asian societies prefer long-term horizons and expect outcomes to be realized in the long term. Brazil offers the only point of reference for this dimension in Latin America. Table 6.1 shows that Brazilians are slightly oriented to the long term, but not as much as those in Asian countries such as Japan and China.

The results of this comparative analysis of Latin America and selected countries appear in Figure 6.1.

Latin American Business Culture According to Trompenaars

Trompenaars uses seven cultural dimensions to characterize cultures. Some of these dimensions are the same as those already discussed under Hall and Hofstede's frameworks and therefore will not be elaborated fully. The first dimension is universalism or particularism, which describes whether rules and agreements apply to all or depend on the relationship or context (low or high context in Hall's framework). This concept is similar to personalism in Latin America. The second dimension contrasts individualism and collectivism in a culture, a topic already discussed in Hofstede's framework. The third dimension is the relationship with the environment and describes whether individuals have control of the environment. The fourth dimension contrasts neutral and affective relationships and refers primarily to the verbal or nonverbal display of internal feelings and thinking to others. The fifth dimension is specific or diffuse relationships. This dimension refers to individual values of privacy (e.g., separation of work and private life) against a preference for a large and social public life. The sixth dimension is related

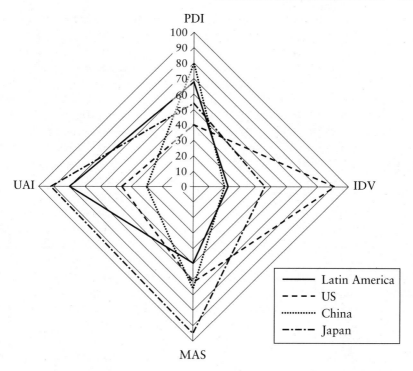

Figure 6.1 Cultural Profiles Based on Hofstede's Value Dimensions
Source: Authors' elaboration.

to achievement or ascribed motivation. Societies that reward accomplishments resulting from personal effort exhibit an achievement orientation. Ascribed values are predominant in societies where rank, status, or advancement is based on social class or level of education. The seventh and final dimension is time orientation, which is similar to Hall's dimension with the exception that Trompenaars distinguishes among past, present, and future orientation (Trompenaars, 1994).

On the basis of these variables, Trompenaars identifies several cultural groups and the countries that are part of each one. Among these cultural groups are the Anglo-Saxon, Germanic, Nordic, Latin European, and Middle Eastern. Trompenaars clearly indicates that Latin America has developed its own particular managerial culture. Finally, Trompenaars argues that Brazil, Japan, India, and Israel cannot be grouped with other cultures. This conclusion suggests that these countries have developed unique cultures and behaviors (Trompenaars, 1994).

Latin America Business Culture According to the GLOBE Study

The GLOBE study is yet another cross-cultural framework that can be used to contrast Latin American business culture with those of other regions. The

GLOBE study was designed to examine the relationships between culture and leadership effectiveness. The GLOBE study of leadership in 62 countries revealed nine cultural dimensions, several of which are the same as those in the other cultural frameworks reviewed earlier. These nine dimensions are uncertainty avoidance, power distance, institutional collectivism, in-group collectivism, gender egalitarianism, future orientation, performance orientation, and humane orientation. For parsimony's sake, this section will comment only on those dimensions that have not been previously discussed (House et al., 2004).

Institutional collectivism refers to how the degree of collective distribution of resources is rewarded. In-group collectivism refers to the degree to which individuals express pride, loyalty, and cohesiveness with regard to their society. Gender egalitarianism is the degree to which a society minimizes gender differences. Assertiveness is the degree to which individuals are assertive, confrontational, and aggressive in social relationships. Performance orientation refers to how individuals are rewarded in society. Humane orientation is the degree to which individuals are rewarded for being fair, altruistic, and kind. Uncertainty avoidance is the extent to which society relies on social norms, rules, and procedures to reduce the unpredictability of the future (similar to Hofstede's uncertainty avoidance dimension, but the scale is reversed in interpretation).

On the basis of data obtained through more than 17,000 standardized surveys in organizations of 62 countries, the GLOBE study collected data on respondents' perceptions across 10 dimensions of cultural values and practices. These dimensions are shown in Table 6.2 and Figures 6.2 and 6.3. The cultural value-perception measured respondents' views of which values should predominate in an ideal society. The inquiry about current practices measured respondents' views of which values are actually practiced in their society across the same 10 dimensions. These perceptions were measured on a scale from low (1) to high (7). More often than not, values-perception scores were higher than scores for values actually practiced, as aspirations typically run higher than current reality.

The GLOBE study identified 10 cultural clusters. Latin American countries constitute a distinct cluster; the United States fits into the Anglo cluster, and Japan and China are in the Confucian Asia group. Table 6.2 provides the average and country-specific society values and practice scores for nine Latin American countries and the average for the region. For cross-cultural comparison reasons, we have included scores on the same variables for the United States, China, and Japan.

The Latin American cluster is described as being high in practice scores for in-group collectivism and low for performance orientation, uncertainty avoidance, future orientation, and institutional collectivism. The GLOBE interpretation of Latin American culture is that it tends to take life as it comes; unpredictability is a fact of life, individuals are not overly worried about results, and there is less concern with institutional collective goals (House et al., 2004).

The GLOBE study for Latin America provides yet another insight into Latin America business culture in contrast with the cultures of the United States and Asia. Next, we elaborate on the results of the GLOBE study for Latin America.

Table 6.2 GLOBE Study Scores for Latin American and Other Selected Countries

	Uncertainty Avoidance		Power Distance		Institutional Collectivism		In-Group Collectivism		Gender Egalitarianism		Assertiveness		Future Orientation		Performance Orientation		Humane Orientation	
	Practices	Values	Practices	Values	Practices	Values	Practices	Values	Practices	Values	Practices	Values	Practices	Values	Practices	Values	Practices	Values
Argentina	3.65	4.66	5.64	2.33	3.66	5.32	5.51	6.15	3.49	4.98	4.22	3.25	3.08	5.78	3.65	6.35	3.99	5.58
Bolivia	3.55	4.7	4.51	3.41	4.04	5.1	5.47	6	3.55	4.75	3.79	3.73	3.61	5.63	3.61	6.05	4.05	5.07
Brazil	3.6	4.99	5.33	2.35	3.83	5.62	5.18	5.15	3.31	4.99	4.2	2.91	3.87	5.69	4.04	6.13	3.66	5.68
Colombia	3.57	4.98	5.56	2.04	3.81	5.38	5.73	6.25	3.67	5	4.2	3.43	3.27	5.68	3.94	6.42	3.72	5.61
Costa Rica	3.82	4.58	4.74	2.58	3.93	5.18	5.32	6.08	3.56	4.64	3.75	4.05	3.6	5.2	4.12	5.9	4.39	4.99
Ecuador	3.68	4.67	5.6	2.3	3.9	5.41	5.81	6.17	3.07	4.59	4.09	3.65	3.74	5.94	4.2	6.32	4.65	5.26
El Salvador	3.62	5.32	5.68	2.68	3.71	5.65	5.35	6.52	3.16	4.66	4.62	3.62	3.8	5.98	3.72	6.58	3.71	5.46
Guatemala	3.3	4.88	5.6	2.35	3.7	5.23	5.63	6.14	3.02	4.53	3.89	3.64	3.24	5.91	3.81	6.14	3.89	5.26
Mexico	4.18	5.26	5.22	2.85	4.06	4.92	5.71	5.95	3.64	4.73	4.45	3.79	3.87	5.86	4.1	6.16	3.98	5.1
Venezuela	3.44	5.26	5.4	2.29	3.96	5.39	5.53	6.17	3.62	4.82	4.33	3.33	3.35	5.79	3.32	6.33	4.25	5.31
Latin America Average	3.641	4.93	5.328	2.518	3.86	5.32	5.524	6.058	3.409	4.769	4.154	3.54	3.543	5.746	3.851	6.238	4.029	5.332
US	4.15	4	4.88	2.85	4.2	4.17	4.25	5.77	3.34	5.06	4.55	4.32	4.15	5.31	4.49	6.14	4.17	5.53
China	4.94	5.28	5.04	3.1	4.77	4.56	5.8	5.09	3.05	3.68	3.76	5.44	3.75	4.73	4.45	5.67	4.36	5.32
Japan	4.07	4.33	5.11	2.86	5.19	3.99	4.63	5.26	3.19	4.33	3.59	5.56	4.29	5.25	4.22	5.17	4.3	5.41

Source: House et al. (2004).

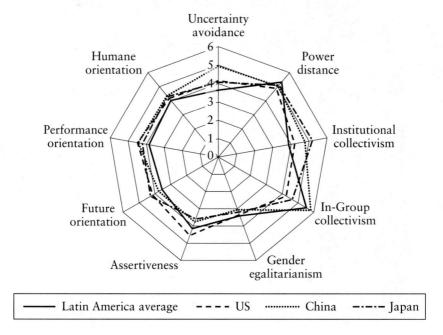

Figure 6.2 Culture Profiles Based on GLOBE Practices

Source: Authors' elaboration.

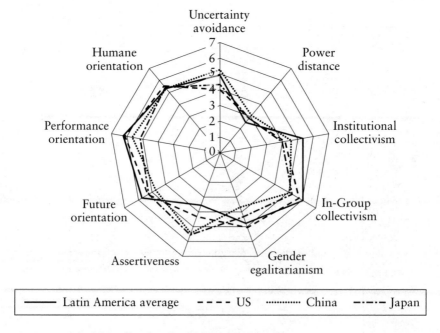

Figure 6.3 Cultural Profiles Based on GLOBE Social Values

Source: Authors' elaboration.

With regard to uncertainty avoidance, Latin America scores in actual practice are lower than those of the United States and the Asian countries. A lower score suggests that Latin Americans rely more on informal networks and norms and are less calculating when taking risks than their US and Asian counterparts, who rely more on policies, procedures, and formalities to deal with uncertainty. The social score for this dimension was higher than the cultural practices score. The interpretation of this difference is that Latin Americans prefer more formal and rule-based societies. One would expect that the recent period of macroeconomic stability in the region would help to make the future more predictable in Latin America. It is interesting to note that in the case of Japan and the United States, the scores for social values are lower than those for current practice, which may indicate that these societies have already reached a level of practices and policies that is satisfactory and effective.

The results for the power distance dimension support the conclusions of other cultural frameworks that Latin America is a society with substantial power differences and concentration of power. The average score for this dimension is than the score for other three countries shown in Table 6.2. The expectation that this situation will change is clear not only for Latin America but also for the United States, Japan, and China, as noted by a substantial drop in the scores for social values on these dimensions.

GLOBE's results on institutional collectivism reveal an unexpected finding for Latin America. Latin Americans obtain a low average score on this dimension. A high score is an indication that society expects more reliance on collectivism and group effort. A low average score based on current practice in this dimension suggests that Latin Americans perceive an environment that does not rely on institutions for individual benefits and encourages greater individualism. In contrast, Japan, China, and even the United States score higher on this dimension. According to social values scores, however, Latin Americans believe that their culture in the future should be more collectivistic. As for the United States, Japan, and China, lower social values scores in this dimension indicate that these societies expect their future to be more individualistic.

The analysis of in-group collectivism supports the Latin American cultural trait of *familism*, mentioned in the first section of this chapter. Both China and Latin America score high on this dimension. The main difference is that Latin Americans indicate that a reliance on group relations should be even greater in the future, whereas the Chinese would prefer that it diminish.

Scores for gender egalitarianism show that all of the regions perceive that their societies have low levels of gender equality—as noted in Table 6.2, the practice scores for all regions are lower than the mid-range of the scale. the average for Latin America is higher than those for the other countries in the analysis, an indication of higher achievement in equality. Both Latin America and the other countries expect that equality should improve in the future, with the United States expressing a higher increase in expectations.

Both Latin America and the United States have higher scores on assertiveness than Japan and China. Assertiveness seems to be a Western cultural trait.

Whereas Latin Americans and the United States express a belief that their societies should have lower levels of assertiveness, the Asian countries anticipate an increase in this characteristic in the future. With respect to performance orientation, Latin America is different from the other countries in the analysis. The current reality is that performance orientation is not part of Latin American business culture, but there is a desire for it to become a larger component in the future. In contrast, a performance orientation is part of the culture of the United States and the Asian countries studied, and this should continue or increase in the future.

With regard to future orientation, the GLOBE study shows low practice scores for Latin America, which suggests a greater tendency to live in the moment, consume, and prefer immediate gratification. This result may be congruent with the rise in consumer confidence explored in chapters 4 and 5. A similar result can be observed for China, suggesting that a focus on the here and now may be a cultural trait of emerging economies. Such cultural trends seem to contrast with the long-term orientation for which Japan is well known. Nevertheless, Latin Americans state that their society should have a more long-term orientation.

On humane orientation, Latin America, the United States, Japan, and China have similar mid-range practice scores. In all cases, respondents suggested that the future should be better in terms of supporting a society with more interest in the welfare of the individual, increased sensitivity toward social issues, and greater social responsibility.

In sum, the GLOBE study enhances our understanding of cultural values in Latin America. Most important, the GLOBE study also provides a glimpse at expectations for the future for this region. So far, we have analyzed Latin America as a whole. In the next section, we explore differences in business culture within this region.

6.3   Roots and Fragmentation of Latin American Business Culture

Historical Roots of Latin American Business Culture

Latin American culture in general and business culture in particular are assumed to be different from those of other regions but homogeneous within Latin America. This assumption is based on the perception that most countries, with the exception of some Caribbean countries, share the same historical and language roots. In this section, we explore expressions of national business culture in the region.

A common historical factor and a large influence on the region is its colonial heritage. Four centuries of colonial rule have exerted a strong influence on Latin American society, particularly its legal and political systems. Except for the Caribbean, which was ruled by Britain, the region was under either Spanish or Portuguese rule. Although both colonial masters were European, one author argues that their ambitions and empire building approaches were different enough to have left substantial differences in the business culture in Spanish- and Portuguese-speaking Latin America. According to Behrens (2009), Spain imposed its rule through superior military power, centralization, and a hierarchy based on aristocracy. Under this system, courage, honor, and loyalty to the imperial power were highly valued and rewarded. To sustain the system, colonial Latin America developed competencies to organize state finances, accumulate wealth, and tax the colonies. This command-and-control approach is still prevalent in contemporary economic and political organizations in Spanish-speaking Latin America. For instance, the expansion of multinationals from Spanish-speaking Latin America has been based on a strategy of fully controlled investments and acquisitions.

Behrens (2009) argues that Portugal took a different approach to empire building. As a small European country, Portugal focused on the discovery and exploration of alternative routes to Asia. Thus, colonial Portugal became a merchant empire, in the process discovering Brazil and leaving a legacy there that instills values based on trade such as negotiation, collaboration, and flexibility, rather than the confrontational and combative approach taken in the Spanish colonies. As a result, Behrens contends that Brazilians have developed a more mercantile approach to business and search for global opportunities based on trade rather than on the accumulation of power.

Business Culture in Brazil-led and Mexico-led Economic Cultures

These historical roots may explain how Brazil was more ready to adapt to the changing world economic order explained in chapter 2. Brazilian businesses explored global business opportunities in Asia and other emerging countries and employed managerial skills and styles attuned to exploit these opportunities mostly through trade. Business firms from the Mexican cluster focused almost exclusively on trade and economic relations with North America and Europe.

We have explored differences in business culture between the two economic clusters identified in chapter 2, and the results are shown in Table 6.3 and Figures 6.4 and 6.5. Figure 6.4 shows the results for Hofstede's cultural framework. The differences are minimal in this case, with the Brazil-led cluster showing slightly higher individualism and levels of masculine values, greater uncertainty avoidance, and the same levels of power distance. In the GLOBE study, the two country clusters also exhibit similar results. On practice values, the Mexico-led cluster shows slightly higher scores on performance orientation value and the Brazil-led cluster a higher score on humane orientation. On expectations of what society should be, the reverse is observed. More Brazilians indicate that their business environment should be performance driven than do respondents in the Mexico-led cluster. The Mexico-driven cluster, on the other hand, perceives that societies should have a more humane orientation, with an average score slightly higher than that of the Brazil-cluster.

Tables 6.3 Hofstede's Scores in Brazil and Mexican Economic Clusters

Cluster	Country	Power Distance	Individualism	Masculine/ Feminine	Uncertainty Avoidance
Brazil	Argentina	49	46	56	86
	Brazil	69	38	49	76
	Chile	63	23	28	86
	Colombia	67	13	64	80
	Ecuador	78	8	63	67
	Peru	64	16	42	87
	Uruguay	61	36	38	100
	Venezuela	81	12	73	76
	Average	66.5	24	51.6	82.2
Mexico	Costa Rica	35	15	21	86
	El Salvador	66	19	40	94
	Guatemala	95	6	37	101
	Jamaica	45	39	68	13
	Mexico	81	30	69	82
	Average	65.75	22.1	47	75.2

Source: Authors' elaboration.

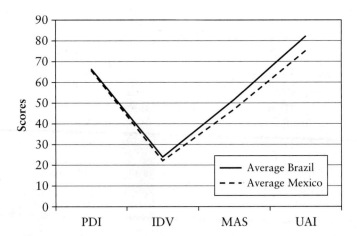

Figure 6.4 Hofstede's Cultural Dimensions by Economic Clusters in Latin America
Source: Authors' elaboration.

National Business Cultures in Latin America

Globalization, economic reforms, the pressure to compete with global multinationals in their own national markets, integration with world supply chains, and ambition to become more international have forced many Latin American companies to abandon many of the traditional business culture traits identified in the previous sections.

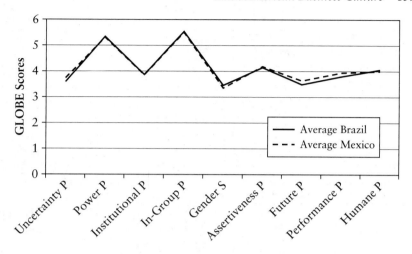

Figure 6.5 GLOBE Pratice Scores in Brazil and Mexico-led Clusters
Source: Authors' elaboration.

The economic reforms and liberalization programs that spread throughout Latin America in the 1990s changed the rules of the game and created a different set of opportunities and competitive environments for business. Latin American companies adapted to these changes and took advantage of new business opportunities such as privatizations and regional integration. The timing and types of reforms, however, have varied across the region. Argentina and Chile were the first countries to introduce deep reforms in the early 1990s. Chilean companies were among the first to adapt to these reforms and transform their business cultures and managerial systems to become very competitive first in their national markets and then in regional markets. This early exposure to economic reforms honed competencies that were later key to the success of the regional expansion of Chilean multilatinas (Del Sol, 2010). In contrast, Brazil was a late and cautious economic reformer. Economic reforms started with the first administration of Fernando Henrique Cardoso, in 1994, and continued under Luiz Inácio Lula da Silva's first administration, in 2002. Brazilian companies had a long time to gradually transform themselves and become global competitive champions, as is covered in Chapter 9. The nature of the opportunities created by reforms and globalization also varied throughout the region. As explained in chapter 2, Brazil and other Southern Cone countries focused on growing opportunities in natural-resource sectors and the growing Asian market. In contrast, Mexico and other northern Latin American countries focused on opportunities in the United States and in manufacturing. Clearly, these different orientations required not only different business competencies but also different cultural mindsets. Economic reforms also created domestic market opportunities, and some Latin American companies pursued opportunities only in domestic markets. The focus on domestic market opportunities also shaped a different variety of business competencies. In this case, business competencies attuned to the particular preferences of domestic consumers and the development of excellent relationships with the government and regulators were important.

Some aspects of national business cultures in Latin America remain constant despite the influence of economic reforms and globalization. In most countries, family business groups are powerful players, with the founding family exerting a great deal of control. There is a high degree of centralization at the core of ownership. Also, strong and good relationships with the government continue to be important.

Although Latin American countries share a number of similarities in their business cultures, the different economic development paths and the impact of globalization mentioned earlier have left an imprint that is unique in each country in the region. These differences have led some studies to conclude that business and managerial styles are quite diverse (Lenartowicz & Johnson, 2001). To illustrate the differences and similarities of business culture in the region, we discuss one example of Spanish (Argentina) heritage and one of Portuguese (Brazil) heritage.

Argentine Business Culture

Argentina was an early economic reformer. The administration of Carlos Menem initiated a whole program of economic liberalization and privatizations, which changed the business landscape for decades to come. The recent administrations of Néstor Carlos Kirchner and Cristina Fernández de Kirchner have reversed some of these reforms but with minor impacts on the transformed business culture of the early 1990s. According to one study, Argentine business groups adapted to the reformed economic environment in four different ways, according to whether they focused on domestic or international business opportunities and their degree of relatedness of their business portfolio (Fraccia & Mesquita, 2006). This study focused on business culture and competencies for the following four groups:

a.   International Focus and Unrelated Businesses. Argentine firms in this group took an aggressive response and pursued international business opportunities. They exhibited flexibility and quick responses to and anticipation of market changes. They focused on leveraging synergies of competencies across diverse businesses. They employed a long-term vision and devoted great effort to their business reputation and brand image. They also encouraged entrepreneurial initiatives within their organizations. Examples of these companies are Argentine industrial groups such as Perez Companc and Techint, which are global corporations in the energy industry and steel transformation. First a ship-building company, Perez Companc pursued opportunities created in the process of deregulation and privatization of the oil industry in the early 1990s to expand into a large holding company that ventured into other businesses such as petrochemicals, agribusiness, and food processing, in Argentina and abroad.

The ownership control of Perez Companc rests with the second generation of the founder's family (Kock & Guillén, 2001).

b.   International Focus in Related Businesses. The business culture of this group is focused on building economies of scale in domestic and international markets that allow them to compete in efficiency. These business groups have made significant investments in upgrading industrial processes and in technology to achieve world-class standards. The influence of the founder is felt through the emphasis on excelling in the industrial transformation process. An example of an Argentine business in this group is Arcor, one the world largest confectionary manufacturers and exporters. A strong government relationship is important to facilitate the international trade activities of the firm.

c.   National Expansion in Unrelated Business. Companies in this group were the dominant form of the traditional Latin American business groups, which thrived under a closed and protected economy. With the reforms, these groups pursued further diversification to seek new opportunities created by economic liberalization and to compensate for sectors that became competitive as a result of the entry of global multinationals after the implementation of the reforms. The opportunities taken were in sectors that were of no interest to global multinationals and in which government relationships were important. There is a strong paternalistic business culture in this group; the founder or corporate leader is the public face in negotiations with the government and regulators. The Roggio group is an example of a company in environmental engineering, real estate, utility concessions, highway toll concessions, and public waste management, all highly regulated activities. The Roggio business group excels in implementing quality public-service contracts in unrelated business sectors.

d.   National Expansion in Related Businesses. Argentine business groups in this cluster have emerged as market leaders in a particular market segment through specialization, appeal to national identity, and strong government relationships. A culture of strong national identification and charismatic, hands-on leadership permeates the business culture in this case. Examples of Argentine companies in this group are the Eurnekian, Fortabat, and Eskenazi Groups.

In the case of Argentina, the business culture that emerges is one in which competencies are driven by either global or domestic competition. In both cases, scanning opportunities, the family and founder heritage has an impact on the vision and decision making. Also, strong government relations are an important component of the group's business.

Brazilian Business Culture

Brazil is a late economic reformer in Latin America, and the transformation of Brazilian businesses has been gradual. Traditional Brazilian business was characterized by centralized decision making, short-term vision, and reactive management in which finding creative solutions to an ever-changing economic environment was valued. With greater macroeconomic stability and increasing global market opportunities, Brazilian companies have invested in developing managerial skills and processes that allow them to become part of a more global competitive world. Thus, the business culture for this group of globally competitive companies is characterized by flexibility, constant monitoring of external conditions, adoption of world-class standards, a greater customer orientation, adaptation to diverse international markets and cultures, and development of innovation, marketing, and sophisticated financial and risk-management competencies for global operations (Fleury & Fleury, 2011).

The transformation of the business culture in Brazil took a different approach than in other countries, mostly because of the different historical roots that were explained earlier in the chapter. As mentioned earlier, Trompenaars observed this particularism of Brazilian business culture and concluded that Brazil is a unique culture that cannot be grouped with other cultural clusters (Trompenaars, 2004). Lenartowicz and Johnson (2001) arrived at a similar conclusion in their study of Latin American managerial values. Business leaders in Brazil carry the Portuguese merchant DNA that brings a zeal for exploration of the unknown, strong negotiating skills, adaptation, and flexibility. These legacy skills, coupled with those of a relationship-based culture and the diversity of origins Brazil's population, have created a unique business culture. Another study states that the essence of this culture is the unique competency of "network capillarity." This competency is described as the ability to build networks of associates on the basis of empathy and the creation of common value (Parente, Cyrino, Spohr, & de Vasconcelos, 2013). As a result, Brazilians are very cognizant of doing business in markets and countries where they can create those networks. The case of Embraer, a global leader in the commuter aircraft market, is an example of such an ability. One key factor in the success of this company is the ability to manage an extensive global network of suppliers of aircraft components. The core of Embraer's business is the design and assembly of the aircraft.

6.4   Summary

Latin American business culture is rooted in its European colonial heritage. This legacy has created long-term organizational and decision-making styles characterized by concentration of power, multilevel hierarchal structures, strong networks of relationships, and paternalism. Spain built a colonial empire aimed at creating wealth through absolute control of the economic activities of its colonies. Portugal aimed at creating wealth through trade and exploration of new territories. These distinctions are important to differentiate the business culture of Brazil from that of Spanish-speaking Latin America.

Historical roots have shaped a set of values in Latin America that is characterized by empathy, familism, trust based on relationship, particularism, and fatalism. These values have nurtured the creation of large industrial groups that are family owned and have a centralized organization and strong government relationships.

Four cultural frameworks identify Latin America as a unique business culture. Latin America is described as a high-context culture in which business organizations exhibit large power distances, collective values, a tilt toward masculine values, and high uncertainty avoidance. Latin American cultures also tend toward in-group collectivism, greater gender egalitarianism, and low trust in institutional collectivism.

Traditional business culture in Latin America has been transformed by economic reforms and liberalization, globalization, and regional integration, which were introduced starting in the 1990s. This transformation has shaped different national business cultures because the timing and extent of these reforms and the opening to globalization varied from country to country.

Within each country, the impact of these changes also varied with the economic sector and the nature of opportunities generated by these reforms and changes. In this chapter, we documented four different types of transformations and business cultures in Argentina. In the case of Brazil, the transformation had the greatest impact on companies seeking greater insertion in the global economy.

In sum, this short review of business culture in Latin America provides the basis for the chapters that follow.

References

Barbosa, L., & Da Matta, R. (2006). *O jeitinho Brasilero: A arte de ser mais igual que os outros*. Rio Janeiro: Elsevier.

Behrens, A. (2009). *Culture and management in the Americas*. Palo Alto, CA: Stanford University Press,

Calvano, J., & Marcus-Delgado, J. (2013). *Latin American women rising*. Retrieved from www.thedialogue.org/page.cfm?pageID=32&pubID=3298.

Del Sol, P. (2010). Chilean regional strategies in response to economic liberalization. *Universia Business Review, 25*, 112–130.

Fleury, A., & Fleury, M. T. (2010). *Brazilian multinationals: Competences and internationalization*. Cambridge: Cambridge University Press.

Fracchia, E., & Mesquita, L. (2006). Corporate strategies of business groups in the wake of competitive shocks. *Management Research, 4*, 81–98.

Hall, E. T. (1959). *The silent language*. New York: Fawcett.

Hofstede, G. (1980). *Culture's consequences: International differences in work-related values*. Thousands Oaks, CA: Sage.

House, R. J., Hanges, P. J., Mansour, M., Dorfman, P. W., & Gupta, V. (2004). *Culture, leadership and organizations: The GLOBE study of 62 societies*. Thousands Oaks, CA: Sage.

Kock, J., & Guillén, M. (2001). Strategy and structure in developing countries: Business groups as an evolutionary response to opportunities for unrelated diversification. *Industrial & Corporate Change, 10*, 1–37.

Lenartowicz, T., & Johnson, J. P. (2003). A cross-national assessment of the values of Latin American managers: Contrasting hues or shades of gray? *Journal of International Business Studies, 34*, 266–281.

Lévi-Strauss, C. (1963). *Structural anthropology*. New York: Basic Books,

Martinez-Nadal, S. (2013). *Women gradually gaining power and influence in Latin America business.* Retrieved from www.nearshoreamericas.com/women-in-business-latin-america-influence/

Mead, M. (1964). *Continuities in cultural evolution.* New Haven: Yale University Press.

Osland, J., De Franco, S., & Oslan, A. (2007). Organizational implications of Latin American culture: Lessons for the expatriate manager. *Economiae Gestao, 7,* 109–120.

Parente, R., Cyrino, A. B., Spohr, N., & de Vasconcelos, F. C. (2013). Lessons learned from Brazilian multinationals' internationalization strategies. *Business Horizons, 56,* 453–463.

Schein, E. H. (1992). *Organizational Culture and Leadership.* San Francisco, CA: Jossey-Bass.

Trompenaars, F. (1994). *Riding the waves of culture: Understanding cultural diversity in global business.* Burr Ridge, IL: Irwin.

Wardrope, W. (2005). Beyond Hofstede: Cultural applications for communicating with Latin American businesses. *Proceedings of the 2005 Association for Business Communication,* Irvine, CA. Retrieved from http://74.220.215.89/~businfm5/wp-content/uploads/2011/04/13ABC05.pdf..

7   Management in Latin America

Introduction

Competing for talent is now a reality for firms from around the world. The ability to recruit, develop, and retain skilled employees and effective leaders is a source of competittive advantage. For Latin American organizations, acquiring this capability will be essential in their pursuit for global competitiveness, and revisiting attitudes and practices toward women and leadership must be part of that process. For firms from outside Latin America, the challenge will be to understand how central culture is to the practice of human resource management in the region, and adopting culturally appropriate practices will have a direct impact on organizational performance.

In this chapter we describe and analyze issues related to leadership, organizational behavior, talent management, and negotiating in Latin America. The chapter highlights the influence of cultural norms and values in the management of organizations in the region. The goals of the chapter are to (a) identify the leadership styles that effectively respond to the cultural and competitive realities of the region, (b) to recognize the influence of culture on organizational behavior and the negotiation process, and (c) to understand the needs, challenges, and best practices related to recruiting and growing talent in Latin America.

The chapter is composed of five sections. The first section discusses leadership styles that best suit the cultural characteristics of the region, while highlighting changes to these leadership styles in response to global competititve dynamics. The second section focues on the influence of culture on various organizational behaviors such as communication, power dynamics, motivation, and teamwork. The next section identifies best practices for negotiating in the region, which incorporate an understanding of sociocultural norms and values. The fourth section describes the needs, challenges, and best practices related to recruiting, developing, and deploying talent in Latin American firms. The final section presents a summary of key concepts and managerial implications for firms inside and outside the region.

7.1   Leadership Styles

In chapter 6 we became familiar with cultural norms and values in Latin America and examined how these impact business culture. In this chapter we focus on leadership and human capital management. Culture remains an important variable to consider as we examine leadership and management in Latin American organizations, one that needs to be considered alongside the effects of competition and the regulatory environment discussed in the first three chapters of the book.

Leadership Styles and Cultural Values

Understanding leadership in Latin American organizations requires that we first review leadership theories. We then discuss how these leadership theories apply to the reality of Latin American national cultures and organizations. Table 7.1 summarizes selected leadership theories.

Douglas McGregor's Theory X and Y proposes that leadership and management styles vary according to assumptions about human nature (McGregor, 1960). Theory X is based on the belief that people are primarily evil and cannot be trusted to self-monitor or self-manage. Theory X assumes that people dislike work and prefer to avoid it and thus require constant supervision and

Table 7.1 Summary of Selected Leadership Theories

Theory X and Y	• *Theory X*: Belief that people are primarily evil and cannot be trusted to self-monitor or self-manage. Assumes people prefer to avoid hard work and require constant supervision and direction.
	• *Theory Y*: Assumes workers are self-motivated and capable of undertaking complex work with little supervision and oversight.
Weber's Theory of Leadership	• *Charismatic*: Based on devotion to the specific or exemplary character of an individual person.
	• *Traditional*: Based on an established belief in the sanctity of a traditionally ascribed position of authority.
	• *Rational*: Calls for obedience to the legally established impersonal order.
Contingency Model of Leadership	Leaders adapt their behaviors to fit the national culture of their followers, the position of power of the leader, and the task at hand.
Benevolent Paternalistic Leadership	Father figure or patriarch within an organizational hierarchy that commands respect and loyalty from employees in exchange for protection (personal and professional). Benevolent authoritative figure makes decisions on behalf of others for their own good.
Transformational Leadership	Transformational leaders provide vision and inspiration and create the necessary conditions for employees to willingly and enthusiastically contribute to the goals of the organization.

Source: Authors' elaboration.

direction. Theory Y has a more optimistic view of human nature. It assumes that work is a natural human process that can provide personal satisfaction and that workers are self-motivated and capable of undertaking complex work with little supervision and oversight. In the context of Latin American organizations, management practices and labor relations are more aligned with Theory X (Paige & Wiseman, 1993). In general, Latin Americans have a more pessimistic view of human nature; there is, for instance, a strong belief that people cannot be trusted until they earn that trust through actions. This belief is well aligned with the assumptions that underlie Theory X, and leaders that share these assumptions tend to be more controlling and directive. Moreover, the high power distance that characterizes Latin American cultures results in followers being more satisfied with autocratic leaders and their perceiving participative leaders—those that adopt a theory Y-based leadership style—as less competetent because they expect their leaders to openly display their expertise and power.

Weber's tripartite model of authority (defined as power accepted as legitimate by those subjected to it) identifies three bases for leaders' legitimacy: traditional, rational, and charismatic authority (Weber, 1947). In Latin America we find both traditional and charismatic leadership styles. Traditional authority, based on established beliefs in the sanctity of a traditionally ascribed position of authority, is consistent with the high degree of masculinity and formality present in the region. Charismatic authority, based on the devotion to the specific or exemplary character of an individual person, is also observed in Latin American organizations, especially when one studies the political history of Latin American populist leaders (the image of caudillos comes to mind). In many ways, these two bases of legitimacy are intertwined in Latin America, through the predominant preference for a paternalist leadership style. As Behrens (2010, p. 21) explains, the "style of charisma acceptable to Latin Americans stems from the notion of paternalism." Paternalism is defined as "hierarchy within a group, by means of which advancement and protection of subordinates are expected in exchange for loyalty, usually to a father or patriarch, who makes decisions on behalf of others for their good, even if this may be against their wishes. . . . Where patriarchalism rules, its legitimacy has seldom been questioned in organizations." Exploratory research conducted by Behrens on leadership style preferences in Brazil shows that paternalistic leaders are in fact preferred by the majority of Brazilians (although less so in the case of knowledge-based industries). He further concluded that the tendency of US multinationals in Brazil to appoint subsidiary managers whose style matches the preferred US style of leadership is so ineffective that these managers are rarely able to make the transition to local organizations.

Finally, a contingency perspective of leadership suggests that effective leaders need to adapt their behaviors to fit the national culture of their followers Thus, cultural values will have a significant impact on what followers regard as "good" or "bad" leadership (Hofstede, 1980; House, Hanges, Javidan, Dorfman,

& Gupta, 2004; Muczik & Holt, 2008). Hofstede's cultural values of power distance, collectivism, and uncertainty avoidance are particularly useful in understanding followers' expectations of leaders in the region. In Latin American countries, which are characterized by high power distance, followers are comfortable accepting the authority of leaders, as defined by a well-established hierarchy, and there is an expectation of social distance between leaders and followers. Subordinates prefer to depend on others (Lenartowicz & Johnson, 2002) and are more likely to prefer a directive and paternalistic leadership style (Dorfman et al., 1997; Hofstede, 1980; Recht & Wilderom, 1998). Leaders from outside the region may find that overly casual and informal management and more participative or consultative leadership styles do not work as well in Latin American organizations, as followers will have a more traditional perspective on their leaders (i.e., an authority figure who is not like them and who should command respect). However, the presence of collectivism alongside high power distance leads to a form of "benevolent paternalism" that has been well documented (Davila & Elvira, 2012; Martinez, 2003, 2005). Moreover, high scores on uncertainty avoidance lead followers to expect that these benevolent but authoritarian leaders will also provide clear direction and structured processes to enable followers to do their jobs effectively (Hofstede, 1980). Abarca, Majluf, and Rodriguez (1998) observed a preference for well-defined rules to guide behavior within organizations.

A high degree of uncertainty avoidance in the region is also associated with employees' low assertiveness and reluctance to make decisions and accept responsibilities. Research conducted by Abarca et al. (1998) in the context of Chilean organizations found this to be true; however, they found that low assertiveness and risk aversion diminished among managers with higher levels of education and at higher levels in the organization. High degrees of uncertainty avoidance combined with high degrees of collectivism are also reflected in followers' aversion to conflict and confrontation. Thus, actions such as pointing out an employee's mistakes in front of others will be detrimental to the overall organizational climate.

Over the past few years, the GLOBE project has sought to develop a more in-depth understanding of the impact of cultural variables on leadership and organizational practices. New insights into the culturally contingent nature of leadership in Latin America have emerged from this research, pointing perhaps to some changes to Latin American values as they pertain to today's global and highly dynamic organizational context. The findings from this study show a relatively homogeneous Latin American culture that values in-group collectivism, is humane, feminine, and present-oriented but also more individualistic and achievement-oriented than previously shown. The achievement orientation would be consistent with the high degree of masculinity present in the region, while the humane orientation could be explained by the high degree of collectivism and moderate levels of feminine values observed in some countries in the region. In the organizational context, the traits that were universally associated with effective leadership included being trustworthy, collaborative, diplomatic, performance-oriented, skilled at administration, visionary, humane, and effective as a team builder. Traits that were seen as hindering effective leadership include being autocratic, self-centered, a face-saver, and malevolent, although the intensity of negative perceptions regarding these traits varied by country. The findings of the GLOBE project that autocratic, self-centered leaders are seen as less effective is consistent with the well-established preference among Latin Americans for leaders whom they see as a "benevolent patrón," rather than as an abusive autocrat. In terms of specific leadership styles, the study found that charismatic/value-based and team-oriented leadership styles were preferred by Latin Americans. As would be expected, participative, individualistic, and autonomous leadership styles were rated less favorably (House et al., 2004; Ogliastri et al., 1999).

Our discussion on leadership styles and culture seems to indicate that a benevolent paternalistic leadership style is preferred and likely to be more effective in the context of Latin American organizations. Benevolent paternalism relies on an unspoken social contract that rules the interactions between managers and employees in today's business organizations. Subordinates expect their managers' protection in exchange for loyalty; thus, there is a sort of "dependency-based" relationship between leaders and followers. Subordinates expect their managers to take care of their personal and family needs; they also expect to be treated with a minimum level of dignity and respect (Greer & Stephens, 1996). Similarly, managers see the organization as a "family" for which they need to provide, and any actions that violate this "duty" will result in employees feeling betrayed. Some researchers have found that this expectation is primarily associated with top-level management and not with those in direct supervisory roles; employees often bypass their immediate supervisors and take their problems or concerns to the top (Page & Wiseman, 1993). A corresponding concept of "fraternalism" (brotherhood) has been identified instead for the role expectations of lower-level supervisors (d'Iribarne, 2002; Martinez, 2003). Behrens (2010) found that this leadership style may be less predominant in knowledge-based industries. This paternalistic leadership style is also consistent with Latin Americans' expectations for egalitarianism, a balance between what d'Iribarne (2001, p. 28) describes as "equals that do not cooperate" and "authority that intimidates." Attempts by foreign leaders to adopt a more "transactional" leadership style, with its underlying expectation that workers will perform their jobs in exchange for a wage, are likely to have disappointing results. Employees in Latin America will not engage with the organization's goals or "give their best" if they feel the organization, through its leaders, does not care about them and their families.

In today's global organizations, though, it is more common to find transformational leaders than charismatic ones. Transformational leaders provide vision and inspiration and create the conditions necessary for employees to willingly and enthusiastically contribute to the goals of the organization (Bass &

Avolio, 1994). Over the next few years, it will be interesting to observe whether any changes to leadership style preferences emerge in Latin American organizations. By all accounts a transformation is already under way in Latin America between the old and the new styles of leadership. For one, some of the largest family businesses in the region are being passed on to the younger generation. This new generation has been educated in some of the best business schools in the United States and Europe, is fluent in English, and is technologically savvy. In the best-planned succession cases, they have not only worked abroad outside the family business but have also spent many years learning their own businesses from the bottom up and thus are extremely knowledgeable about their industries and their national markets. Analysts familiar with the management of family groups in the region expect this new cadre of leaders to be more in tune with the needs of consumers, more open to internationalization, and more likely to look to Asia for growth, in addition to the United States and Europe. They are also more aware of their companies' social and environmental responsibilities and are more willing to embrace modern human resource practices (Brenes, 2012; Long, 2013).

Women as Leaders

There is abundant research that shows that the presence of women in executive positions and in boards of directors improves organizational performance. We have certainly seen gains in the number of women occupying positions at the top, yet the gap between genders remains in all regions, and Latin America is no exception (Artigas, Callegaro, & Novales-Flamarique, 2013; McKinsey & Co., 2010; Moreno, 2013; United Nations, 2010).

Looking at Hofstede's measures of masculinity, we find that Mexico and countries in the Andean region tend to be more masculine, while those in Central America and the Southern Cone are more feminine. In the organizational context, one would expect gender inequality to be higher in countries with a more masculine culture; in Latin America this gender gap is, in fact, present, even for countries with slightly lower masculinity scores. Latin American companies are very patriarchal, and senior executive positions are notoriously male dominated. A McKinsey & Company (2010) survey shows that Latin America lags behind the rest of the world in gender diversity. Among Latin American respondents, only 21% indicated that their companies include gender diversity as a top-10 agenda item, whereas 27% in Europe, 28% in North America, and 35% in the Asia-Pacific region do so. For the top-performing companies in their study, gender diversity is a top-three agenda item, with 87% of these respondents reporting that more than 15% of their C-level[1] executives are women, against 55% for all respondents.

As cited by Moreno (2013), the percentages of women on boards in Latin America ranges from 1.9% in Chile and 5.1% in Brazil to 6.8% in Mexico and 10% in Colombia. A study of board members in the 50 largest firms in

Colombia shows almost half the firms do not have a single woman on their boards. Yet, some encouraging trends are emerging. In many cases, the few women in boards of directors are there because they are members of the family that owns the company, as in the case of FEMSA, a large holding beverage company in Mexico. This is also the case in large family businesses where the patriarch is close to retirement age and daughters rather than sons are inheriting the reins of their companies. Examples include Maria Asuncion Aramburuzabala, who took over Grupo Modelo (the maker of Corona) in the 1990s; Pilar Zabala, the head of Chile's 30-company conglomerate Pie de Monte since 2006; and the empire left behind in Brazil by Dirce Navarro de Camargo, which includes cement, real estate, and energy companies, to her daughters, Regina, Renata, and Rosana (Long, 2013).

The talent shortages now common in many countries of the world make the gap between men and women in senior management positions untenable. Incorporating qualified women into the top leadership positions will help companies fill this urgent talent shortfall (Barsh, Cranston, & Craske, 2008). But gender diversity at all levels of the organization has benefits that go beyond filling a talent shortage.

Early research sponsored by the International Women's Forum (Rosener, 1990) showed that women are more likely than men to use transformational leadership. Women were also more likely than men to use power based on charisma, work record, and contacts (personal power), rather than power based on organizational position, title, and the ability to reward and punish (structural power).

McKinsey & Company has been conducting global surveys on gender diversity and its impact on corporate performance since 2007. This research has consistently shown that gender diversity (including having three or more women in C-level positions) is indeed a driver of corporate performance, measured in terms of return on equity, operating results, and stock price growth. The findings also show that gender diversity strengthens organizations' ability to recruit and retain talent and raises productivity and employee morale. For example, a study by the European Commission found that 58% of companies with diversity programs reported higher productivity and improved employee motivation; 62% reported easier recruitment and retention of highly talented people (Desvaux, Devillard-Hoellinger, & Meaney, 2008). Another study found that having at least one woman on the board of directors of a company reduces by 20% the chance of the firm going bankrupt (Women on Boards, 2011).

Although Latin American firms remain reluctant to consider women for governance positions, minor signs of improvement are evident. McKinsey (2010) found that Latin American firms that are deliberately trying to recruit, retain, and develop women are doing so by providing more flexible working conditions, supporting programs and facilities to reconcile work and family life, and encouraging female networking and mentoring (Artigas et al., 2013; McKinsey & Co., 2010). There is also increasing acceptance of women as directors, primarily in banking and the retail sector. To the extent that women are acquiring the same sets of skills and competencies as men and are becoming more experienced, they are more likely to be considered for these positions. Among Latin American firms, the main benefits associated with having women on their boards of directors include strengthening organizational diversity; gaining a better understanding of the marketplace, where women are now more important consumers; balancing men's and women's perspectives in the decision-making process; and developing more open organizational cultures (Moreno, 2013).

The incorporation of women across all levels of the organization, but especially in top leadership positions, will help Latin American firms achieve, at a minimum, competitive parity in the global market. McKinsey's extensive research has revealed that one of the keys to improving gender diversity is to make it a top-three agenda item. Other actions that seem to make a notable difference are "visible monitoring by the CEO; skill-building programs aimed specifically at women; and encouraging or mandating senior executives to mentor junior women" (McKinsey & Co., 2010, p. 5). To attract and retain women, Latin American firms will have to implement policies and programs that enhance women's presence, resilience, and sense of belonging, including helping them be more assertive, take risks, be adaptable, develop social networks, and adopt a more positive framing (Barsh et al., 2008).

7.2   Culture and Organizational Behavior

In this section we focus on how culture impacts selected aspects of organizational behavior, namely delegation, communication, motivation, and teamwork.

Delegation

The primarily hierarchical nature of organizations in Latin America leads to limited delegation of tasks and a highly centralized power structure. Too much delegation can be perceived as undermining authority, and even when tasks are delegated, decision-making power and resource control remain in the hands of a few executives at the top. This high degree of centralization also results in organizations that are rather opaque, with little information shared with those at the bottom of the organization. The concentration of power and information in the hands of so few makes implementing empowerment initiatives difficult; this diminishes the ability of front-line employees to respond to consumers' needs in a timely fashion.

Communication

As briefly described in chapter 6, Latin Americans are predominantly high-context cultures. Indirect communication that conveys information while saving face and preserving the relationship is the norm in Latin American organizations. In addition, personal communication is very important in the region. Creating friendly and warm personal relationships among managers and employees (Abarca et al., 1998) and an organizational environment of respect and consideration (Greer & Stephens, 1996) is one of the most important tasks for managers in Latin American organizations.

Frequent face-to-face communication and social interactions allow managers and subordinates to bridge the power distance inherent in Latin American organizations by establishing a social connection. Also, it allows managers to gain a rich understanding of what is happening at all levels of the organization, an imperative in highly centralized organizations. Moreover, personal interactions are key to building trust, loyalty, and a sense of solidarity and reciprocity across all levels of the organization; these are essential in achieving high levels of performance and strengthening organizational agility and flexibility.

Motivation

Maslow's pioneering work on motivation led to his development of the concept of a hierarchy of needs. The theory assumes that people's behavior is motivated by their desire to satisfy lower-order needs (e.g., physiological) and then moves up toward the fulfillment of higher-order needs (e.g., self-realization) (Maslow, 1970). In the context of the wide social and economic gaps present in Latin America, one would expect employees to be motivated by lower-order needs. This is in fact evident in the importance placed by employees on financial compensation and rewards that yield job security, protection for themselves and their families, and a sense of belongingness or affiliation. Lenartowicz and Roth (2001) found that in the context of Brazil, security, followed by enjoyment and self-direction, were the most important motivators of performance. Yet, Latin Americans are very status conscious; thus, motivators that raise their self-esteem also have a positive effect on performance. For instance, job titles are very important to individuals because they assert the person's status within the organization, and it is not unusual to see important-sounding titles that do not match the level of decision-making power or skills of the title holder (Flynn, 1994). Perks such as reserved parking spaces, a company phone, and so forth are also highly valued as symbols of high social standing.

Herzberg's theory of motivation identified two types of factors. *Hygiene* factors, which are considered extrinsic to the job, must be attended to in order to avoid employees' dissatisfaction. *Motivators* are factors that are intrinsic to the employee and are likely to lead to superior performance (Herzberg, 1966). In the context of Latin American organizations, reasonable wages and working conditions are considered hygiene factors. Not allowing employees to express their religiosity in the workplace (e.g., the wearing of crosses, displaying images of the virgin or saints) or publicly criticizing or reprimanding an employee are deterrents to even basic levels of performance.

In terms of reinforcement theory, the application of positive versus negative reinforcements, Abarca et al. (1998) found that Chilean managers paid more attention to poor performance, and although they indicated a preference for positive reinforcement, they admitted to using sanctions more frequently than rewards (79% versus 72%). Sanctions were also more formally established than rewards, a practice that has also been observed in the case of Mexican organizations (Kras, 1991).

We discuss motivators in greater detail in the section on performance appraisal and compensation.

Teamwork

Hofstede (1991) found that power distance and collectivism are positively correlated: when people are highly dependent on each other, they are also dependent on authority figures. Thus, management in a collectivist society is about managing groups, not individuals (Davila & Elvira, 2005). Teamwork is both consistent with highly collectivist societies and also a way to bridge the high power distance present in Latin American cultures. Loyalty to the group in particular has been found to be an important organizational value (Lenartowicz & Johnson, 2002), and team-based leadership is also preferred by Latin American employees. There are exceptions, however, such as in the case of Chile, which is characterized by a high level of individualism and a corresponding reduced preference for team work (Abarca et al., 1998).

However, the combination of high power distance and collectivist behaviors makes implementation of self-managed teams problematic in Latin America. In high-power-distance Latin America, employees may be reluctant to express their opinions freely, or their opinions may not be favorably received. Moreover, in collectivist societies, employees tend to evaluate the performance of those in their in-group more positively than that of those in the out-group. Thus, to achieve the level of active participation and objective performance evaluations associated with self-managed teams, adjustments may be needed for firms operating in Latin America (Gomez & Sanchez, 2005).

Managing multicountry and virtual teams also presents challenges in Latin America. First, the importance of perceived in-group membership determines Latin Americans' willingness to collaborate and share information within a team. The inherent physical and cultural distances of multicountry and virtual teams may also create communication problems because of both the region's high context and Latin Americans' aversion toward conflict and confrontation. Identifying ways to increase the amount of face-to-face communication between team members, establishing clear team structures and norms, and identifying group goals will go a long way in improving team performance.

7.3   Managing Talent in Latin America

In 1998, McKinsey's article "The War for Talent" brought attention to the shortage of executive talent faced by US firms, a shortage that was expected to intensify. Follow-up research conducted in 2001 showed the shortage was a fact of life for organizations in the United States and in others parts of the globe (Axelrod, Handfield-Jones, & Welsh, 2001; Chambers, Foulon, Handfield-Jones,

Hankin, & Michaels, 1998). The main factors driving this talent shortage are increased competition for talent from small and medium-size businesses and from companies from emerging economies; an increasingly aging population; a higher degree of job mobility; and the paucity of women in executive positions. Moreover, today's business organizations require a more sophisticated, globally minded, and technologically savvy manager, a type that is in short supply. We first describe the scope and implications of a shrinking talent pool and then present selected best practices related to recruiting and developing talent in Latin American firms.

Talent Needs in Latin America

Talent shortages, also described as skill gaps, have been identified as one of the main challenges faced by global leaders, including those from Latin America, and this situation will continue (Axelrod et al., 2001; Chambers et. al, 1998; Ready, Hill, & Conger, 2008; Schwalje, 2011). Skill gaps have a particularly strong impact on small and medium-size businesses, which identified these shortages as a major or severe obstacle to their growth—42% and 39%, respectively, against 18% of large firms (Schwalje, 2011). Difficulties in recruiting and retaining qualified employees were identified as the second most important concern among Latin American managers (CFOSurvey.com, 2013). A lack of executive talent was also identified as a major competitive weakness for Latin American firms (Haberer & Kohan, 2007), with the skills gap extending to all organizational levels and industries (Schwalje, 2011). Research indicates that middle-income countries, such as those in Latin America, are especially affected by skills gaps, since their rapid development is usually associated with more sophisticated technology adoption, export-oriented industries, and the presence of foreign investment. These conditions result in a higher demand for highly skilled workers who are performance and competitiveness oriented (Lall, 2000; Porter, Sachs, & McArthur, 2001; Schwalje, 2011). Table 7.2 shows the level of the skills gap in Latin American countries.

Table 7.2 Skills Gaps in Latin America

% of Firms with a Major or Very Severe Skills Gap	Countries
> 15%	Costa Rica, Mexico, Nicaragua, Panama
15%–35%	Bolivia, Chile, Colombia, Ecuador, El Salvador, Guatemala, Honduras, Peru, Uruguay, Venezuela
< 36%	Argentina, Brazil, Jamaica, Paraguay
20.3%	Average, Latin America and the Caribbean
24%	Average, Middle East and North Africa
15%–16%	Average, East and South Asia

Source: World Bank Enterprise Surveys 2002–2010.

Developing Talent in Latin America

In this section, we borrow extensively from the research on work values and human resource management reported by Davila and Elvira (2005), which is based on the premise that Latin American organizations have adopted hybrid management systems that integrate global and local management practices. Our reseach in preparation for this book supports their assertion that Latin American firms increasingly combine the old and the new in the policies and processes that guide their management and development of human capital. We also discuss several best practices for attracting, motivating, and retaining talent in today's global organizations.

Recruitment and Selection

Recruitment and selection practices are influenced by the long-term goals of the organization, local laws, traditional recruitment practices, and cultural differences. As described earlier, a strong sense of collectivism in Latin America leads to a preference for those considered members of the in-group (Hofstede, 1980). Thus, when there is a job opening, managers are most likely to recruit from within their affiliation groups, be it family, friends, university peers, or members of their current employees' families (Flynn, 1994; Gomez & Sanchez, 2005).

In terms of selection, the criteria used are likely to reflect the hybrid management system referenced earlier. Although skills, merit, and experience are given due weight in the evaluation of an applicant, the social network of the applicant and personal characteristics such as gender, age, and physical appearance also play a significant role; this is especially true in the selection of top executives (Abarca et al., 1998). Those in the in-group will be more trusted and seen as more reliable, and the availability of more personal information about them may facilitate assessing how an applicant will fit into the organization. In addition, the sense of solidarity and reciprocity mentioned earlier is likely to impact a manager's decision to choose someone referred by a relative or friend over someone unknown.

Development and Promotion

Organizational needs for training and development vary by country and are highly dependent on the quality of the country's educational systems. Companies operating in Latin America are faced with unskilled and semiskilled labor pools, and companies are not always in a position to offer remedial training and education (Davila & Elvira, 2005; Schwalje, 2011). However, companies are recognizing the need for training and have engaged in internal (e.g., Cementos Mexicanos-CEMEX) and cooperative training initiatives (e.g., the PREJAL project, a public private partnership for promoting youth employment in Latin

America, trained more than 17,000 young people in five countries between 2005 and 2010) (CFOSurvey.org, 2013; PREJAL Project, 2012).

Promotions are also influenced by an employee's social network and personal characteristics, although the influence of these factors is less marked in such cases than it is during the selection process (Abarca et al., 1998).

Performance Appraisal and Compensation

The dislike for conflict and confrontation characteristic of Latin Americans makes performance appraisals and evaluation as conducted in the United States and other Western countries impractical and unacceptable in the region. The collectivist nature of the culture may lead employees to take an "everyone is accountable, and thus no one is accountable" position. Power distance also plays a role in performance evaluations. Lower-level employees may perceive performance appraisals as unfair. Since they usually have little control or autonomy over work systems and resources, they may believe that responsibility for performance falls on their supervisors or upper management. Moreover, employees may see performance appraisals as futile exercises, as they have few expectations of social mobility based on merit. Finally, given the high levels of uncertainty avoidance in the region, one might expect employees to be reluctant to engage in self-evaluations or to accept blame for deficiencies in their performance, as these imply a high professional and financial risk.

The financial rewards and fringe benefits valued by employees are affected primarily by socioeconomic conditions, labor practices and regulations, and cultural values. In Latin America, a region with wide income differences between the wealthy and the poor, financial compensation is certainly the most important. This can extend beyond salaries to include subsidized or free food, transportation, medical care, and vacation premiums (Flynn, 1994; Gomez & Sanchez, 2005; Greer & Stephens, 1996). Salaries are also important for those in higher positions as they signal their power and authority to others within the organization. One must also understand that what gives meaning to Latin Americans' work is their need to provide a high quality of life for their families (Davila & Elvira, 2005). Thus, in addition to fair wages, Latin Americans value material and nonmaterial rewards that benefit their families, either directly (e.g., educational subsidies for children; health insurance that covers parents) or indirectly (e.g., providing training for the employee that results in promotion possibilities). Moreover, compensation and rewards, including salary increases, vacation time, and promotions, are primarily linked to seniority (Davila & Elvira, 2005). Table 7.3 summarizes the various types of rewards that are valued by employees in Latin American organizations.

Latin American firms' ability to recruit and retain talented managers can become a valuable competitive advantage. McKinsey's extensive research on talent shortages, especially managerial talent, reveals some best practices that Latin American firms should consider implementing (Axelrod et al., 2001;

Table 7.3 Rewards Valued by Employees in Latin America

Type of Rewards	
Financial	Fair wages and fringe benefits.
	Especially valued: Financial rewards that extend to family (spouse, children, parents). Common benefits include health insurance, school supplies, and educational subsidies.
Security	A great deal of security in terms of predictable salary, benefits, and future employment.
Affiliation	Social interactions with colleagues.
	Sense of pride from belonging to a well-respected organization.
Status	Rewards that raise the individual's prestige within the group (e.g., promotions, job titles, larger office, reserved parking spaces, use of company car or phone).
Lifestyle	Time and flexibility to pursue other important aspects of an individual's lifestyle (e.g., family, leisure, education).
Authority	Opportunity to manage and direct other people.

Source: Authors' elaboration.

Chambers et al., 1998; Guthridge, Komm, & Lawson, 2008; Ready et al., 2008). These practices include making talent management a top strategic priority; developing a clear company value proposition and brand (i.e., communicating to prospective employees why they should work for your company rather than a competing firm); and offering a good "product" (i.e., jobs that provide meaning, freedom, and/or opportunities for advancement) and a fair "price" (i.e., compensation and lifestyle that meet the needs of employees).

7.4   Culture and Negotiation

Negotiation is a part of everyday business activities. In cross-cultural settings, misunderstandings occur as a result of one party ascribing erroneous meaning to the other party's words and behaviors. These misunderstandings can be amplified by differences in language, communication, and negotiation style. Firms interested in doing business in Latin America need to understand how cultural values and norms impact the negotiation process and strategies of Latin Americans so that they can prepare for and adapt to them. In addition to Hofstede's cultural dimensions, a discussion of negotiation necessarily incorporates three of Trompenaars's dimensions—particularism, emotional expression, and diffuse relationships. Time orientation and formality are also important cultural considerations.

Latin American managers' perceptions of negotiations exhibit the same hybrid nature of management practices mentioned earlier. More traditional managers in the region are likely to see negotiations as win-lose (zero-sum) situations, while those that adopt a more modern approach will see negotiations as a win-win (positive-sum) opportunity. For managers from outside the region, predicting whether their Latin American counterpart will approach negotiations from a traditional or a modern perspective will depend on four key factors: Sector, Age, Locale, and Education (SALE), with younger, urban, more educated businesspeople from technologically advanced, higher-growth sectors being more likely to approach negotiations as a win-win (Becker, 2011).

In addition to their overall approach to negotiations, Latin American managers place the utmost importance on personal, trust-based relationships, more than on the specifics of a business deal. In countries with high levels of economic and political instability, weak legal and judicial systems, and high degrees of uncertainty avoidance, self-enforcing or relational governance mechanisms (e.g., reputation, trust, goodwill) are more reliable and effective than detailed and lengthy written contracts. In most cases, Latin Americans enter into business deals only with those they like and trust; thus, time and effort must be allocated to building strong relationships with potential business partners (Katz, 2008). The preference for doing business with trusted partners is very much aligned with Latin Americans' strong inclinations toward particularism and diffuse relationships and with their high levels of collectivism and uncertainty avoidance.

In terms of the negotiation process, Latin Americans are more responsive to a foreign counterpart's proposals if they can determine his or her ability to fit in and to become a long-term partner. In this context, adapting to the region's hierarchical structures, cultural norms, and social etiquette and having a strong social network are instrumental in negotiating a deal and maintaining a long-term business relationship.

Latin Americans are less concerned about time and deadlines, and thus negotiations should not be rushed. Patience is key to understanding the bargaining positions of Latin American counterparts, and this information can be useful for handling negotiations in a respectful and culturally sensitive manner. Latin Americans can be expressive and sometimes loud during negotiation exchanges; however, care should be taken to avoid open conflict, confrontation, or criticism. Finally, although kind and friendly, Latin Americans are more comfortable if initially approached with a certain level of formality (e.g., being punctual, dressing in formal business attire, addressing people by title and last name). Table 7.4 presents a summary of how culture impacts negotiation in the region.

Morris's (2005) research suggests that minimizing the reliance on cultural schemas during the negotiation process can lead to better decision making. Cultural schemas can be triggered by a number of factors. First, attention pressures such as distractions, multitasking, or deadlines can drive people to ascribe cultural biases to their counterparts' behaviors; it is easier to rely on cultural biases when one is distracted than to engage one's critical thinking to assess a situation objectively. Second, emotional stressors push people to revert to their own cultural schemas during the negotiation process, and thus reaching consensus may be more difficult as people become less flexible in their approach to negotiations. Finally, cognitive factors can also trigger one's use of cultural schemas during the negotiation process. For instance, the expectation that one will be

Table 7.4 How Culture Impacts Negotiation in Latin America

Cultural Value Dimension	Negotiation Style and Process	Best Practices
Power distance/ hierarchy	• Respecting hierarchy is critical. • Those in higher power positions expect to be treated in a manner consistent with their power status. • Sellers have lower status than buyers.	• Identify the top manager who has actual power to make decisions. • Send a top-ranking executive to negotiate; especially important for sellers and small companies. • Select a team that matches the expected positions of the Latin American team. • Use physical appearance (of person and facilities) to communicate power.
Collectivism	• In-group relationships are more valued than out-group relations. • Becoming part of the in-group is critical.	• Take the time to become a member of the in-group (e.g., secure an introduction from a third party; leverage initial contacts to build a relationship). • Appeal to Latin Americans' collectivist nature by highlighting aspects of your deal that would benefit *the group.*
Trust-based relationships	There is a preference to deal with trusted partners.	• Allocate enough time to build personal relationships. • Follow through on your promises.
Uncertainty avoidance	• Prevalent attitude is "nothing gained; nothing ventured." • Risk aversion and discomfort with uncertainty make high-gamble deals less appealing.	• Be open to less-detailed written agreements; rely more on relationships and the value placed on honor and prestige to resolve contractual conflicts when they arise. • Be flexible in the management of contingencies.
Particularism	People are more important than rules. Latin American managers will give preferential treatment to members of their in-groups.	• Do not show your frustration or annoyance at being bumped by a friend or relative. • Strive to become part of the favored in-group by making social interactions an integral part of doing business in the region.
Formality	Expectations of respect and deference to a person's level of authority, education, social status, and age.	• Always use titles and address Latin American counterparts with deference. • Respect age, seniority, and class status.

Cultural Value Dimension	Negotiation Style and Process	Best Practices
Emotional expression	Latin American counterparts are likely to speak loudly and display drama, anger, and visceral responses to negotiating terms.	Respond with calm; ignore outbursts of emotion and move conversation to a different topic; ask Latin counterpart to explain concerns.
High-context communication	What is not said is as important as what is said.	• Learn to be a careful observant and a good listener: leverage cues from nonverbal behavior, silence, and indirect verbal communication. • Show empathy and respect when communicating bad or unpleasant news.
Temporal orientation (Polychronic)	• For Latin Americans, time is fluid and cyclical; time allocations are based on priorities given to affinity groups and desired quality of life. • Negotiations will progress slower, will take more time. • Punctuality is expected at business meetings, although you may be made to wait. • Frequent interruptions may occur during a meeting.	• Always arrive on time to business meetings, even if you expect delays. While waiting, engage the receptionist, executive assistant, or others in the waiting area. • Do not show annoyance or irritation for being made to wait. • Lunch meetings are recommended. • Plan for lengthy negotiation periods that account for relationship-building activities.

Source: Authors' elaboration, based on Becker (2011) and Volkema & Chang (1998).

held accountable for one's decision making can make people rely on cultural values and principles that can be easily supported when explaining one's decision-making process. Or, priming effects that trigger associations with an individual's own culture (e.g., language in which negotiations are conducted) can result in an individual relying more heavily on her own cultural schemas during the negotiation process. This all means that we can both prepare for and shape the impact that culture has on a negotiation involving people from other cultures. Carefully planning the setting, teams, and negotiation agenda can minimize cultural misunderstandings and ensure a more open, flexible, and collaborative negotiation process. Managers from both inside and outside the region should be mindful of these considerations when engaging in business negotiations.

7.5   Summary

In this chapter we examined the leadership styles that are most consistent with Latin American cultural values and are most preferred by followers. We find that a benevolent paternalistic style is consistent with followers' preferences, which are shaped by the prevalence of high power distance, masculinity, collectivism, and uncertainty avoidance in the region. We then described the state of women in top executive positions in Latin America. Latin America lags behind other regions of the world in the acceptance and presence of women in top positions, although this is slowly changing due to internal successions in large family-owned business groups. Research shows that firms that have women in top executive positions enjoy a competitive advantage in the market and improve their overall performance; Latin American firms are well advised to adopt best practices aimed at recruiting, retaining, and development women talent. This is especially critical given the increasing talent shortages facing today's organizations.

The chapter also reviews various organizational behavior aspects, including communication, delegation, and motivation. We focus primarily on the influence of culture on organizations and find that Latin American organizations are characterized by high centralization of power and decision making, opaque information sharing, bureaucratic internal systems and processes, and an emphasis on personal communication. In terms of motivators, it is important for the reader to remember that Latin American workers have an expectation of protection and reciprocity from their employers (in exchange for loyalty and commitment to the organization's goals), and therefore, financial incentives aimed to individual employees alone will not be sufficient. Fringe benefits that extend to families and that provide security and a balanced lifestyle are most valued by employees in Latin America.

Our final section focuses on negotiating in Latin America. Those doing business in the region should consider adopting a negotiation process that allows enough time to build rapport and trust, using a win-win approach, and following through on commitments and contracts. In sum, respecting the importance of hierarchy, engaging in highly personal relationships, and embracing the collectivist nature of Latin Americans and their expectations for reciprocal employer-employee relations are the most critical aspects for effectively managing organizations in the region.

Note

1. C-level is an adjective used for describing top-level executive positions such as CEO (chief executive officer), COO (chief operating officer), and CFO (chief financial officer).

References

Abarca, N., Majluf, N., & Rodriguez, D. (1998). Identifying management in Chile: A behavioral approach. *International Studies of Management and Organizations, 28*(2), 18–37.

Artigas, M., Callegaro, H., & Novales-Flamarique, M. (2013). Why top management eludes women in Latin America, 1–7. *McKinsey & Company*. Retrieved from www.mckinsey.com.

Axelrod, E. L., Handfield-Jones, H., & Welsh, T. A. (2011). War for talent, part 2. *The McKinsey Quarterly, 2*, 9–11.

Barsh, J., Cranston, S., & Craske, R. (2008). Centered leadership: How talented women thrive. *The McKinsey Quarterly, 4*, 35–48.

Bass, B. M., & Avolio, B. J. (Eds.). (1994). *Improving organizational effectiveness through transformational leadership*. Thousand Oaks, CA: Sage.

Becker, T. H. (2011). *Doing business in the new Latin America*. 2nd ed. Santa Barbara, California: Praeger.

Behrens, A. (2010). Charisma, paternalism, and business leadership in Latin America. *Thunderbird International Business Review, 52*(1), 21–29.

Brenes, E. R. (2012). Latin America's new breed of corporate leaders. *Latin Trade* (July–August), 14.

CFO Survey.com. (2013). CFOs: Latin American outlook bright for 2013. *Duke University News* (January 2). Retrieved from www.cfosurvey.org/13q1/PressRelease_ Latin America.pdf.

Chambers, E. G., Foulon, M., Handfiled-Jones, H., Hankin, S. M., & Michaels III, E. G. (1998). The war for talent. *The McKinsey Quarterly, 3*, 44–57.

D'Iribarne, P. (2001). Administración y culturas políticas. *Gestión y Política Pública, 10*(1), 5–29. Cited in M. M. Elvira and A. Davila (Eds.) (2005), *Managing human resources in Latin America*. London: Routledge.

D'Iribarne, P. (2002). Motivating workers in emerging countries: Universal tools and local applications. *Journal of Organizational Behavior, 23*(3), 243–256.

Davila, A., & Elvira, M. M. (2005). Culture and human resource management in Latin America. In M. M. Elvira and A. Davila (Eds.), *Managing human resources in Latin America*. London: Routledge.

Davila, A., & Elvira, M. (2012). Humanistic leadership: Lessons from Latin America. *Journal of World Business, 47*, 548–554.

Desvaux, G., Devillard-Hoellinger, S., & Meaney, M. C. (2008, September). A business case for women. *The McKinsey Quarterly*, 1–8.

Dorfman, P. W., Howell, J. P., Hibino, S., Lee, J. K., Tate, U., & Bautista, A. (1997). Leadership in Western and Asian countries: Commonalities and differences in effective leadership processes across cultures. *Leadership Quarterly, 8*(3), 233–274.

Flynn, G. (1994). HR in Mexico: What you should know. *Personnel Journal, 73*(8), 34–41.

Gomez, C., & Sanchez, J. I. (2005). Managing HR to build social capital in Latin America within MNCs. In M. M. Elvira and A. Davila (Eds.), *Managing human resources in Latin America*. London: Routledge.

Greer, C. R., & Stephens, G. K. (1996). Employee relations issues for US companies in Mexico. *California Management Review, 38*(3), 121–145.

Guthridge, M., Komm, A. B., & Lawson, E. (2008). Making talent a strategic priority. *The McKinsey Quarterly, 1*, 49–56.

Haberer, P. R., & Kohan, A. F. (2007). Building global champions in Latin America. *The McKinsey Quarterly*, special edition, 1–9.

Herzberg, F. (1966). *Work and the nature of man*. Cleveland: World.

Hofstede, G. (1980). *Culture's consequences: International differences in work-related values*. Abridged ed. Beverly Hills, CA: Sage.

Hofstede, G. (1991). *Cultures and organizations: Software of the mind*. Cambridge: Cambridge University Press.

House, R. J., Hanges, P. J., Javidan, M., Dorfman, P. W., & Gupta, V. (Eds.). (2004). *Culture, leadership, and organizations*. Thousand Oaks, CA: Sage.

Katz, L. (2008). *Negotiating international business: The negotiator's reference guide to 50 countries around the world*. Charleston, South Carolina: Booksurge.

Kras, E. S. (1991). *La administración mexicana en transición* [The Mexican administration in transition]. Mexico D.F., Mexico: Grupo Editorial Iberoamérica.

Lall, S. (2000). Skills, competitiveness and policy in developing countries. *QEH Working Paper Series*, Working Paper No. 46. Retrieved from www3.qeh.ox.ac.uk/pdf/qehwp/qehwps46.pdf.

Lenartowicz, T., & Johnson, J. P. (2002). Comparing managerial values in twelve Latin American countries: An exploratory study. *Management International Review, 42*(3), 279–307.

Lenartowicz, T., & Roth, K. (2001). Does subculture within a country matter? A cross-cultural study of motivational domains and business performance in Brazil. *Journal of International Business Studies, 32*(2), 305–325.

Long, G. (2013). Dynasties' silent revolution. *Latin Trade*. Retrieved from http://latintrade.com/2013/05/dynasties-silent-revolution.

Martinez, P. G. (2003). Paternalism as a positive form of leader-subordinate exchange: Evidence from Mexico. *Management Research, 1*, 227–242.

Martinez, P. G. (2005). Paternalism as a positive form of leadership in the Latin American context: Leader benevolence, decision-making control and human resource management practices. In M. M. Elvira and A. Davila (Eds.), *Managing human resources in Latin America*. London: Routledge.

Maslow, A. H. (1970). *Motivation and personality*. New York: Harper & Row.

McGregor, D. (1960). *The human side of enterprise*, New York: McGraw-Hill.

McKinsey & Co. (2010). *McKinsey global survey results: Moving women to the top*. Retrieved from www.mckinsey.com.

Moreno, A. (2013). Women on board. *Latin Trade*. Retrieved from http://latintrade.com/2013/4/women-on-board.

Morris, M. W. (2005). When culture counts—and when it doesn't. *Negotiation* (June), 1–5.

Muczic, J. P., & Holt, D. T. (2008). Toward a cultural contingency model of leadership. *Journal of Leadership & Organizational Studies, 14*(4), 277–286.

Ogliastri, E., McMillen, C., Altschul, C., Arias, M. E., Bustamante, C., Davila, C., et al. (1999). Cultura y liderazgo organizacional en 10 países de América Latina: El estudio Globe. [Culture and organizational leadership in 10 Latin American countries: The GLOBE study.] *Academia, Revista Latinoamericana de Administración, 22*, 29–57.

Page, N. R., & Wiseman, R. L. (1993). Supervisory behavior and worker satisfaction in the United States, Mexico and Spain. *Journal of Business Communication, 30*(2), 161–181.

Porter, M. E., Sachs, J. D., & McArthur, J. W. (2001). The Global Competitiveness Report 2001–2002: Executive summary. *World Economic Forum*. New York: Oxford University Press.

PREJAL Project. (2012). Retrieved from www.ilo.org/wcmsp5/groups/public/—dgreports/—xrel/documents/publication/wcms_193809.pdf.

Ready, D. A., Hill, L. A., & Conger, J. A. (2008). Winning the race for talent in emerging markets. *Harvard Business Review* (November), 63–70.

Recht, R., & Wilderom, C. (1998). Latin America's dual reintegration. *International Studies of Management & Organization, 28*(2), 3–17.

Rosener, J. B. (1990). Ways women lead. *Harvard Business Review* (November–December), 119–125.

Schwalje, W. A. (2011). The prevalence and impact of skill gaps on Latin America and the Caribbean. *Globalization, Competitiveness, and Governability Journal, 5*(1), 16–30.

United Nations. (2010). *The world's women 2010: Trends and statistics.* New York: United Nations Department of Economic and Social Affairs.

Volkema, R. J., & Chang, S. (1998). Negotiating in Latin America: What we know (or think we know) and what we would like to know. *Latin American Business Review, 1*(2), 3–25.

Weber, M. (1947). *The theory of social and economic organization.* Translated by Talcott Parsons. New York: Free Press.

Women on Boards. (2011). *Department of Business, Innovation, and Skills.* Retrieved from www.gov.uk/government/publications/women-on-boards-review.

Part III

Strategies for Latin Markets

8 Company Strategies for Firms from Outside the Region

Introduction

Multinationals assess the importance of opportunities in Latin America in relation to opportunities in other emerging markets. On the basis of this assessment, they allocate resources to build their presence in the region. These companies also identify key country markets in which to concentrate their effort and investments and adapt their global strategies to Latin American managerial styles. This chapter presents a framework for formulating such a strategy for multinational companies from outside the region.

The chapter focuses on several aspects of formulating a regional strategy for multinationals (MNCs) from outside the region. The first section discusses the challenges for strategy formulation in regional markets and elaborates on the advantages and disadvantages of MNCs in Latin America. The next section introduces a framework for a regional strategy for MNCs and describes a path of regional expansion for these companies. The following section describes the extent of replication and adaptation of MNCs in the region. The chapter ends with examples of regional strategies of these MNCs in Latin America.

8.1 MNCs Challenges and Competitive Advantages in Latin America

As we have discussed in chapters 4 and 5, countries in Latin America have vastly different buying power, consumer markets, cultures, and managerial styles. Different countries in the region also present unique vulnerabilities and risks. These differences present challenges to the formulation of a regional strategy. At the same time, despite these differences mentioned, Latin American countries share a number of similarities. Their core markets are based on robust vibrant middle-class markets with affordability as the key factor in success. These similarities present MNCs with a similar set of market opportunities and solutions.

To understand the strategy of multinational companies from outside the region, we need to identify first their strengths and weaknesses as competitors in Latin American markets. In formulating their regional strategies, MNCs leverage their advantages and try to compensate for their disadvantages. MNCs possess strong global brands, innovative products, and proven production processes. With a global presence, MNCs enjoy large economies of scale that bring a strong cost advantage in local markets. With a presence in different types of economies, MNCs also benefit from the ability to leverage the different comparative advantages of the countries in which they operate. This flexibility to leverage advantages gained in different world locations is also known as *arbitrage*. Furthermore, MNCs in Latin America bring to bear a wealth of resources and technology from their global parent corporations and the subsidiaries in other parts of the world.

On the other hand, MNCs suffer from a number of competitive disadvantages. For one, MNCs tend to have higher costs of operation than local competitors. They lack the deep understanding of the business culture that local companies have. Initially, MNCs do not have access to local supply networks, and they may be driven to build their own, at a high cost of development. In the relationship-driven cultures of Latin America, MNCs may also need to invest (at a cost) in building strong relationships with business and government.

8.2   MNC Regional Strategy in Latin America

Nonregional MNCs have a long history of presence in Latin America. Multinationals that entered the region many decades ago were attracted by the mineral and natural resources of the region. Other early pioneer multinationals were attracted by incipient domestic consumer markets, particularly those for packaged foods and cosmetics. In this chapter, we focus on this latter group.

Today, the presence of non–Latin American multinationals is felt in almost every economic sector of the region. Twenty-four non–Latin American MNCs are among the 100 largest companies in Latin America (see Table 8.1). These companies are in the retail, automotive, energy, telecom, food processing and beverages, and mining sectors. However, the largest companies in the region are Latin American firms in the extractive energy sectors; Petrobras (Brazil), Pemex (Mexico), and PDVSA (Venezuela) have annual revenues in excess of US$100 million. The largest non–Latin American multinational, Wal-Mart Latin America, had revenues of US$51 billion in 2012—almost half the revenue of the top Latin American giants.

Traditional Strategy

Historically, the strategy of multinationals can be described as involving three stages: initial penetration, regional market expansion, and consolidation. In the first stage, multinationals target two or three large regional markets and with global brands focus on premium market segments only. A second stage is the gradual expansion of the multinational into markets in other countries as well as deeper penetration into the initial country markets. Several strategies are utilized to carry out expansion. Acquisitions of local companies and brands allow multinationals to expand their offerings to other market segments. Expansion to secondary and tertiary market segments within a country is another expansion

Table 8.1 Non–Latin American MNCs among the 100 Largest Companies in the Region (2012)

Rank	Company	Country	Industry	2013 Revenues in US$ Mill	Subsidiaries
6	Telefónica	Spain	Telecom	40,255	Argentina, Brazil, Chile, Colombia, Central America, Ecuador, Mexico, Peru, Puerto Rico
11	Wal-Mart-Mexico	USA	Retail	32,242	Argentina, Brazil, Chile, Central America, Mexico
14	Casino	France	Retail	25,391	Brazil, Colombia
16	Volkswagen	Germany	Automotive	24,152	Argentina, Brazil (M), Bolivia, Chile, Ecuador, Mexico (M), Paraguay, Peru, Uruguay, Venezuela, Central America, Caribbean
22	Carrefour	France	Retail	18,695	Argentina and Brazil
27	Telefonica/Vivo	Spain	Telecom-mobile	16.604	See Telefonica
28	Nestle	Switzerland	Food	16,541	All 24 Latin American countries
29	Carrefour-Brazil	France	Retail	16,540	See Carrefour
31	AB Inbev	Belgium	Beverages (Beer)	15,772	
35	Fiat	Italy	Automotive	14,590	Argentina, Bolivia, Brazil (M), Chile, Colombia, Mexico, Paraguay, Peru, Uruguay, Venezuela, Central America, Caribbean
37	Endesa	Spain	Energy	14,228	Argentina, Brazil, Chile, Colombia, Peru, Central America
44	Wal-Mart Brazil	Brazil	Retail	12,690	See Wal-Mart
48	Fiat	Brazil	Automotive	11,720	See Fiat

(*Continued*)

Table 8.1 (*Continued*)

Rank	Company	Country	Industry	2013 Revenues in US$ Mill	Subsidiaries
51	AES	USA	Energy	11,550	Argentina, Brazil, Chile, Colombia, Guatemala, Mexico, Peru, Uruguay
59	Ford	USA	Automotive	10,880	Argentina, Belize, Brazil, Chile, Colombia, Central America, Venezuela
61	GM	USA	Automotive	9,470	Mexico, Central America, Argentina, Brazil, Chile, Colombia, Ecuador, Paraguay, Peru
65	Caterpillar	USA	Equipment	8,936	Brazil (M), Mexico (M), Argentina, Chile, Panama, Peru, Venezuela
69	GN Fenosa	Spain	Natural Gas	8,380	Argentina, Brazil, Colombia, Costa Rica, Dominican Republic, Guatemala, Mexico, Panama, Puerto Rico, Peru
73	SAB Miller	UK	Beverages (beer)	7,821	Brewing: Argentina, Chile, Colombia, Ecuador, El Salvador, Honduras, Panama, Peru
74	PepsiCo	USA	Food & Beverages	7,780	Argentina, Belize, Bolivia, Brazil, Caribbean, Central America, Chile, Colombia, Ecuador, Guyana, Mexico, Paraguay, Peru, Suriname, Uruguay, Venezuela,
77	Schulumberger	USA	Energy	7,554	Argentina, Colombia, Ecuador, Brazil, Mexico, Peru, Trinidad-Tobago

Rank	Company	Country	Industry	2013 Revenues in US$ Mill	Subsidiaries
80	Anglo/ American	USA/UK	Mining	7,527	Chile, Brazil, Colombia, Peru
86	Dow	USA		7,060	Regional Centers: Argentina, Brazil, Mexico Sales: Chile and Peru
91	Southern Copper	USA	Mining	6,669	Mining, Smelting & Refinining: Mexico, Peru
98	NII Holdings	USA	Technology	6,086	Argentina, Brazil, Chile, Mexico
99	Iberdola	Spain	Energy	6,077	Bolivia, Brazil, Honduras, Venezuela
100	Wal-Mart Chile	USA	Retail	6,044	See Wal-Mart

Source: Latin Trade (2013).

strategy. In the third stage of consolidation, multinationals reassess their competitive situation in several Latin American markets and, if necessary, withdraw from uncompetitive market situations. In addition, in this third stage multinationals also focus on rationalizing production, marketing, and financial activities. Thus, production will occur in one or two countries to serve the regional markets. For instance, manufacturing facilities in Brazil might supply Southern Cone markets whereas Mexico might be the supplier for the northern areas.

One important characteristic of the traditional multinational regional strategy is its focus on global brands aimed at affluent market segments. Aiming at the top of the market allowed multinationals to fully leverage their advantages and nullify any competitive threat from local companies. Global and premium brands were a good fit with more affluent and cosmopolitan customers.

One disadvantage of this strategy is the narrow customer base of the affluent market segment. To enter other attractive market segments, MNCs did not have the products or distribution. Another disadvantage of the traditional strategy is that the initial premium-price strategy was challenged by local competition over time. Local companies learned fast and developed their own versions of premium brands at lower cost. In most cases, MNCs were forced to lower their prices, and a price war evolved as even discount products entered into the fray. The only ways out of this vicious circle of price erosion were the introduction of more innovative products in the premium segment or, as mentioned, the acquisition of local products and brands for the mass markets.

A New Regional Strategy

Emerging market conditions in Asia and Latin America have challenged in many ways the traditional MNC strategy explained in the preceding section. The new strategy for MNCs is to focus on large mass markets and to consolidate their competitive position in a few country markets in the region. As was discussed in chapters 4 and 5, the emergence of middle classes has made possible the creation of large mass markets. This increase has been very large in Brazil and Mexico but also in midsize countries such as Colombia and Peru. In many countries, these consumers have migrated from the bottom of the pyramid and have no experience with or relevance to the global premium brands of multinationals.

The new strategy requires either extensive adaptation or innovation for large middle-class market where affordability is a key factor. In this respect, MNCs often have a cost disadvantage. Therefore, their new strategy has focused on improving efficiency and lowering costs. One way to lower costs is to hire local human resource talent to lead innovation, quality, and efficiency improvement and new product initiatives. This approach has been aided by the availability of large pools of qualified human resource talent in Mexico, Brazil, Colombia, and Argentina. In their new strategy, MNCs designate some of these large markets as leaders in businesses in which cost arbitrage possibilities make sense. For instance, Arcos Dorados, the master franchise for McDonald's in Latin America, has set up a center of excellence in distribution and quality control in Brazil for the purpose of improving the food supply for its restaurants and managing its regional supply chain (Industry Today, 2013). Nestle Latin America is another example of a multinational committed to finding better nutritional products for the region. One initiative is to add iron, calcium, and vitamins to Nestle's Nido milk powder brand for low-income consumers throughout Latin America. Nestle has also introduced snacks with reduced sugar and fat under the Nestle Fitness brands in six countries in Latin America, as well as low-salt bouillon, seasonings, and soups under the Maggi, Benebien, and Equivele brands in Dominican Republic, Argentina, and Chile respectively (Nestle, 2013).

8.3   A Regional Strategy Formulation Framework

A regional strategy is embedded within a multinational's global strategy and organization. In this section, we discuss the regional strategy only. The main assumption is that the multinational has presence in three or more country markets in Latin America.

Within this global strategy, a new regional strategy has four essential components (Lasserre & Schutte, 2006). The first component is regional ambition, which requires the determination of the strategic importance of the Latin America region in the global business portfolio of the multinational. A second component is strategic thrust, which is the identification of regional targets of opportunities. The third component is the building of the infrastructure and assets of the regional strategy. The final component focuses on the operational

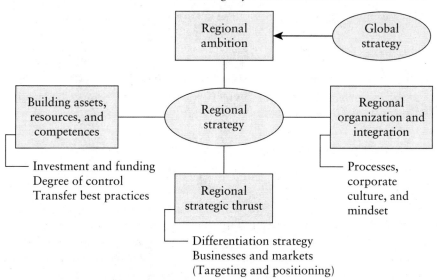

Figure 8.1 Regional Strategy Framework

Source: Adapted from Lasserre & Schutte (2006).

aspects and, in particular, the regional mindset that provides the personality of the firm in the region. These components are visualized in Figure 8.1. We elaborate on these four components next.

Regional Ambition

Regional ambition has two components. One part is shaping the regional vision. This part of the strategy requires visualizing the role of the region in the future of the company. This aspect of ambition entails deciding whether the company wants to be an important player in the region. If so, what is the level of assets and resources that must be dedicated to this region for the company to become a viable player? Finally, as there will be risks and challenges, ambition should address how the company will attempt to minimize them.

The second part of ambition is very straightforward. This aspect defines more specifically the importance of the region as a market and/or platform of production. This component defines more precisely the level of importance within the global corporate realm. For instance, a company may designate Brazil as one of the top five sources of global revenues and profits in the future.

A second element of regional ambition is strategic importance, determined by the range of opportunities that a region offers. These opportunities range from domestic market demand to natural resources and/or cost-effective service or manufacturing platforms. Latin America offers all of these opportunities. Large countries such as Brazil and Mexico offer a mix of opportunities, as they offer large internal markets and are endowed in rich natural resources. For example, Brazil and Mexico are manufacturing bases for General Motors, Ford,

Volkswagen, and Fiat. Smaller countries such as Costa Rica and Uruguay offer educated and bilingual labor forces at competitive costs for a range of service outsourcing. Panama offers very efficient logistics services and financial services. Thus, a multinational has to formulate a regional strategy that integrates the diversity of comparative and competitive advantages that Latin American countries offer and identify each country's contribution to the overall regional strategy and, in some cases, to the global strategy.

Concept of Proportionality

The strategic importance of a region can be used for important corporate decisions such as resource allocation. Using a simple example based on regional market size, we illustrate in Figure 8.2 the concept of proportionality. The horizontal axis measures the contribution of the region to an economic indicator. For instance, if we were to use population as our base of comparison, Latin America's share of the world's population is about 10%. Asia's share is about 50%. If we were to use share of GDP, Asia accounts for 26% of the world's GDP and Latin America, 6%.

In the vertical axis of Figure 8.2, we present the region's contribution to the multinational's global revenues. For instance, assume that Asia represents 30% of multinational global revenues. If Asia accounts for 50% of the world's population, we may argue that Asia is underrepresented in the global business portfolio of a multinational. If Latin America contributes 10% percent of global revenues, the region is on target in realizing its potential because that is its population's proportion of world population. The best alignment of a region's performance is the diagonal line in Figure 8.2, which assumes equal representation.

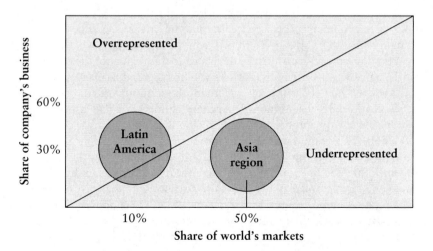

Figure 8.2 Concept of Proportionality

Source: Authors' elaboration.

Firm Worldwide Sales = 18.4 units	World GDP = 100%
Home market = 5/5 = 1 unit	Home GDP = 5%
Rest of region = 27/5 = 5.4 units	Rest of region GDP = 27%
Home region = (5+27)/5 = 6.4 from home region	Home region GDP = 32%
Rest of the world = 68/5 = 12 units	Rest of world = 68%

Figure 8.3 An Example of Proportionality

Source: Authors' elaboration.

A further example illustrates numerically how to estimate regional representation. In this example, the world's GDP is depicted on the right column and multinational sales by region in the left column. In this example, the region is NAFTA, which comprises the United States, Canada, and Mexico. Thus, the example shows that the home market economy in the United States generates 5% of the world's GDP. The rest of the region, Canada and Mexico, accounts for 27% of the world's GDP. The NAFTA region thus constitutes 32% of the world's GDP. The rest of world accounts for 68% of the total world's GDP. Applying the rule of proportionality to the firm, we would expect that for any one unit of sales in the home market, the firm should sell 5.4 units in NAFTA and 12 in the rest of the world.

Regional Strategic Thrust

A second component of regional strategy is regional strategic thrust. To develop thrust, the multinational identifies key strategic country markets, businesses, and particular market segments. The multinational also identifies countries in which to access the strategic resources to support a regional strategy. Finally, the multinational formulates a strategy of differentiation from competitors in those key country markets.

The key regional markets in Latin America should offer the largest business market opportunities in the region. More likely than not, these markets are Brazil and Mexico. A third market among the top three regional opportunities should be a medium-size market such as Argentina or Chile. A second tier of regional markets comprises countries with good potential but not as matured. Examples of these second-tier markets are Colombia, Peru, Uruguay, and the countries of Central America.

Another aspect of formulating strategic thrust is a strategy for regional market development beyond the first tier of opportunities. Multinationals with long presence in Latin America have already achieved good penetration of the primary markets in the first-tier countries and even the second-tier group. These companies have already achieved a strong presence in the largest urban concentrations with populations of 1 million or more.

These companies are now expanding into secondary and tertiary cities in the first- and second-tier markets. The third level consists of mostly rural areas and small cities of 100,000 inhabitants or less. Brazil has 13 cities with populations of more than 1 million inhabitants, 17 cities with more than 500,000 but fewer than 1 million inhabitants, and 70 cities with more than 200,000 but fewer than 500,000 inhabitants (Citymayors-Brazil, 2013). Similarly, Mexico has 10 cities with 1 million or more inhabitants, 11 cities with 500,000 or more but fewer than 1 million inhabitants, and 42 cities with fewer than 500,000 but more than 200,000 inhabitants (Citymayors-Mexico, 2013). The strategic thrust for the three levels of market potential within a country may need to be adapted to reflect differences in consumer sophistication, buying power, and local competition. This logic of strategic thrust is illustrated in Table 8.2.

Table 8.2 Regional Strategy Expansion

Market Tiers	Countries	1st-Tier City Markets (1 million+) Examples	2nd-Tier Cities (500K–1 million) Examples	Smaller Cities (> 500K) Examples
Top three (three of four)	Brazil	Rio de Janeiro, Sao Paulo, Brasilia	Campinas, Salvador, Monterrey, Guanajuato	Santos
	Mexico	Mexico City, Guadalajara, Monterrey	Queretaro, Hermosillo	Veracruz, Matamoros
	Argentina	Buenos Aires, Cordoba, Rosario	La Plata, Mar del Plata, Tucuman	Parana, Formosa
	Chile	Santiago	Valparaiso	Concepcion
Second Tier	Colombia	Bogota, Cali, Medellin, Barranquilla	Cartagena, Cucuta, Bucaramanga	Pereira, Santa Marta
	Peru	Lima	Arequipa, Trujillo, Chiclayo, Piura	Iquitos, Cuzco
	Venezuela	Caracas, Maracaibo, Maracay, Valencia	Barquisimeto, Ciudad, Guayana	Barcelona, Maturin
Rest of the region	Ecuador, Central America, Caribbean	Guayaquil, Quito, Santa Cruz (Bolivia)	San Jose, Panama City, La Paz, Kingston (Jamaica)	Cuenca, Sucre (Bolivia), New Kingston (Jamaica)

Source: World Population Review (2013).

Building Assets, Resources, and Competencies

A third component of regional strategy is building the regional infrastructure of assets, resources, and competencies. Building such infrastructure requires financial resources as well as physical infrastructure. In addition to physical assets, firms also must assemble human resources and build social capital in the region.

Take, for instance, the Latin American regional strategy for Chevron. This giant oil multinational has built an infrastructure network for its downstream operations in countries with oil reserves in the region, namely Argentina, Brazil, Colombia, and Venezuela. The company also operates a network of upstream operations with refinery, petrochemical, and marketing assets, which include retail stations in the Caribbean under the Chevron and/or Texaco brands and Smart Mart convenience stores (Chevron, 2013).

Organization and Integration

The final component of regional strategy is organization and integration. There are two parts to organization and integration. On the one hand, the firm has to develop policies, processes, and systems to function effectively and integrate the region with global operations. In addition to the organization and integration aspects, another aspect of regional strategy is nurturing a regional cultural mindset. A lot has been written about the need to have a global mindset to operate successfully in today's globalized world (Gupta & Govindarajan, 2002). The same is true at the regional level. As part of their regional strategy, multinationals provide a regional culture imprint to their operations in terms of imbuing their staff and decision making with a Latin American personality.

8.4 Regional Strategy Replication and Adaptation

Over time, MNCs transfer and adapt their advantages and competencies to different regions and cultures. This experience provides MNCs with advantages of transferability and replication. In this section, we discuss how MNCs have replicated and adapted their strategies to the particular context of Latin American markets. We identify particular adaptation strategies and explain their effectiveness in particular market contexts.

An example of replication is Danone's regional strategy for bottled water, explained in chapter 5. The Bonafont bottled-water brand has its origin in Mexico, where Danone acquired the locally owned brand and transformed it into a national brand leader. In 2013, Bonafont commanded about 27% market share of the Mexican bottled-water market (*Forbes,* 2012). In Mexico, Bonafont targets the female consumer segment with an appeal to lose weight, drink "light water" frequently, and keep hydrated. Clever advertising showing the svelte silhouette of a female athlete promotes a fashionable image in this country.

In 2008, Danone replicated the Mexican strategy with the introduction of the Bonafont brand in Brazil. Targeting primarily the urban areas of southern Brazil, Bonafont achieved a 20% market share in the important Sao Paulo market in 2013. The targeting and positioning strategy used in Mexico was duplicated in Brazil: ads targeted women seeking to maintain social status and physical attractiveness. The brand differentiation in Brazil, however, is different. Advertising messages for Bonafont in Brazil emphasize its low sodium content, lower than that of rival brands, and its role in the reduction of bloating, associated with water intake (Datamark, 2012). In Argentina and Uruguay, Danone uses a different strategy altogether. Since acquiring the local water brands Villavicencio, in 1999, and Villa del Sur in Argentina and Salus in Uruguay, Danone has kept the local brand identities and marketing.

Another example of adaptation is McDonald's. The core menu follows the global approach for all restaurants, but the adaptation of the menu takes a national approach. McDonald's offers *dulce de leche* (caramelized milk) ice cream and wine in Argentina, *pao de quejo* (cheese bread) in Brazil, *arepas* (cornmeal flatbread) in Venezuela, and *gallo pinto* (rice and beans) in Costa Rica. Beyond adaptations to the menu, the company has introduced ecologically friendly restaurants in Costa Rica, Argentina, and Mexico and reduced-sodium, -sugar, and -calorie menus throughout Latin America (Industry Today, 2013).

8.5   A Case of a Global MNC Regional Strategy in Latin America

In this section, we illustrate the formulation of a regional strategy within the context of the fast-food industry, with Subway as our example.

The Global Fast-Food Market

The global fast-food market is estimated to have a value of $608 billion in 2012 (Euromonitor, 2013). Most of the growth is driven by expansion in emerging and developing countries—most notably in Asia-Pacific and Latin America. North America accounts for 37% of the market, followed by Asia-Pacific with 33% and Latin America with 8% (see Table 8.3). The two regions with the fastest growth in fast-food revenues are Asia-Pacific and Latin America, with compound annual growth rates (CAGR) of 13.5% and 11.1%, respectively for the period 2007–2012. In contrast to these rates, North America CAGR was a weak 2.5% and Europe's a mere 0.7%.

The Latin American Fast-Food Market

With increased discretionary income, Latin American consumers are attracted to fast-food restaurants because of their convenience, price, and value. Increasingly, consumers are seeking better nutritional value and diversity of options. Young consumers use fast-food outlets as places to socialize and meet friends at any time of the day. Furthermore, increased urbanization, an increase in the number of women entering the workforce, and an increase in the number of single-parent households are changing traditional meal patterns and home cooking. The traditional long lunch has given way to short lunch breaks that are driving demand for fast food.

Table 8.3 Global Fast-Food Market Size and Growth

Region	2012 US$Bn	% of Total World Revenues	2010–2011 Annual Growth %	2011–2012 Annual Growth %	2007–2012 CAGR %
World	608.2	100	9.7	4.7	6.3
Asia-Pacific	200.7	33	15.6	8.6	13.5
Australasia	16.3	3	16.3	2.7	9.2
Eastern Europe	15.3	2.5	15.3	6.5	6.0
Latin America	49.4	8	14.6	7.1	11.1
Middle East and Africa	21.4	3.5	8.3	4.9	7.3
North America	225.6	37	4	4.3	2.5
Western Europe	79.4	13	8.4	−4.3	0.7

Source: Euromonitor International (2013).

As the middle class and urban populations continue to increase, the market can only grow larger. In fact, Latin American countries are at the top of the list of countries with the greatest fast-food-store density. A recent report on global fast-food density shows Peru as the number one country. On average, a Peruvian travels 0.6 mile to find a fast-food establishment. Using the same indicator of density, Ecuador, Guatemala, and Mexico rank fourth, fifth, and sixth worldwide. Other top-ranked Latin American countries are El Salvador, Venezuela, Honduras, Colombia, Brazil, the Dominican Republic, and Argentina (Bloomberg, 2013).

The high density of fast-food restaurants is an indication that Latin American consumers love to eat out. The food quality and sanitary conditions maintained by the food chains and the affordable prices are very attractive to consumers in the region. Fast-food establishments in Latin America are mostly in large metropolitan areas such as Lima, Buenos Aires, Mexico City, and Sao Paulo. Increasingly, fast-food operators are penetrating secondary and tertiary markets.

Country Markets

Brazil is the largest fast-food market in the region. The Brazil market for eating out in all types of outlets reached $122 billion in 2012. The fast-food market category for that year was $21.7 billion, an increase of 11% over the figure for 2011 (see Table 8.4). The market is very fragmented, with independent food outlets representing the bulk of stores. Only 1.1% of the total stores are chain restaurants; of these, 63.1% are fast food.

Table 8.4 Latin American Fast-Food Market Size and Growth

Country	Consumer Food Service Market 2011 Local Currency	Consumer Food Service Market 2011 US$ Bn*	Fast-Food Market Size 2011	Annual Growth % 2012/11	Total Outlets	Chain Outlets	Chain Fast Food	% Chain/Total	% Fast-Food/Chain
Argentina	ARS billion 85.1	19.8	ARS 10.2 billion (US $2.3 billion)**	13	67,963	5,618	3637	8.2	64.7
Brazil	R$ billion 251	144	R$ billion 21.7 (US$ $9.1 billion)**	11	978,006	16,235	10259	1.6	63.1
Chile	CLP billion 3051	5.8	n.a.	13.5	22,648	1,830	1033	8.0	56.4
Colombia	COL$ trillion 24.9	1.3	n.a.	9.8	57,107	2,437	1618	4.2	66.3
Mexico	Mx$ billion 651.3	57	Mx$ billion 84.4 (US$ 6.5 billion)***	3.3	799,446	26,055	2665	3.2	10.2
Peru	NS billion 18.9	7	n.a.	12.1	155,517	1,204	669	0.7	55.5
Venezuela	VEB billion 46.2	10.3	n.a.	25.4	32,671	2,094	1278	6.4	61.0

* Exchange rates for selective countries from www.irs.gov/Individuals/International-Taxpayers/Yearly-Average-Currency-Exchange-Rates
** Chain outlets
*** Fast food only
Source: Euromonitor International (2012).

The market is very competitive, and the industry is starting to consolidate with acquisitions and the emergence of multibrand fast-food holding groups. The top five leading groups account for 53% of sales in the fast-food category. These top five groups are Arcos Dorados (McDonald's), Brazil Fast Food Corporation (Bob's, KFC, and Pizza Hut), Doctor's Associates (Subway), Al Saraiva Empreendimentos (Habib's Ragazzo, Box 30), and Restpar Alimentos (Giraffa).

The multibrand model brings many synergies in cost sharing and economies of scope. Fast-food operators are able to share real estate and distribution costs of their different brand outlets and integrate their management. As a result, multibrand operators increase efficiency and offer more competitive prices. Some groups, such as the Al Saraiva group, are vertically integrated, growing and producing their food inputs for their different brands. This vertical integration allows lower costs and imposes common quality-control standards. The food is processed partially in central kitchens and is delivered to stores for finishing, thus reducing the need to refrigerate food in stores (Euromonitor International, 2012). Single-brand operators also compete in Brazil. For instance, the Brazilian private-equity group 3G Capital Management acquired the Burger King worldwide franchise in 2010 (Burger King, 2013).

Mexico is the second largest market in Latin America, with an estimated $57 billion in consumer food expenditures in all types of outlets in 2012. The fast-food market is estimated to be $6.5 billion (Companies and Markets, 2012). The market is predominantly dominated by a very large number of independent food operators. Chain operators represent 3.2% of all of the food outlets, and only 10.2% of this group is made up of fast-food chains. The lunch market is the most important market segment in Mexico. Given the size of the large cities and their congestion, most Mexicans opt to eat breakfast and dinner at home and eat out at lunchtime. As is traditional in many Latin American countries, breakfast at home is light, consisting of coffee and toast. In contrast to inhabitants of other Latin countries, many urban commuters grab a quick bite of traditional Mexican food from street vendors that sell around bus or metro stops. With this supplemental meal, Mexicans can work continuously to past midday. It is not uncommon to see Mexicans eating lunch at 2 P.M. For low-paid office workers, affordability and speed are important. Business executives and more affluent families prefer full-service restaurants. In addition, the accelerated pace of life in large cities and consumer insecurity have made delivery of food a very popular option.

Argentina is another important fast-food market. The most important consideration for Argentines is the total price of the meal. Thus, Argentines tend to prefer the affordable full, inclusive meals (*menu del dia*) in restaurants, self-service food service restaurants, and meal packages in fast-food outlets.

With the improvement of the economy in recent years, Argentines are returning to their usual busy and intense social lifestyle, although this impetus is being moderated by increased inflation in recent years. Inflation has had an impact on the price of beef, the preferred food option. Consequently, Argentines are embracing other types of cuisines, particularly Asian and Peruvian. Furthermore, Argentines are showing increasing interest in healthier meals. Fast-food chains have responded to these trends with the introduction of healthier meals, with reduced-fat and low-sodium options on their menus.

As socialization and entertainment are very important to Argentines, coffee shops and pastry chains are a strong category of growth. Coffee culture stems from the Argentine appreciation of European lifestyles. This trait has been noticed by Starbucks, which is providing Argentines a relaxed place where they can meet friends or family or browse books, read a newspaper, or listen to poetry. Prepared foods, takeout, and home delivery are other growth categories in Argentina. The diversity and sophistication of prepared food for takeout rivals the experience of full-service restaurants. Argentines rely on these establishments for dinner and snacks during the day. It is not unusual to call for a delivery of an order of *empanadas* (turnover or filled pastry) in the middle of the day; the cost of the meal is cheap, and so is the delivery. Fast-food mini-outlets embedded in retail networks are also growing in Argentina.

Venezuela is another important Latin American market. In 2012, the country's consumer expenditures in full-service restaurants increased by 25%. The fast-food category achieved a reasonable 6.4% share of all expenditures, of which 61% represented fast food. These results are remarkable considering the dire economic difficulties that the Venezuelan economy is enduring. With the highest levels of unemployment and inflation in the region, Venezuela's buying power is being reduced, yet citizens find the time and money to eat out. With a poor business environment, increasing government intervention, and labor unrest, foreign and local fast-food operators are keeping their investments to the minimum. In this environment, the global fast-food operators dominate the market, particularly McDonald's, Burger King, Wendy's, and Subway.

Chile is a mature midsize fast-food market with a total consumer food service market of $5.8 billion and an impressive annual growth of 13.5% in 2012. With the proliferation of shopping malls and food courts, the fast-food industry grew rapidly. Of all of the total food outlets in the country, chain restaurants accounted for 8%, of which 56.4% served fast food.

Chile is among a group of countries with high obesity rates (*Economist*, 2013). Chilean society is becoming more health conscious, and there is a trend toward healthier lifestyles and the consumption of healthier foods. Healthier menu options and innovative menu options are becoming a major draw for the Chilean consumer; fast-food companies have introduced salads, wraps, healthy sandwiches, diet yogurts, and natural fruit. Juice bars offering a variety of natural fruit juices and smoothies are also popular. Health-and-wellness self-service outlets are popular options for business lunch. Locations near work centers and in shopping areas are two other key successful factors for fast-food operators.

A highly consistent quality of product results in better presentation of food servings to customers. Fresh foods are also perceived as of higher quality but tend to be more expensive. Competitive pricing is important to Chilean consumers. The dynamism of the Chilean market is attracting operators from other South American countries. Juan Valdez, from Colombia, and Argentina's Havanna's cafés have entered the strong but competitive specialty coffee chains that also offer food alternatives and compete with Starbucks and its Chilean version, Starlight, as well as Brazil's Bob's Burger chain, which entered the Chilean market in 2010 (Euromonitor, 2012).

Other Latin American markets of importance are Colombia, Peru, and the countries of Central America. In Colombia, eating out historically was mostly restricted to lunch breaks due to security concerns and a strong tradition of going home for a family meal. This has changed with increasing prosperity and a lower threat of terrorism. Colombians are catching up economically and adopting hectic work lifestyles aggravated by long commutes from home to work. These factors are driving the demand for convenience and time-saving meals. Home delivery is expanding quickly and growing in sophistication. Colombia's consumer food service grew at an annual compound rate of 9.8% between 2006 and 2011; 4.2% of all outlets are chain networks, of which 66.3% served fast food (Euromonitor, 2012).

Eating out in Peru is frequently a gourmet experience. The diversity and quality of Peruvian cuisine has been praised by food critics worldwide. As mentioned before, Peru has the distinction of having the highest concentration of fast-food restaurants in the world. As a result, Peruvians eat out very frequently during the workday and on weekends. Peruvians are very conscious of the health impact of food intake and prefer seafood and vegetarian options. Asian and especially Japanese cuisine are popular among Peruvians for these reasons. The Peruvian fast-food market grew at the annual rate of 12.1% in 2012. Peru resembles Brazil and Mexico in terms of the large number of independent food stores. Chain stores represent a mere 0.7% of all food stores (Euromonitor, 2012).

Central American fast-food country markets are small and, given their similarity, can be considered as a single subregional market. Central Americans' favorite food when eating out is barbecue-grilled chicken accompanied by rice and beans, fried cassava, or plantains. In recent years, this style of preparing chicken has been exported to nearby countries and faraway markets—including the United States.

Competition

Table 8.5 identifies the most important global fast-food competitors in Latin America. As shown in Table 8.3, the region accounts for 8% of global fast-food market revenues. Using the proportionality rule explained earlier, the number of units deployed in the region by any fast-food company should be proportional to this share. Domino's Pizza and Subway come close to achieving this proportionality. For other global fast-food companies shown in Table 8.5, Latin America is underrepresented in their global portfolio. Asia is clearly the most attractive region for global fast-food companies; KFC, for instance, has more

Table 8.5 Largest Global Fast-Food Companies by Outlets and Region (2012)

Brand	Africa	Asia-Pacific	Europe	Latin America & Caribbean		Middle East	Canada	United States		Total	Global Revenues US$ bn	Sales Growth
	Units	Units	Units	Units	% of Total Units	Units	Units	Units	% of Total Units	Units		
McDonalds	258	8,613	7,385	2,085	6	586	1,417	14,157	41	34,501	88.29	2.9
Subway	35	3,596	4,163	3,207	7.8	373	3,020	26,339	64	40,733	18.1	6.7
Burger King	n.a.	1,010	2,909	1,390	6.3	212	293	7,183	57.6	12,997	15.8	3.9
KFC	787	6,545	522	598	3.4	249	650	4,558	33.5	13,568	11.6	4.6
Pizza Hut	94	1,774	3,881	251	1.8	252	305	6,209	47.5	11,060	7.4	4.4
Starbucks	23	3,294	1,681	594	3.2	228	1,181	11,128	61.5	18,066	13.3	7.0
Dominos Pizza	27	2,148	1,847	811	8.3	126	368	4,928	48	10,255	7.4	5.3
Dunkin Donuts		1,047		162	1.6	n.a.	n.a.	7015	69.5	10,083	6.9	3.9

Source: Authors' Compilation from Corporate Sites and Annual Reports.

stores in Asia than in the United States and proportionally more outlets than the 33% share of global revenues that this region generates for KFC. For most global fast-food chains, the home market (the United States) is still an important generator of revenues. The North America market should account for 37% of the world total; only KFC seems to have achieved this level.

Global fast-food competitors face strong challenges from local fast-food champions. These challenges vary with the country. In Mexico, the global fast-food chains collectively are the market leaders, although no single global fast-food operator holds dominant market leadership. In Brazil, McDonald's is the largest network of restaurants in the country, with 1,277 units and a dominant 28% of the total food service market. A Brazilian competitor, Bob's Burger, is also large, with 764 units and a 7.1% market share. McDonald's also dominates the Venezuelan market with 26.2% market share in a market where global fast-food players are wary of making more than minimal investments. In other Latin American markets, the market is fragmented. In Peru and Colombia, local fast-food operators have achieved significant market shares with companies such as Bembos and El Corral. In Chile, hot-dogs-and-sandwich formats are popular with local consumers, and the local company Doggies is a market leader. In Argentina, where a coffee culture is prevalent, fast-food chains that combine food, coffee, pastry, and ice cream offerings have a strong appeal and have grabbed substantial market share. Bakery is also a good basis for local fast-food chains. This is the case with the Pao de Queijo chain in Brazil, which has transformed the very popular cheese bread snack into a chain of establishments with a full offering of food and drinks.

The global fast-food companies operate in Latin America in many different ways. For instance, a single private investment group, Arcos Dorados, holds and operates the McDonald's franchise in Latin America. The company is one of the largest employers in Latin America and trades on the New York Stock Exchange. Arcos Dorados is organized into four regions: Brazil is one operational unit, Latin America South is another (Argentina, Chile, Colombia, Peru, and Ecuador), Latin America North is a third unit (Mexico, Costa Rica, and Panama), and the Caribbean, which includes Puerto Rico, is the fourth (Industry Today, 2013). McDonald's is the market leader in Brazil and Venezuela (see Table 8.6). In Venezuela, despite the lack of investment and expansion, McDonald's achieves market leadership with a 26.2% market share. Another example is Starbucks, with 643 stores in the region. Starbucks operates through joint ventures with local investors.

National champions are formidable competitors of global fast-food chains in Latin America. Brazilian Habib's is the world's largest fast-food chain serving Middle Eastern cuisine, not in the Middle East but in Brazil. Some 12 million Brazilians are of Arab descent, and Habib's founder recognized the opportunity to cater to this large population. The company's strategy is rather simple: a very low price strategy for decent quality food. The company has a network of 318 franchises in Brazil, half of which are owned by the company (Industry Today,

Table 8.6 Global Chained Fast-Food Companies in Latin America (2012)

Brand	Argentina		Brazil		Chile		Colombia		Mexico		Peru		Venezuela	
	# Outlets	Share	# Outlets	Share	# Outlets	Share	# Outlets	Share	# Outlets	Share	# Outlets	Share	# Outlets	Share
McDonalds	145	14.6	1,308	28	69	9.7	65	11.6	398	4.2	22	2.7	139	26.2
Subway	41		795	4.9	22		160	0.7	780	2.8	16	0.1	176	4.8
Burger King	65	4.2	224	2.6	32	2.5	28		431	4.2	19	2.0	63	7.1
KFC	1	n.a.	19	n.a.	45	4.5	13	0.5	296	3.0	68	10.6	17	1.2
Pizza Hut			58	1.6	24	1.4	Opening in 2014		172	2.4	44	4.4	9	n.a.
Starbucks	66	1.3	53	0.3	41	1.7			337	3.0	34	1.4		
Dominos Pizza							22	0.7	573	3.8	24	0.4	n.a.	2.4
Papa Johns											16	2.0	20	

Sources: Euromonitor (2012) and Annual Reports.

Table 8.7 Top Latin American Fast-Food National Companies by Country

Country	Brand	Category	# Outlets	Share
Argentina	Grido	Ice cream	999	6.3
	Havanna Café	Bakery	165	3.6
	Bonafide	Bakery and coffee	167	3.5
Brazil	Bobs	Burgers	764	7.1
	Casa do Pao	Bakery	438	1.9
	Habibs	Middle Eastern	318	8.4
Chile	Doggis	Hot dogs	170	8.6
	Tele-Pizza	Pizza	130	6.7
	Domino	Sandwich	33	2.2
Colombia	El Corral	Burgers	160	11.6
	Crepes & Waffles	Crepes, ice cream, and salads	63	11.3
	Kokoriko	Roast chicken	110	8.5
Mexico	Hawaiian Paradise	Crepes, pizzas, ice cream, and coffee	755	1.3
	Taco Inn	Mexican food	123	1.2
	Gorditas Dona Tota	Mexican food	201	1.2
Peru	Norkys	Chicken	75	10.4
	Bembos	Burger, chicken	51	6.3
	Pardos	Chicken	23	3.4
Venezuela	Arturos	Chicken	76	6.2
	Pollos a la Broaster	Chicken	57	2.4
	Dog and Ball	Hot dogs	62	2.1

Sources: Euromonitor (2012) and Annual Reports.

2013). A strategy of vertical integration and centralized kitchens allows Habib to achieve a low cost position. Habib offers a menu of 56 items of traditional Lebanese-Syrian foods, including the popular *esfishas*, flat bread topped with beef, chicken, or cheese. Habib's also offers hamburgers, chicken sandwiches, pizzas, French fries, and ice cream (Isto é, 2013). Habib's garnered annual sales of 2 billion Brazilian reals (US$890 million) in 2012, second only to McDonald's in Brazil. The low-price strategy reflects its menu choice of foods that are cheap to produce. An *esfisha* at Habib's, for example costs less than one-third as much as an original McDonald's hamburger and less than half as much as either a hot dog or a *pao de quejo* (cheese bread), two popular foods sold by street vendors. Habib's Middle Eastern fast-food model has been extended to Italian food under the Ragazzo brand name and into bakery under the Box 30 brand name.

Another example of a local champion is Peru's Bembos, a hamburger specialist. Bembos is a blend of a standard fast-food hamburger joint with a little spice of Peruvian flair. Bembos integrates a variety of local ingredients into its offerings, and customers are able to assemble their own burgers and also choose from a large variety of salad choices. Bembos's market strategy is to stay fairly local and affordable. The chain prides itself on the quality of its burgers and increases accessibility by offering online ordering. Like Brazil's Habib's, Bembos is vertically integrated. Such creativity and adaptation come with a price; Bembos's burgers are expensive by Peruvian standards (*Semana Económica,* 2013).

Subway in Latin America

Subway's success is based on a strong brand and a unique value proposition stressing healthy eating. The company's low-cost franchising strategy has allowed Subway to flourish both domestically and overseas. The success of this strategy has led to sales of $18.1 billion in 2012 and 40,000 stores in 2012 (Franchise Times, 2013).

Global Strategy and Regional Vision. Subway's goal to be the largest global fast-food network in the world has already been achieved as the company took the number one position from McDonald's in 2012 (*Franchise Times,* 2013). Subway extends its ambition in Latin America with an aggressive expansion to become the largest fast-food operator in the region (see Table 8.6) and expects to reach a goal of having 45,000 stores worldwide in 2015 and more outlets in international markets than in the United States. One important component of this strategic vision is to achieve rapid expansion in nontraditional locations that require small spaces (Euromonitor International, 2012). Latin America is an important part of this expansion as it has the world's second highest annual growth rate in fast-food sales.

Regional Strategic Thrust. Subway's successful strategy can be explained by the following four pillars: formulating a unique value proposition, targeting an underserved customer segment, structuring an aggressive franchising model, and expanding internationally.

Subway's global strategic thrust remains constant in Latin America. Subway fully capitalizes on the perceived healthiness and freshness of its products, which aligns well with the trend toward healthy lifestyles in Latin America. Its marketing slogan, "Live Fresh, Eat Fresh," demonstrates clearly and simply the company's approach to the market. Quality is a major component of the sandwich chain's core values and brings the added benefit that its products have a higher perceived value than other fast-food options.

Increasing obesity in Latin America has also been a driver of Subway's appeal to customers in the region. Subway attracts health- and weight-conscious consumers, largely young people and urban professionals. This is reflected in the layout of Subway's restaurants; spaces are small, and seating is minimized to encourage takeout business.

Building Assets, Resources, and Competencies. The franchise network is the most valuable asset for Subway. Structuring an aggressive independent franchising model has been the key to its international expansion. One reason is low start-up costs; Subway's estimated costs to open a single franchise unit range from $84,800 to $258,300, with a franchising fee of $15,000. The start-up costs at other global fast-food chains are approximately $959,000 to $2.1 million per unit, with franchise fees of $45,000 (Yahoo Finance, 2013). The cost of running Subway franchises is also low. Subway restaurants require far less equipment than a typical restaurant, needing only a counter, a small countertop oven in which bread is baked, a refrigerator, and a microwave. Real estate costs are lower because the lack of a complete kitchen gives Subway access to a greater number of locations without having to meet complex zoning requirements. Subway operates many "nontraditional units" in areas such as airports, hospitals, military bases, convention centers, gas stations, and convenience stores. Operating costs are lowered further because Subway stores have fewer food items on the menu and need far fewer staff to run the operations. Most stores can operate at off-peak times with one staff member, very different from the situation at other fast-food restaurants. Subway has an added benefit from not pre-making sandwiches, because it eliminates the waste associated with trying to predict short-term demand.

Subway's core concept of an assembled sandwich is left unchanged in international markets. The flexibility of this formula allows Subway to include a variety of local options that meet the religious and cultural preferences of every country in which it operates.

Regional Organization and Integration. Subway operates exclusively through independent franchising worldwide. Franchisees play an important role and are organized to support themselves by means of common advertising and purchasing of inputs; they also generate new ideas and operating solutions (Euromonitor, 2012).

Subway's regional expansion in Latin America has been supported by the use of "development agents" to push franchisee growth. Development agents are responsible for recruiting franchisees and helping them grow. These agents are paid part of the franchise fee and one-third of ongoing royalties to keep their incentives in line with those of the franchisees. Development agents are independent entrepreneurs, not employees of Subway.

Challenges for Subway in Latin America. Subway is not the market leader in Latin America. McDonald's is still the market leader with a 26% share of global markets; Subway, in contrast, has a 5% share. Thus, the challenge for Subway is to catch up with the regional market leader. Another challenge is to improve its average revenues per store. Subway lags on this indicator when compared to other global fast-food chains. In this respect, McDonald's revenue is 5.4 times Subway's global average of $426,000 (Euromonitor, 2012). Thus, the challenge for Subway in Latin America is to increase same-store sales in the future. This increase should come from expanding daytime offerings beyond the traditional lunch. The breakfast option is less attractive for expansion, because Latin Americans do not typically go out for breakfast. Capturing the midmorning flow for snacks and coffee is, however, a good option. Dinner menus also offer potential. Furthermore, converting in-store demand to home delivery and the use of online ordering may be other avenues to growth. Finally, allowing local operators to test new sandwich concepts based on local food preferences will improve market penetration.

8.6   Summary

Latin America has attracted many multinationals interested in participating in the growing domestic markets in the region. The rich and abundant natural resources and increasingly efficient manufacturing costs vis-à-vis those in Asia are also attractive to multinationals.

These multinationals bring a wealth of resources and advantages to the region. They also integrate their global value supply chains to either receive inputs or serve the domestic markets.

Non–Latin American multinationals entered the region with expectations of replicating their competencies and adapting their strategies to achieve greater market penetration. Given the diversity of market opportunities and resource advantages that the region offers, multinationals focus on key country markets to sustain their viability. In most cases, this multicountry strategy includes the largest economies, Brazil and Mexico, and a few additional country markets.

The multinationals' strategy for Latin America is highly integrated with their global strategy but with substantial adaptations to the local market conditions. This regional strategy has four components: (1) regional ambition, (2) regional strategic thrust, (3) efforts to build assets, resources, and competencies; and (4) a regional organization and culture.

Regional ambition is the effort to assess the strategic importance and contribution of Latin America to the multinational's global strategy and performance. According to the concept of proportionality, Latin America's importance and contribution range from 6% to 10% of a given indicator, whether revenues or assets. Such an assessment may affect the strategic decisions of resource allocation and investments. Multinationals may decide to focus more on other emerging regions such as Asia and underperform in Latin America, as in the cases of Starbucks and KFC, discussed in this chapter. On the other hand, the case of Subway illustrates an equal representation of Latin America in this multinational global business portfolio in terms of number of outlets.

Regional strategic thrust focuses on leveraging the multinationals' advantages in the region. Global brands, marketing competencies, and technology advantages are bases for differentiation. Starbucks is a good example of the ability to penetrate markets where the coffee culture is strong by enhancing in-store customer experience in a region where the product is good but the experience is poor.

Building strategic resources and assets can be accomplished in many different ways. Some multinationals, such as Subway, utilize franchising systems where local investors build the regional network independently under strict guidelines from Subway. Others, such as Spain's Telefónica, have built telecommunications networks organically and through acquisitions.

Non–Latin American multinationals organize their Latin American activities by grouping countries in a particular way. Brazil is sometimes handled by a separate organization, as are the Southern Cone and the Andean countries. Mexico and Central America are combined to form a third unit. The Caribbean becomes a fourth unit.

Organizational and marketing adaptations are common in the implementation of regional strategies in Latin America. Adaptation to address local preferences is important in markets where national culture is strong. Multinationals have found similarities across regional markets and replicated successful business models from one market to another; an example is the case of Danone's bottled water, Bonafont, in Mexico and Brazil.

Despite their overwhelming advantages, multinational companies face strong competition from national companies. As the case of the fast-food market illustrates, global fast-food brands dispute market leadership with entrenched national operators, which offer local favorites and identity that are very appealing to Latin American consumers. Given the strong market fundamentals of the region, one would expect that multinationals would deepen their efforts to be more aggressive and innovative in the future.

References

Bloomberg. (2013). *KFC rules in Peru, as nation is bastion of US fast food.* Retrieved from www.bloomberg.com/news/2012–10–15/kfc-rules-in-peru-as-nation-is-bastion-of-u-s-fast-food.html.

Burger King. (2013). *3G Capital completes acquisition of Burger King Holdings, Inc.* Retrieved from http://investor.bk.com/conteudo_en.asp?idioma=1&tipo=43682&conta=44&id=165749.

Chevron. (2013). *Chevron corporate sites.* Retrieved from www.chevron.com/countries/.

Citymayors-Brazil. (2013). *Almost three quarters of Brazilians live in cities.* Retrieved from www.citymayors.com/gratis/brazilian_cities. html#Anchor-Brazil's-49575.

Citymayors-Mexico. (2013). Retrieved from www.citypopulation.de/Mexico-Cities.html.

Companies and Markets. (2013). *The Mexican fast food industry increased by 6% in 2012.* Retrieved from www.companiesandmarkets.com/.

Datamark. (2012). *After leading turning Bonafont SP, "waters that make you look thinner," locking rack duel.* Retrieved from www.datamark.com.br/en/news/2012/11/after-leading-turning-bonafont-sp-waters-that-make-you-look-thinner-locking-rack-duel-135280/.

Economist. (2013). Obesity in Latin America: Battle of the bulge. Retrieved from www.economist.com/news/americas/21582273-waistlines-grow-so-does-fight-against-junk-food-battle-bulge/print.

Euromonitor International. (2012). *Passport consumer foodservice reports for Argentina, Brazil, Chile, Colombia, Peru and Venezuela.* Retrieved from www.euromonitor.com/countries.

Euromonitor International (2013). *Consumer Foodservice: Euromonitor from trade sources/national statistics.* Retrieved from www.euromonitor.com/countries.

Forbes. (2012). Mexico's water war. Retrieved from www.forbes.com/sites/ivancastano/2012/02/22/mexicos-water-war.

Franchise Times. (2013). Top 200 franchise times. Retrieved from www.franchisetimes.com/Store/Franchise-Times-Top-200/index.php?previewmode=on.

Gupta, A. K., & Govindarajan, V. (2002). Cultivating a global mindset. *Academy of Management, 16*, 116–126.

Industry Today. (2013). *Arcos Dorados Latin America.* Retrieved from http://industrytoday.com/article_view.asp?ArticleID=2861.

Isto é. (2013). *A formula do Habib's.* Retrieved from www.istoedinheiro.com.br/noticias/118289_A+FORMULA+DO+HABIBS.

Lasserre, P., & Schutte, H. (2006). *Strategies for Asia Pacific: Meeting new challenges.* New York: Palgrave-Macmillan.

Latin Trade. (2013). http://latintrade.com/wp-content/uploads/2013/07/Latin500-2013-Eng.pdf.

Nestle. (2013). *Insight: Meeting our commitments in Latin America.* Retrieved from www.nestle.com/media/newsandfeatures/insight-chris-johnson.

Semana Económica. (2012). Bembos del Peru. Retrieved from http://semanaeconomica.com/escala-global/2012/08/21/bembos-del-peru/.

Subway. (2014). *Explore our world.* Retrieved from www.subway.com/subwayroot/exploreourworld.aspx.

World Population Review. (2013). Retrieved from http://worldpopulationreview.com.

Yahoo Finance. (2013). *What it takes to start a fast food franchise.* Retrieved from http://finance.yahoo.com/news/what-it-takes-to-start-a-fast-food-franchise-222831956.html.

9   Global Latinas and National Champions

Introduction

This chapter looks at the rapid rise of the "multilatinas"—Latin America–based firms that expanded intraregionally largely from the late 1990s to the early 2000s—as well as the development of the "global latinas," Latin America–based firms that initially may or may not have expanded intraregionally but that now have a presence in at least one other world region outside Latin America and that have sales of $500 million or more per year (Casanova, 2009; Casanova, et al., 2009).

The Latin American firms' path to internationalization is described in this chapter. We first examine the historical and economic drivers that led to their creation, followed by a description of their unprecedented rise to regional and global prominence. In the final section of this chapter, we identify the sectors in which the multilatina and global latina firms tend to predominate and the countries in which they are based. We also analyze their competitiveness at present and draw some conclusions about their prospects for growth in years to come. State-owned global latinas and national champions are also discussed. Finally, the chapter finishes by focusing on the 2012 merger of two Latin giants: LAN Airlines (Chile-based) and TAM Airlines (Brazil-based) to form the LATAM Airlines Group.

9.1   Drivers in the Development of Multilatinas and Global Latinas

Early Drivers of Internationalization

The final decades of the 20th century in Latin America were characterized by significant economic reforms that created the perfect backdrop for the creation and development of local Latin American firms with a regional and global orientation.

For much of the 20th century (1930s to 1980s), Latin American countries adopted an economic policy of import substitution. In order to encourage national self-sufficiency through the consumption of locally produced goods, governments protected domestic producers through protectionist trade policies, the heavy use of subsidies, and, in some cases, nationalization. The 1980s gave rise to the debt crisis in Latin America, and many of the countries that could not repay their foreign debts found themselves resorting to the International Monetary Fund in an attempt to resolve their debt crisis. (Mexico, Argentina, and Brazil were among the countries that sought the help of the IMF at that time.) The IMF loans were accompanied by strict austerity measures that limited government spending and required that structural reforms aimed at introducing free-market-like competition (and the elimination of the protectionist policies of the past) be implemented within the Latin American economies. Latin American countries at the time had little choice but to bring their economies more in line with the economies of the developed world, and the region began its integration into the world economy. The Latin American experience gradually demonstrated that trade opening (along with opening to foreign direct investment) could provide the means to promote economic growth and poverty reduction. Yet the period of transition from protected economies to more open economies proved to be a difficult one for Latin America, leading some to refer to the 1980s as Latin America's "lost decade." This term referred to the decline in growth rates and living standards at that time.

The transformation of the Latin American economies in the 1980s and 1990s had profound implications for firms in Latin America. Many of the firms that had previously enjoyed government protections had to reinvent themselves and devise new strategies to survive. Firms unable to make the changes either closed down or were acquired by more competitive local firms or international firms that had invested in inward foreign direct investments at the time. Others devised survival strategies in such a way that national champions were created. Some of these national champions subsequently became regional champions and eventually developed into global champions. The reduction (or elimination) of government protections and the influx of international firms into their own domestic markets forced these Latin American firms to focus on innovation and cost-competitiveness to compete more effectively with other firms in their domestic markets and on the global stage. The new competitive pressures led some firms in Latin America to develop unique competitive advantages that facilitated their expansion into new international markets, giving rise to a period in the late 1990s and early 2000s when there was increased intraregional foreign direct investment. For many companies, the regional (albeit limited international) expansion gave them the confidence or the experience needed for broader international expansion, often leading to the creation of more significant core competencies that could be implemented on a broader, global stage. This gave rise to the development of the global latinas.

The international expansion of emerging market firms into the global scene has attracted renewed research focus on emerging market firms and their international activities (1980s–1990s). The global expansion activities of Asian firms first caught (and held) researchers' attention. Research on Latin American multinationals was a subject of research much later, in the early 2000s. When emerging market firms began their international expansion in earnest, research focused on their need to overcome the "liability of foreignness," in which the liability of foreignness was defined as a series of costs associated with operating in unfamiliar environments, dealing with administrative and cultural differences, and coordinating operations over geographical distances, among others (Zaheer, 1995). These views led to a discussion among business and academic communities of the challenges facing emerging-market multinationals. They were often viewed as weaker competitors with weak institutions that could not easily rival developed-market multinationals in the global arena. The first decade of the 21st century showed that emerging-market multinationals could achieve global leadership status in many industries and often did so in a relatively short time.

While multilatinas and global latinas attracted some research attention in the last two decades of the 20th century, the speed of their global expansion accelerated from 2000 to the present (United Nations Conference on Trade and Development [UNCTAD], 2012). The scope of their global reach has expanded, and the list of the home country participants in international expansion has also increased. The rise of prominent firms on the global stage has not been limited to firms from key Latin American markets such as Brazil, Mexico, and Chile. Instead, Latin American multinationals have emerged from many other Latin American countries because of the region's integration into the world economy. Admittedly, multinationals from Brazil, Mexico, and Chile have a more significant presence on the global stage. Multinationals from other Latin American countries such as Colombia and Peru are also sharing that stage. Not only has there been an increase in the number of countries participating in international activities and not only has the pace of global expansion picked up, but, according to UNCTAD (2012), the speed with which firms achieved global status has accelerated from 2000 to the present.

Latin America's favorable external conditions, rising domestic opportunities in the 1990s and early 2000s, embracing of pro-market reforms, and the region's recent favorable performance have led to economic prosperity for Latin American consumers (as noted in chapter 4) and the transformation of Latin American businesses. In many instances, the multinational firms in Latin America not only benefited from the economic bolstering within the region but in fact underpinned the region's economic transformation.

More Recent Drivers of Internationalization

Natural Resources

In addition to the structural reforms, many other factors have contributed to the enhanced competitiveness of Latin American multinationals. First, Latin American countries are rich in natural resources, and the growth of their firms paralleled an era characterized by rising prices for natural resources. The rise in the demand for natural resources, driven largely by China's purchases, has given rise to a number of resource-based Latin American multinationals such as Brazil's Vale, which exports iron ore. While China had experienced annual double-digit GDP growth in the early 2000s, its economy also slowed in tandem with the global economic downturn that began in 2007; more recently, it showed an annual increase in GDP of about 7.5% (UNCTAD, 2013). As a result, China has maintained its demand for natural resources, albeit at lower levels, and commodity prices are expected to remain stable. This is likely to vary across commodities; for example, petroleum prices are projected to stay roughly the same for the foreseeable future, while copper and iron ore prices may dip as a result of China's slowdown (*Economist,* 2013). Stability of current commodity prices may support the continued global participation of Latin American multinationals in the natural-resources sector.

Technological Advancements

Latin American firms have also made technological advancements in the extractive industries that have led to the development of core competencies that will allow them to compete more readily in global markets. The skills can be "exported" to other world regions rich in natural resources. For example, several of Brazil's large mining firms (e.g., Vale), as well as several Brazilian construction and materials firms (e.g., OAS Construtora, Andrade Gutierrez), now have a presence in Africa, where they have undertaken horizontal foreign direct investments and are demonstrating a willingness to share their technological know-how with host-country nationals. China also has a significant presence in Africa, with much of it concentrated in the natural resources sector as well. Chinese horizontal FDI in the mining sector in Africa has, however, come under scrutiny for several human resource management issues, including the practice of "importing" mine workers from China. Host African countries perceive that Chinese investments offered lower benefits to their countries than Brazilian investments in terms of net job creation and transfer of technological know-how. Brazil's apparent willingness to share technological know-how with its African counterparts may give Brazilian firms a competitive advantage in the region, further enhancing their competitiveness in this sector.

Education

Latin America has also made great strides in education, particularly with regard to technology and engineering education. The readily available talent pool, and at significantly lower salaries than one might find in developed countries, has likely contributed to new product development and advances in firms' innovation capabilities. Progress in both these areas enhances Latin American competitiveness in various sectors, including the extractive industries (as mentioned before) but also manufacturing, telecommunications, and electric and power generation, among others. These sectors have also likely been the beneficiaries of the advancements in education.

Knowledge Spillovers

Low costs in the region vis-à-vis those in developed markets have also attracted multinational firms into Latin American markets. The presence of large multinationals has likely led to knowledge spillovers as a result of industry clusters created in Latin American markets. This leads to greater sharing not only of technological know-how but also of managerial know-how, skills often needed to make the difference in creating and delivering strong core competencies.

Economic Prosperity

The region's economic prosperity in recent years contributed to the growth of the middle class. The presence of a middle class can result in more demanding consumers that pressure local firms to innovate to more readily meet their needs. These product innovations can then be transferred to other locations where the local consumer base may not have pressured the firm to innovate but that may be equally interested in purchasing the innovative product.

Firm-specific Advantages

In addition to the location specific advantages outlined earlier, internationalization has resulted in additional firm-specific advantages that would not have been possible in the firms' home markets alone. Multilatinas and global latinas benefit from international expansion through improvements in economies of scale, thus lowering unit costs of production and creating barriers to entry for other competing firms. Furthermore, internationalization gives these firms easier access to capital on the global markets and lowers their currency risk through market diversification.

9.2 Multilatinas and the Global Latinas

This section highlights the various sources and methodologies that are available to identify the largest Latin America–based multinational firms. This is followed by a discussion of the competitiveness of the multilatinas and global latinas.

What are the multilatinas and the global latinas? The answer to this question depends on which source is used and on the variables used in generating these lists. As there is some overlap in these lists, a core of firms is likely to appear in all lists. However, there are also other firms that may appear in only one or two of these lists. This is a result of the fact that in addition to size (e.g., sales or assets), other measures, such as geographic dispersion, are used to try to differentiate between the regionally and globally focused firms.

Four potential sources of Latin America–based multinationals were identified. The methodology that is used for each of these sources is briefly described in the following sections; we then present a table showing the latest list of firms based on each methodology.

Forbes Global 2000

Forbes Global 2000 list consists of a ranking of the "world's largest and most powerful" firms. *Forbes* uses a composite score to generate its ranked list, in which four metrics are equally weighted: sales, profits, assets, and market value.

The 2013 list contained a total of 69 firms from Latin America (see Table 9.1 for details on the list of firms, their home countries, and the four metrics). The number of firms in the latest list has not risen by much (only by five firms) since 2008; however, the Latin American firms have steadily moved higher in the rankings, suggesting that they are becoming even more global.

Table 9.1 *Forbes* Global 2000 List of Multilatinas by Country of Origin (2013)

Rank	Company	Country	Sales $ Billions	Profits $ Billions	Assets $ Billions	Market Value $ Billions
20	Petrobras	Brazil	144.1	11.0	331.6	120.7
42	Itau Unibanco Holding	Brazil	70.5	6.2	453.6	82.0
45	Bradesco	Brazil	78.3	5.6	417.5	71.6
67	Banco do Brasil	Brazil	69.0	6.0	552.2	37.9
87	Vale	Brazil	45.7	4.8	130.4	92.7
173	Itausa	Brazil	27.8	2.2	172.4	25.4
597	Cemig	Brazil	9.5	2.2	19.4	10.7
614	Grupo Pão de Açúcar	Brazil	24.9	0.5	16.8	14.1
656	JBS	Brazil	38.9	0.4	24.3	10.4
671	CSN	Brazil	8.9	2.0	24.2	7.2
734	BRF-Brasil Foods	Brazil	13.9	0.4	14.7	19.2
819	Oi	Brazil	12.3	0.4	38.0	6.1
836	CPFL Energia	Brazil	7.7	0.6	15.2	10.4
910	Sabesp	Brazil	5.5	1.0	12.8	10.5
935	Eletrobras	Brazil	17.5	−3.5	84.1	5.0
1,075	Cielo	Brazil	2.6	1.1	4.7	18.9
1,156	Braskem	Brazil	17.3	−0.4	19.6	5.0
1,158	BM&F Bovespa	Brazil	1.0	0.5	11.7	13.4
1,173	Metalurgica Gerdau	Brazil	18.5	0.2	25.0	3.8
1,211	Cosan	Brazil	14.1	0.3	12.2	5.5
1,234	CCR	Brazil	3.0	0.6	7.0	17.3
1,517	Embraer	Brazil	6.2	0.3	9.5	6.3
1,520	BR Malls	Brazil	0.6	0.9	8.7	5.8
1,542	Natura Cosmticos	Brazil	3.1	0.4	2.5	10.5
1,586	Marfrig Group	Brazil	12.3	−0.1	12.0	2.5
1,627	Usiminas	Brazil	6.2	−0.3	15.3	5.3

Rank	Company	Country	Sales $ Billions	Profits $ Billions	Assets $ Billions	Market Value $ Billions
1,811	Lojas Americanas	Brazil	5.5	0.2	5.3	8.9
1,908	Porto Seguro	Brazil	6.1	0.3	8.8	4.4
1,914	WEG	Brazil	3.0	0.3	4.3	8.1
1,989	Klabin	Brazil	2.0	0.4	6.9	6.5
569	Falabella	Chile	11.5	0.8	17.9	26.8
573	Cencosud	Chile	19.1	0.6	19.7	17.4
938	Antarchile	Chile	22.8	0.2	22.3	7.5
1,007	Latam Airlines	Chile	9.7	0	20.6	11.1
1,049	BCI-Banco Credito	Chile	2.7	0.5	31.0	7.9
1,252	SQM	Chile	2.5	0.7	4.4	14.8
1,591	Empresas CMPC	Chile	4.8	0.2	14.0	8.0
1,611	Quinenco	Chile	4.1	0.2	46.3	4.6
1,761	CorpBanca	Chile	2.0	0.2	28.3	4.7
114	Ecopetrol	Colombia	39.0	8.4	64.4	116.2
608	BanColombia	Colombia	5.9	1.0	55.4	13.5
652	Grupo Aval	Colombia	6.1	0.7	57.4	13.2
1,288	Banco Davivienda	Colombia	2.7	0.4	23.2	6.4
1,594	Grupo Argos	Colombia	3.8	0.2	15.2	9.5
1,998	Interconexin Elctrica	Colombia	2.4	0.2	14.6	5.8
100	Amrica Mvil	Mexico	60.2	7.1	74.6	70.7
349	Femsa	Mexico	18.5	1.6	22.6	37.7
440	Grupo Mexico	Mexico	10.4	2.4	18.4	32.3
491	GFNorte	Mexico	7.7	0.8	70.6	18.5
712	ALFA	Mexico	15.6	0.7	11.8	12.7
769	Grupo Modelo	Mexico	7.2	1.0	9.6	29.0
778	Cemex	Mexico	15.3	−0.9	35.9	13.6
818	Grupo Inbursa	Mexico	3.6	0.7	26.2	18.5
918	Grupo Televisa	Mexico	5.4	0.7	12.6	14.9
925	Industrias Peoles	Mexico	7.4	0.8	6.4	17.4
1,106	Grupo Bimbo	Mexico	13.5	0.2	10.1	13.0
1,117	Grupo Carso	Mexico	6.4	0.6	5.9	11.3
1,153	El Puerto de Liverpool	Mexico	5.0	0.5	6.6	15.5
1,192	Fresnillo	Mexico	2.2	0.7	3.3	16.1
1,455	Arca Continental	Mexico	4.4	0.4	4.9	12.0
1,465	Grupo Elektra	Mexico	5.3	−1.5	12.8	9.5
1,469	Mexichem	Mexico	4.9	0.4	7.6	10.8
1,626	Soriana	Mexico	8.0	0.3	5.7	6.8
1,773	Kimberly-Clark de Mexico	Mexico	2.3	0.3	2.2	9.6
338	Carnival	Panama	15.4	1.5	38.7	28.4
796	Credicorp	Peru	3.6	0.8	41	12.7
1,601	Buenaventura	Peru	1.5	0.7	4.5	6.3
1,148	Mercantil Servicios	Venezuela	3.9	1.0	33.2	3.4

*Includes all Latin America–based firms in the latest available ranking of *Forbes's* Largest and Most Powerful Firms. A composite score based on equal weighting of sales, profits, assets, and market value is used to rank-order the firms
Source: *Forbes* (2013).

The Boston Consulting Group (BCG) Global Challengers

The Boston Consulting Group (BCG) publishes its "Global Challengers" list. The first list, published in 2006, included a total of 18 Latin American companies; the list published one year later contained 22 companies, and the most recent listing (2009) contained a total of 100 Latin American companies with either "global reach or global potential."

Table 9.2 Boston Consulting Group Global Challengers (2009)

Argentina (7)	Papel (VCP)	**Mexico (28)**
Arcor	Weg	Alpek
Atanor		Alsea
Grupo Plus Petrol	**Chile (21)**	América Móvil
Molinos Río de la Plata	Antofagasta Minerals	Cemex
Pan American Energy	CAP	Comex Group
Tenaris	Celulosa Arauco y	Corporación
Ternium	Constitución	Interamericana de
	Cementos Bio	Entretenimiento
Brazil (34)	Cencosud	Empresas ICA
Alpargatas	Compañía Cervecerías	Famsa
América Latina Logstica	Unidas (CCU)	Femsa
Andrade Gutierrez	Compañía General de	Grumas
Brasil Foods	Electricidad (CGE)	Grupo Bal
Braskem	Compañía Sud Americana	Grupo Bimbo
Coteminas	de Vapores (CSAV)	Grupo Cementos
CSN	Embotelladora Andina	de Chihuahua
Embraer	Empresa Nacional del	Grupo Condumex
EMS Sigma Pharma	Petróleo (ENAP)	Grupo Iusa
Gerdau	Empresas Carozzi	Grupo Lala
Globo Comunicao e	Empresas CMPC	Grupo Mexico
Participcoes	Falabella	Grupo Modelo
Grupo Camargo Correa	Farmacias Ahumada	Grupo Salinas
Grupo Queiroz Galvao	LAN Airlines	Industrias CH
Grupo Votarantim	Madeco	Mabe
Iochpe-Maxion	Masisa	Mexichem
Itautec	Molibdenos y Metales	Nemak
JBS-Fribol	(Molymet)	Sigma Alimentos
Klabin	Sigdo Koppers	Televisa
Magnesita Refratarios	Sonda	Telmex
Marcopolo	SQM	Verzatec
Marfrig Group		Xignux
Minerva	**Colombia (5)**	
Natura Cosméticos	Argos	**Peru (3)**
Odebrecht	Avianca	Allcorp
Petrobras	Grupo Nacional de Chocolates	Grupo Gloria
Random	Organización Terpel	Southern Copper Corp
TAM Linhas Aéreas	Salud Coop	(SCC)
Tigre		
Tramontina		**Venezuela (1)**
Ultrapar	**El Salvador (1)**	Petróleos de Venezuela
Vale	Grupo Taca	
Votarantim Celulosa		

Source: Boston Consulting Group, 2009.

To make their selections for the multilatina firms, BCG first compiled a list of 471 nonfinancial companies in the region that in 2007 had sales greater than $500 million. BCG analysts analyzed a series of publicly available sources, including company websites, annual reports, and press reports, to build a database of firms. The database characterizes companies according to their revenues, net equity, number of employees, and EBITDA and considers factors such as the nationality of the company's equity controller, the sectors and countries in which the company is present, the business model, and company strategies. According to BCG, all 100 multilatinas in the 2009 list have Latin American equity control, and all have significant assets/operations in multiple countries.

América Economía

América Economía, an economics publication that has ranked Latin America's largest firms since 1987, calculates a multilatina index based on firm sales, number of countries and geographic areas in which it is present, percentage of international sales, percentage of international employees, geographic coverage, and growth potential (*América Economía*, 2013).

Table 9.3 shows the top 50 multilatinas in 2013 and reveals that the mix of multilatinas is a varied one, representing a wide array of industries: food, beverages, steel/auto parts, petroleum, telecommunications, shipping, energy, petrochemicals, construction/engineering, cement, and airlines.

Latin Business Chronicle

Latin Business Chronicle, a leading business publication focused on Latin America, also publishes an annual list of the top multilatinas. It calculates a multilatina index based on total revenue.

Regardless of the list used to identify global latinas or the variables used to generate the rankings of the largest firms, it is clear that they represent a diverse mix of sectors, ranging from natural-resource and agricultural-resource firms, airplane manufacturing, and airlines to shipping, chemicals, energy, cement, pulp and paper, food, beverages, and manufacturing. This industry variety makes it difficult to draw conclusions about these firms, but the following section attempts to do so by identifying some of the factors that accounted for their growth.

9.3   Competitiveness of Multilatinas and Global Latinas

The competitiveness of Latin America–based multinationals is intertwined with outward investment flows from the individual home countries. Between 2011 and 2012, for example, outward FDI originating from Latin America and the Caribbean increased by 18% for a total of $49.1 billion. This annual flow is 5% higher than the previous high in outward flows, set in 2010 (United Nations Economic Commission for Latin America [ECLAC], 2012). According to ECLAC, the Latin America–based multinationals have benefited from the

Table 9.3 Multilatinas

Ranking 2013	Ranking 2012	COMPANY NAME	Country of Origin	Primary Sector	Sales 2012 (MM US$)	N° countries	N° Geographic Areas	% Intl Sales 2012	% Intl Employees 2012	Investment	Geog. Covg	Growth Potential	Multilatina index
1	4	CEMEX	MX	CEMENT	15,196.6	50	8	77	69	60	100	91	81.0
2	1	GRUPO JBS-Friboi	BR	FOOD	34,856.9	15	8	84	56	66	77	99	79.8
3	2	BRIGHTSTAR (1)	USA/BO	TELECOMM	4,448.6	46	9	55	67	65	97	93	79.7
4	5	TENARIS	AR	METALS	10,834.0	11	5	86	74	82	75	75	79.1
5	7	GRUPO ALFA	MX	MULTISECTOR	13,053.1	17	6	60	28	77	84	93	77.0
6	–	LATAM	CL/BR	AIRLINES	13,379.6	16	5	57	25	80	80	91	76.0
7	11	IMPSA (1)	AR	ENERGY	1,442.8	30	7	67	50	82	94	64	75.1
8	6	TELMEX	MX	TELCOMM	10,109.2	8	3	96	91	51	60	92	75.0
8	10	AJEGROUP	PE	BEVERAGES	1,666.7	16	4	80	78	68	76	75	75.0
10	0	TERNIUM	AR	METALS	8,734.7	10	4	74	70	70	59	84	73.2
11	12	ODEBRECHT (1)	BR	CONSTRUCTION	49,892.9	35	7	42	31	55	91	97	71.4
12	13	GRUPO BIMBO	MX	FOOD	13,353.4	19	6	46	40	70	77	79	69.3
13	9	GERDAU	BR	METALS	20,346.0	14	6	63	50	58	72	83	68.9
14	18	ISA	CO	ENERGY	2,438.0	8	2	70	66	87	53	57	68.6
15	8	VALE	BR	MINING	45,760.5	36	9	17	22	52	92	100	68.1
16	25	MEXICHEM	MX	PETROCHEM	4,889.6	18	6	61	72	35	76	87	66.0
17	15	SIGDO KOPPERS	CL	CONSTRUCTION	2,786.4	25	9	41	20	65	89	71	65.0
18	–	GRUPO BELCORP (1)	PE	CHEM	2,000.0	17	5	80	72	60	73	52	64.3

		Company	CO/SV	Sector									
19	21	AVIANCA-TACA	CO/SV	AIRLINES	4,293.7	22	4	78	71	30	74	80	**63.9**
20	20	MARFRIG	BR	FOOD	11,227.9	21	8	35	42	40	85	88	**63.7**
21	23	SUD. DE VAPORES	CL	SHIPPING	3,431.8	5	5	93	63	45	58	72	**63.3**
22	17	PETROBRAS	BR	PETROLEUM	137,694.9	25	7	37	9	40	84	99	**63.2**
23	14	LAB. BAGÓ(1)	AR	CHEM	1,500.0	22	6	23	45	70	77	63	**62.6**
24	16	AMÉRICA MÓVIL	MX	TELECOMM	59,778.0	18	4	39	55	34	70	94	**62.3**
24	–	ANTO. MINERALS	CL	MINING	6,469.9	7	7	94	26	40	63	83	**62.3**
26	24	INTEROCEÁNICA	CL	SHIPPING	970.4	5	5	93	54	59	59	56	**62.0**
27	29	CENCOSUD	CL	RETAIL	19,116.3	5	1	59	54	50	44	87	**61.9**
28	31	SONDA	CL	TECHNOLOGY	1,423.3	10	3	57	72	43	58	66	**58.2**
29	–	SQM	CL	CHEM	2,429.2	11	5	86	4	25	74	87	**58.0**
30	33	GRUMA	MX	FOOD	4,960.5	18	7	66	63	20	84	71	**57.9**
31	–	RECALCINE	CL	CHEM	575.9	16	4	76	69	32	66	64	**57.5**
32	26	BRASIL FOODS	BR	FOOD	13,955.2	20	6	40	16	21	86	93	**57.4**
33	30	WEG	BR	MANUFACTURING	3,021.2	38	8	44	20	25	91	82	**57.1**
34	22	GRUPO NUTRESA	CO	FOOD	2,950.6	15	5	23	23	75	62	57	**56.8**
35	27	FIBRIA	BR	PULP/PAPER.	3,021.5	8	4	51	4	30	73	90	**56.5**
36	39	VOTORANTIM (1)	BR	CEMENT	12,115.3	10	4	24	24	50	67	76	**56.3**
37	32	ARAUCO	CL	PULP/PAPER.	4,280.3	10	6	90	24	24	64	76	**54.8**
37	44	FALABELLA	CL	RETAIL	11,297.1	4	1	33	44	45	40	84	**54.8**
39	38	GRUPO MODELO	MX	BEVERAGES	7,658.4	22	3	53	5	16	82	90	**54.3**
40	34	V. CONCHA Y TORO	CL	BEVERAGES	938.5	12	6	80	21	20	77	69	**52.8**

(Continued)

Table 9.3 (Continued)

Ranking 2013	Ranking 2012	COMPANY NAME	Country of Origin	Primary Sector	Sales 2012 (MM US$)	N° countries	N° Geographic Areas	% Intl Sales 2012	% Intl Employees 2012	Invest- ment	Geog. Covg	Growth Potential	*Multilatina index*
40	–	**MASISA**	CL	PULP/PAPER	1,349.3	5	2	81	81	15	45	73	**52.8**
40	42	**EMBRAER**	BR	AEROSPACE	5,885.3	6	4	83	7	27	66	74	**52.8**
43	40	**CMI (P. CAMPERO) (1)**	GT	FOOD	2,247.2	12	7	75	77	13	70	61	**52.3**
44	37	**GRUPO ARGOS**	CO	CEMENT	323.5	3	3	52	41	33	44	79	**52.2**
45	35	**CMPC**	CL	PULP/PAPER.	4,848.8	9	2	33	44	31	57	77	**52.0**
46	–	**EMB. ANDINA**	CL	BEVERAGES	2,449.4	4	2	66	73	25	40	70	**51.5**
47	–	**XIGNUX**	MX	METALS	2,523.1	5	4	54	22	30	54	78	**51.3**
48	43	**TIGRE (1)**	BR	CONSTRUCTION	1,514.4	9	2	24	27	44	61	62	**49.5**
49	53	**FEMSA**	MX	BEVERAGES	18,379.8	9	3	42	43	20	53	79	**49.2**
50	47	**ARCOR (1)**	AR	FOOD	3,500.0	16	6	15	35	27	75	68	**48.8**

Source: Compiled by authors, on the basis of information from *América Economía* (2013).

region's economic gains and the investor confidence that emanates from the region. ECLAC indicates that as firms from other world regions held back, Latin America–based multinationals continued investing with newfound vigor in international markets—in both developing and developed markets. For example, global latinas capitalized upon the availability of acquisition targets made available by European firms that decided to shed assets in 2012 (in Europe and in other markets). However, many of the assets that were sold by European firms were regarded by the sellers as tangential or nonstrategic assets and were sold to improve their financial position or to facilitate the purchase of other investments.

Mexican firms were the 2012 regional leaders in Latin American–led outward investments. Outward investments from Mexico in 2012 totaled $25.6 billion, more than twice the prior year's level. This was driven in large part by América Móvil's diversification strategy of moving more aggressively into new markets outside Latin America. América Móvil's 2012 acquisitions were largely in European markets. See Table 9.4 for details on the main cross-border acquisitions made by Latin American firms in 2012.

Chilean firms took second place with outward investments in 2012 totaling $21.1 billion. This was also a record year for Chile with regard to the scale of its outward investment. Chilean firms, however, are largely multilatinas. Examples of this regional focus include Chile's retailing giants, Cencosud and Falabella. Both of these retailers have a strong presence throughout Latin America. Cencosud extended its presence even further with more acquisitions in 2012 in Argentina, Brazil, and Colombia. While Chilean firms have made recent acquisitions in the United States and in Europe, Chilean firms can best be described as having a strong pan-regional presence.

One large merger that occurred between two prominent multilatinas in 2012 was that of Chile-based LAN with Brazil-based TAM, giving rise to LATAM Airlines Group. This $6.5 billion transaction created the region's largest carrier. This case is examined more closely at the end of this chapter.

Unlike their Chilean counterparts, Brazilian firms are generally global latinas. They tend to have a wider geographic presence than Chilean firms, often in several world regions. Global latinas in mining, construction, agriculture, and even consumer packaged goods (e.g., cosmetics) have an increasing presence in Africa (*Economist*, 2012). Vale and Petrobras, two of the largest global latinas, are present in most world regions. Large Brazilian companies in the agricultural sector, such as Embrapa, have provided technical assistance to cotton farmers in several West African countries.

Specific company names provide anecdotal evidence of the geographic dispersion of Brazilian firms; however, a broader measure of the extent of assets held abroad is the value of a country's FDI stock. Brazil has the highest FDI stock of any Latin American country–in excess of $200 billion. This is far greater than Mexico's stock of approximately $130 billion or Chile's of approximately $100 billion (ECLAC, 2012). Brazil's global latinas continue to solidify

Table 9.4 Main Cross-border Acquisitions by Trans-Latinas (2012)

Company	Country of Origin	Assets Acquired	Seller Located in	Sector	Amount US$ Millions
1 LAN & TAM	Chile & Brazil	Merger	Chile & Brazil	Transport	6,502
2 Camargo Correa	Brazil	CIMPOR Cimentos (40%)	Portugal	Cement	4,097
3 América Móvil	Mexico	Koninklijke KPN (23%)	Netherlands	Telecom	3,380
4 Techint	Argentina	Usiminas	Brazil	Steel	2,823
5 Cencosud	Chile	Carrefour Colombia	France	Retailing	2,614
6 Grupo Safra	Brazil	Bank Sarasin & Cie	Netherlands	Financial	2,087
7 Iochpe-Mexion	Brazil	Hayes Lemmerz Intl	US	Automotive	1,317
8 Copbanca	Chile	Banco Santander Colombia	Spain	Financial	1,225
9 América Móvil	Mexico	Telekom Austria	Austria	Telecom	1,103
10 Banco Davivienda	Colombia	HSBC in Central Am	UK	Financial	801
11 Cielo S.A.	Brazil	Merchant e-Solutions	US	Financial	670
12 Grupo Elektra	Mexico	Advance America	US	Financial	656
13 CSN	Brazil	Stahlwerk Thueringen	Spain	Iron & steel	632
14 BTG Pactual	Brazil	Celfin Capital	Chile	Financial	600
15 Techint	Argentina	Confab Industrial (56%)	Brazil	Iron & Steel	567

Source: United Nations Economic Commission on Latin America and the Caribbean (2012).

their geographic presence. In 2012, Brazil accounted for 7 out of the 20 largest foreign acquisitions by Latin American firms (see Table 9.4).

Venezuela, Argentina, and Colombia have also shown high levels of outward investment. In Venezuela's case, these investments have largely been made by the state-owned oil company PDVSA. Argentina's outward investments have been spearheaded by its large steelmaker, Techint. Other than the countries mentioned here, outward investment is either not undertaken in any significant amount in Latin America, data on outward flows are not reported, or data are unreliable (ECLAC, 2012).

9.4   National Champions and State-Owned Global Latinas

State-owned global latinas are primarily concentrated in the oil industry, and some have a limited degree of public ownership. For example, more than

200,000 Colombians own shares of Ecopetrol, the Colombian oil company. This helps secure a public interest in the company's ongoing success. There are four state-owned oil companies in the top 10 Latin American companies listed in the *Latin Business Chronicle*'s list of the top 500 Latin American firms in 2012 (see Table 9.5) (*Latin Business Chronicle, 2013*).

Even though state-owned companies are in the top 10 in sales, it is worth noting that they represent only 16% of the sales for the top 500 Latin American firms, indicating a growing diversity of companies with other type of ownership and in other industries. A benefit to Petrobras of being a public company (36% is owned publicly, according to Table 9.5) is its ability to successfully access international capital markets to fund its large expansion programs. For example, in May 2013, it was able to issue $11 billion of 10-year debt at 4.35% (which is probably two percentage points higher than Exxon Mobil would have had to pay for similar debt). On the other hand, being public brings other challenges. In October 2013, Moody's issued a warning to Petrobras, reducing its debt rating to a barely investment-grade level, citing revenue losses resulting from the fuel subsidies given to Brazilian consumers and the large capital requirements for development. The risk to Petrobras is that if it drops below investment grade, the company may lose its capability to borrow at reasonable rates. The pressure from the capital markets on the Brazilian government to reduce fuel subsidies for Brazilian citizens led to a reduction in these subsidies in November 2013.

The importance of maintaining profitability and return on equity is illustrated by market valuation of these companies. In November 2013, the market value of Petrobras was $67 billion, while Colombia's much smaller oil company Ecopetrol was valued at $88 billion. The difference in valuation was due to Ecopetrol's higher profit margins (21.5% versus 7.7% for Petrobras) and its higher return on equity (22.8% versus Petrobras's 6.6%).

The issue of fuel subsidies in Brazil is just one of several issues these national companies face. For example, Pemex (the Mexican oil company) provides about one-third of the Mexican government's budget because it pays 99% of its profits in taxes. It has been unable to retain profits for sorely needed investment. The Mexican oil company has reached a point where its production has been in slow

Table 9.5 Latin American State-Owned Oil Companies

Rank	Company	Country	Revenues $ Millions	Profits $ Millions	% State Ownership
1	Petrobras	Brazil	137,695	10,366	64%
2	Pemex	Mexico	127,019	218	100%
3	PDVSA	Venezuela	124,459	N/A	100%
8	Ecopetrol	Colombia	37,735	8,451	89%

Source: *Latin Business Chronicle* (2013).

but steady decline. This decline is attributed to Pemex's having drilled in easier-to-reach areas until now. In order to access the more challenging sites that remain, the company will need greater investment and new technology. Foreign oil companies may offer the resources—both financial and technical—that will allow Mexican production to increase over current levels. In December 2013, after much contentious debate in the Mexican parliament, President Nieto's initiative allowing foreign companies to invest in the Mexican petroleum industry was approved.

9.5   The Case of LATAM Airlines Group

The case of the merger between LAN Airlines of Chile and Brazil's TAM Airlines in 2012 provides insight into one of the region's more visible multilatina firms, its operations and its strategies.

In 2012 LAN Airlines, based in Chile, completed the acquisition of TAM Airlines, based in Brazil. This merger created the second largest carrier in the world by market value and one ranking just outside the 10 largest carriers by passenger volume. More important, it created the largest airline in Latin America, with a significant presence in Brazil, Latin America's largest and fastest-growing market for airline services. The new airline serves 150 destinations and 22 countries.

LAN has had the reputation of being one of the industry's best operators, with a long track record of profits, while TAM has been less profitable because it has carried more debt and faced higher costs, partly because of Brazil's higher business taxes and complicated regulations. The debt rating on LAN, for example, was an investment grade of BBB, while TAM had a lower rating of B+. Under the terms of the transaction, TAM's controlling shareholders retained 80% voting control of the Brazilian airline in order to comply with Brazilian regulations limiting foreign ownership to 20%. LAN shareholders ended up with about 70% control of LATAM.

One of the goals of the combined airline is to expand more profitable international routes, particularly on the east coast of the United States and in Asia. Another goal is to deal with profit pressures in Brazil stemming from competition, fuel costs, airport fees, and currency losses. This occurred even though passenger volume in Brazil doubled over the past decade.

LATAM appears to be succeeding in achieving its goals. There has been improved performance in the Brazilian market, a key market that accounts for 34% of LATAM's total business. Cost-cutting measures (such as workforce "rightsizing" and reductions in low-load/inefficient flights) aimed at enhancing airline efficiency have been implemented in Brazil. Domestic traffic in Brazil stayed relatively flat, but capacity was reduced, thus increasing the load factor to approximately 80%. Passenger revenue increased by about 10% in the rest of Latin America, a market where LATAM maintained a load factor of about 79%. International passenger revenue (33% of the total) increased by about 3% and the load factor (around 80+ %) stayed steady.

Investors are confident that Mr. Enrique Cueto, with years of experience and success heading LAN as its CEO since 1994, will be able to succeed in running the merged company. In the three months ending September 30, 2013, the operating margin was 7.6%, up from 3.2% one year earlier, roughly beginning with the approval of the merger. This result reflects an increase in operating margins in the quarter ending September 30 for LATAM, although it has yet to match the approximately 10% levels that LAN had achieved in the past on its own.

Improving profitability is a key to managing the LATAM balance sheet so as to reduce exposure to fluctuations in the Brazilian real. This has been done both through operational measures and through financial hedging. Since airlines typically make heavy use of financing, it was important that LATAM was able to issue a seven-year $450 million securitized bond at 6% in November 2013 to reduce its reliance on short-term debt, even though the debt rating for LATAM had been reduced to BB+ after the merger.

Since TAM is a member of the Star Alliance and LAN of OneWorld, a choice had to be made. LATAM chose OneWorld, which improved profitability of routes between Brazil and the United States because it provided passengers with improved connectivity in the United States through American Airlines. LATAM introduced several of LAN's newer aircraft into the TAM fleet, allowing it to ground 10 of its oldest and least efficient planes. LATAM also introduced the LAN model of optimizing use of capacity in the wide-body planes to carry both cargo and passengers.

9.6   Summary

The pro-market reforms of the 1980s and '90s led to the development of the multilatinas and the global latinas, but the firms have accelerated their international expansion in recent years. This was in part due to European divestment efforts in 2012, which led to greater availability of new and appealing acquisition targets for the multilatinas within Latin America and in other world regions. These firms continue to play a vital role in their respective economies (e.g., boosting employment, expanding the knowledge base, creating a favorable balance of payments positions when exports increase), but they also enhance the region's competitiveness.

In chapter 1, we referenced the views of Alberto Ramos, head of the Latin America economic research team at Goldman Sachs, with respect to what Latin American countries may expect over the near term. The reader may recall that Mr. Ramos alluded to the polarization of Latin American countries and their movement along two different paths. In one group are the countries that continue to pursue strategies that reflect free-market ideals; in the other are countries with more populist pursuits, which make predictions about their performance tenuous. He went on to state that Colombia, Mexico, Peru, and Brazil are part of the first, capitalist-oriented group, while Argentina, Venezuela, Ecuador, and Bolivia are part of the second group (Universia Knowledge@Wharton, 2013). He noted that the first group will continue to grow, while the second group's performance is less predictable. The performance projections for multilatina and global latina firms will likely mirror the performance of their home countries, whether they are part of the first or the second group. Multilatinas and global latinas from group one are likely to continue their international expansion and will continue to reap benefits similar to those that have already been described, while the firms based in group two will find it more difficult to start or continue international expansion. Firms from Argentina already find international expansion difficult given the government's efforts to protect its foreign currency reserves and the imposition of strict currency convertibility regulations imposed by Kirchner's government in 2011 (International Financial Law Review, 2012). Institutional challenges such as these will likely continue to affect the competitiveness of Argentinian firms, as well as those from Venezuela, Ecuador, and Bolivia.

References

América Economía. (2013). Multilatinas, las empresas más globales de la región. Retrieved from http://rankings.americaeconomia.com/2013/ranking_multilatinas_2013/index.php.

Boston Consulting Group. (2009). *The 2009 BCG Multilatinas Index. A fresh look at Latin America and how a new breed of competitors are reshaping the global business landscape.* Retrieved from www.bcg.com/documents/file27236.pdf.

Casanova, L. (2009). *Global latinas: Latin America's emerging multinationals.* London, UK: Palgrave Macmillan.

Casanova, L., Golstein, A., Almeida, A., Fraser, M., Molina, R., Hoeber, H., et al. (2009). *From multilatinas to global latinas: The new Latin American multinationals.* Retrieved from www.iadb.org/intal/intalcdi/pe/2009/03415.pdf.

ECLAC. (2012). *See* United Nations Economic Commission on Latin America and the Caribbean (2012).

Economist. (2012, November 11). A new Atlantic alliance: Brazil in Africa. *Economist 405* (8810): 66–67.

Economist. (2013, September 21). China and Africa: Little to fear but fear itself. *Economist 408* (8854): 51.

Forbes. (2013). The world's biggest companies. Retrieved from www.forbes.com/global2000/.

International Financial Law Review. (2012). *Foreign exchange controls in Argentina.* Retrieved from www.iflr.com/Article/3099463/Foreign-exchange-controls-in-Argentina.html.

Latin Business Chronicle (2013, July 30). *Multilatina Index 1st Quarter 2013* (Special Report). Retrieved from www.latinbusinesschronicle.com/app/article.aspx?id=6176.

UNCTAD. (2012). *See* United Nations Conference on Trade and Development (2012).

United Nations Conference on Trade and Development. (2012). *World investment report: Towards a new generation of investment policies.*

United Nations Economic Commission on Latin America and the Caribbean. (2012). *Foreign direct investment in Latin America and the Caribbean.* Retrieved from www.eclac.org/publicaciones/xml/4/49844/ForeignDirectInvestment2012.pdf.

Universia Knowledge@Wharton. (2013). *Finanzas e inversión: Investing in Latin America: Tremendous growth, but not without complications.* Retrieved from http://wharton.universia.net/index.cfm?fa=printArticle&ID=2371&language=English.

Zaheer, S. (1995). Overcoming the liability of foreignness. *Academy of Management Journal, 38,* 341–363.

10   Entrepreneurship in Latin America

Introduction

> *"Be careful that other people's lack of vision does not become your blind spot."*
> —Linda Alvarado, founder/owner/president and CEO of
> Alvarado Construction

These are sound words of advice for any entrepreneur and they come from a highly successful one, Linda Alvarado. Alvarado is the founder, current president, and CEO of Alvarado Construction, a company she founded approximately 35 years ago. Alvarado Construction is a large commercial general contractor firm that is responsible for the construction of multi-million-dollar construction projects in commercial, housing, government, industrial, and utility projects throughout the United States. She was born in 1951 in Albuquerque, New Mexico, to parents who hailed from Mexico and is considered a role model for many: entrepreneurs, Latino entrepreneurs, women, and others. She likely derives her strength and tenacity from her mother's guiding philosophy: "start small, yet think big." Both generations of Alvarado women can clearly inspire and offer guidance to businesspeople and entrepreneurs.

Entrepreneurial inclinations can be found in every single country, yet the challenges facing entrepreneurs vary greatly across countries, including within Latin America. What are the nuances of entrepreneurship in Latin America, and is there any difference between being a Latin entrepreneur and being an entrepreneur anywhere else in the world? This chapter addresses these issues by first providing an overview of the attitudes toward entrepreneurship in Latin America. Yet, as is the case with most if not all of the topics covered in this book, in order to truly understand the entrepreneurial climate in the region, individual nations must also be considered, as entrepreneurial environments vary considerably from country to country.

The second section in this chapter makes a distinction among different types of entrepreneurial ventures and describes various programs that countries have implemented to attract new business ventures within their borders, with particular emphasis placed on a program, known as Start-up Chile, that is aimed at attracting tech entrepreneurs to Chile. This part of the chapter also looks at the interests and concerns of specific groups of entrepreneurs, including local entrepreneurs, international entrepreneurs in Latin America, and women entrepreneurs. The following section focuses on social entrepreneurship, and the final section reflects on the state of entrepreneurship in Latin America today, as well as its prospects for growth.

10.1   Attitudes toward Entrepreneurship

Macroeconomic Views on Entrepreneurship

The creation of new business can have a significant impact on a nation's growth and development. Innovation and new business development are the drivers of economic activity, leading to growth and employment. Capitalist economies strive to build strong local institutions since they will encourage entrepreneurial activity and investment in the local economy. Innovation and entrepreneurism are thus viewed as a means of wealth distribution and as a way to encourage growth in a nation's middle class. And that, in the long run, can lead to other societal changes of significant importance to a country's development, such as greater emphasis on educational reforms and stronger innovative capability, resulting in the creation of larger, scalable start-ups that will further strengthen the cycle of economic development. Entrepreneurism can lead to new levels of innovation and can increase economic growth for those countries that provide fertile ground for its development (Larroulet & Couyoumdjian, 2009; Montealegre, 2012). Yet, while Latin American countries have embraced capitalism (some to a greater extent than others), they have accepted a Latin American style of capitalism, that is, with strong influence from the left. This situation can result in unique challenges for Latin American entrepreneurs, with varying implications for economic growth across countries. In addition, institutions in emerging and developing markets are often weaker than those in developed markets (Díaz Casero, Almodóvar González, Sánchez Escobedo, Coduras Martínez, & Hernández Mogollón, 2013), and, as a result, the start-up environment may not be as appealing as in developed markets. The weaker Latin American institutions may cast a shadow over the local entrepreneur's enthusiasm and willingness to launch a venture.

Recognizing the uncertain climate in Latin America, James Turley, former chairman and CEO of Ernst & Young, reached a seemingly surprising conclusion (Turley, 2010). In the 2010 Ernst & Young report "Entrepreneurship and Innovation: The Path to Growth in Latin America," the company concludes that the appropriate time to launch entrepreneurial ventures is under uncertain market conditions (Ernst & Young, 2013). While this may seem counterintuitive, the report argues that uncertainty spurs innovation—that the difficulties and the uncertainties in the marketplace lead new ventures to develop innovative goods or services that ultimately yield a competitive advantage. This argument is reminiscent of Michael Porter's (1990) work describing why nations develop a competitive advantage in certain industries. In his work on national competitiveness, Porter maintains that there are four elements that can lead countries to develop a competitive advantage in an industry: factor conditions, demanding consumers, the presence of related and supporting industries, and the strategy, structure, and rivalry of firms. He further points out that adverse factor conditions may lead to innovations that can yield competitive advantages (Porter, 1990). This parallels Ernst & Young's conclusions with regard to uncertain market conditions being fertile ground for innovation.

Latin Business Chronicle, a business publication that focuses on the region, uses World Bank indicators and data from the World Economic Forum to generate a Latin Entrepreneur Index (LEI) that is used to rank countries by their attractiveness to entrepreneurs (*Latin Business Chronicle,* 2013). Several factors are taken into account, including the ease of opening up a business (determined by the number of procedures, number of days required, and cost of starting a new business as a percentage of a nation's per capita income), as well as the availability of funding sources (access to loans and venture capital). The LEI scores are used to generate a rank-ordered list of countries in terms of attractiveness to entrepreneurs. The LEI 2013 rankings of Latin American countries are found in Table 10.1. They reveal that Chile, Panama, and Mexico are in the top three spots, respectively, with Colombia in 4th position. Brazil, however, ranks 15th in the LEI rankings (just before Bolivia, in the 16th position). Brazil's LEI ranking reflects the length of time that is required to open a business. This is the sort of issue that policymakers in Brazil will need to address if Brazil is to enhance its competitiveness with entrepreneurs. The LEI reveals another major hindrance to entrepreneurial activity in the region, and that is the lack of funding sources—including low access to loans and venture capital. This is common to all Latin American markets and may be the reason why some entrepreneurs have left the region.

Despite the challenges, entrepreneurism has historically been viewed as a driver of economic growth (Anchorena & Ronconi, 2012; Castellani & Lora, 2013; King & Levine, 1993; Schmitz, 1989; Schumpeter, 1934; Wennekers & Thurik, 1999). Others have suggested that entrepreneurial ventures tend to be more prevalent when there is a large middle class. As Castellani and Lora (2013) state, this results from the fact that "middle-class individuals have the resources and values to postpone gratification and reap the long-term benefits of innovation." Given the growth of Latin America's middle class, one could assume that this has led to increases in entrepreneurism in the region as well as economic growth, prompting Anchorena and Ronconi (2012) to study this issue in Argentina, a country which (like Uruguay) has traditionally had a large middle class. Anchorena and Ronconi (2012) set out to determine whether the presence of Argentina's large middle class translated into entrepreneurial activities that spurred greater economic growth. They made a distinction between two types of entrepreneurs: "necessity" and "opportunity" entrepreneurs. "Necessity"

Table 10.1 Latin Entrepreneur Index (LEI) (2013)

| | | Starting a Business | | | Access to Capital | | |
| | | A | B | C | D | E | |
Rank	Country	Procedures	Time (days)	Cost	Access to Loans	Venture Capital Avg.	LEI Score
8	Argentina	14	26	12.3	1.69	1.82	62.79
16	Bolivia	15	50	74.1	3.57	3.28	146.25
15	Brazil	13	119	4.8	3.11	2.82	144.86
1	Chile	7	8	4.5	3.74	3.21	26.55
4	Colombia	8	13	7.3	3.09	2.82	36.39
11	Costa Rica	12	60	11.4	2.28	2.24	92.88
7	Dominican Rep.	7	19	17.3	2.54	2.18	52.57
13	Ecuador	13	56	29.9	2.80	2.61	107.49
9	El Salvador	8	17	46.7	2.72	2.29	80.69
14	Guatemala	12	40	48.1	3.09	2.67	108.34
10	Honduras	13	14	45.9	2.77	2.45	81.68
3	Mexico	6	9	10.1	2.63	2.62	33.84
17	Nicaragua	8	39	100.6	2.63	2.73	156.24
2	Panama	6	7	8.8	4.14	3.69	27.97
12	Paraguay	7	35	46.8	3.24	2.56	97.00
6	Peru	5	26	10.6	3.64	2.93	49.03
5	Uruguay	5	7	24.3	2.62	2.49	45.19
18	Venezuela	17	144	27.7	2.51	2.19	198.00
	LatAm Avg.	**10**	**38**	**29.5**	**2.93**	**2.65**	**85.99**

Notes:

A = Total number of procedures required to register a firm.

B = Total number of days required to register a firm with minimum follow-up with government agencies and no extra payments.

C = Cost recorded as a percentage of the economy's income per capita. It includes all official fees and fees for legal or professional services if such services are required by law.

D = Ease of access to obtain a bank loan with only a good business plan and no collateral [1 = very difficult; 7 = very easy].

E = Venture capital availability for entrepreneurs with innovative but risky projects [1 = very difficult; 7 = very easy].

Sources: World Bank, *Doing business 2013;* World Economic Forum, *Global competitiveness report 2012–2013;*2 *Latin Business Chronicle* (2013).

entrepreneurs started businesses because they may not have had the skills to be employable in a salaried position elsewhere. The economic growth derived from this form of entrepreneurship is limited. "Necessity" entrepreneurship lies in stark contrast to "opportunity" entrepreneurs, which tend to contribute in a more significant way to economic growth. As a result, Anchorena and Ronconi (2012) argue that there is a difference in the quality and the quantity of entrepreneurs. Quality entrepreneurs are generally "opportunity" entrepreneurs, and these are often middle-class entrepreneurs. While it was expected that the presence of a sizable middle class would spur greater economic growth, Anchorena and Ronconi (2012) concluded that the presence of a large middle class alone was insufficient to lead to increased economic growth from entrepreneurship and that there were other moderating factors in encouraging entrepreneurship, including more favorable government policies. Lack of access to capital relative to the situation in other Latin American markets was cited as an example of government policies that had likely constrained entrepreneurial activity in Argentina. According to World Bank indicators, credit to the private sector in Argentina amounted to 14% of GDP, whereas in Brazil and Chile it represented 53% and 97%, respectively.

Environmental conditions are critical to entrepreneurial development, yet another factor must also be considered: the entrepreneurial mindset. After all, entrepreneurship and innovation are individual experiences, and, as a result, it is important to understand the individuals engaging in these activities (Cromie, 1994; Dodd & Anderson, 2007). A clearer understanding of the entrepreneurial mindset is needed.

Individual Views toward Entrepreneurship

Views on entrepreneurship and differences across countries would be difficult to gauge if it was not for the availability of GEM (Global Entrepreneurship Monitor) studies.[1] These studies describe the current level of entrepreneurial activity and the aspirations and entrepreneurial attitudes among individuals in Latin American countries and for the region overall (wherever possible).

In order to understand attitudes about entrepreneurism and about willingness to engage in entrepreneurial activity, GEM collects data from a random sample of at least 2,000 adults (ages 18–64 years) in each country. Data from a smaller group—a minimum of 36 national experts—aims to gauge perceptions about entrepreneurial conditions prevalent in each country, including factors such as ease of opening a business, availability of financial resources, and extent of entrepreneurship training. The GEM data reveal some marked differences in attitudes toward entrepreneurship across Latin American countries. See Table 10.2 for entrepreneurial attitudes among a cross section of adults in each Latin American country. If one looks at Latin America in general, then the countries with the higher perceived entrepreneurial opportunities were in South America (Argentina, Brazil, Chile, Colombia, Ecuador, Peru, and Uruguay), whereas those with less perceived entrepreneurial opportunities were in Central America (Costa Rica, Mexico, and Panama). According to respondents in Latin America, the most optimistic country with regard to entrepreneurial opportunities was Colombia and the least optimistic was Panama, with Mexico following closely behind. Even though Panama scored the lowest with regard to perceived opportunities, it scored the lowest with regard to "fear of failure" as well. This suggests that if there were better opportunities for entrepreneurship,

Table 10.2 Entrepreneurial Attitudes and Perceptions in Latin America and the Caribbean (2012)

Country	Perceived Opportunities	Perceived Capabilities	Fear of Failure	Entrepreneurial Intentions	Entrepreneurship as a Good Career Choice	High Status to Successful Entrepreneurs	Media Attention for Entrepreneurship
Argentina	50	63	27	29	74	67	63
Barbados	47	70	17	23	–	–	–
Brazil	52	54	31	36	89	86	86
Chile	65	60	28	43	70	68	66
Colombia	72	57	32	57	89	75	69
Costa Rica	47	63	35	33	72	72	79
Ecuador	59	72	33	51	88	84	79
El Salvador	43	59	42	40	73	72	62
Mexico	45	62	26	18	56	54	38
Panama	38	43	17	12	–	–	–
Peru	57	65	30	45	77	73	76
Trinidad & Tobago	59	76	17	37	78	76	64
Uruguay	51	58	27	20	61	59	51
Average (unweighted)	53	62	28	34	75	71	67

Source: Xavier et al. (2012).

Panamanians would likely be willing participants in entrepreneurial ventures, given their low fear of failure—they are risk takers, but the opportunities are not present. There appears to be a slightly different problem in Mexico and Panama in that the perceptual measures (GEM studies) do not align with more objective measures of entrepreneurism (LEI in Table 10.1). For example, Panama and Mexico rank high with regard to ease of doing business (Table 10.1), yet both countries rank low with regard to perceived opportunities in the GEM studies. Is it that the entrepreneurial opportunities do not exist, despite the fact that if they did, it would be easier to set up businesses there than in other Latin American countries? Alternatively, does the misalignment arise because of a lack of awareness of entrepreneurial opportunities? Policymakers armed with this knowledge might increase or alter the promotion of entrepreneurial opportunities to correct a lack of awareness of existing opportunities.

Citizens from countries that are known to provide some support for entrepreneurial ventures (such as Chile, Brazil, and Colombia) tended to have positive attitudes toward entrepreneurship, as reflected in the scores on "entrepreneurship as a good career choice," "high status associated with successful entrepreneurs," and "media attention on entrepreneurship." Mexico stands out for its relatively low value placed on entrepreneurship, although in part this might be explained by the particularly low score with regard to media attention on entrepreneurship. Of all Latin American countries, Mexico scores the lowest with regard to media coverage. Perhaps if the media created greater awareness of entrepreneurship, the perceptions of entrepreneurship would be more positive.

A panel at the 2013 Latin America Conference at the University of Pennsylvania's Wharton School of Business confirmed that attitudes toward entrepreneurship in Latin America appear to be shifting—ever so slightly—in its favor (Knowledge at Wharton, 2013). One of the panel discussants, Juan Carlos García,[2] who is from Mexico and attended the Wharton School of Business in the 1990s, indicated that the majority of his MBA peers had pursued more traditional careers in banking and finance. Very few at the time had followed the entrepreneurial career path, either in the United States or in Latin America. García and other panelists indicated that entrepreneurism is now perceived in a more positive light in Latin America, with growing opportunities and an increase in the number of individuals interested in pursuing this career path.

10.2   Heterogeneity in Entrepreneurial Ventures

In discussing entrepreneurship, it is important to distinguish between different types of entrepreneurial ventures. In Latin America, as in many other countries and world regions, the entrepreneurial heartbeat is discernible simply by walking the streets. Street vendors sell all kinds of products, sometimes in the open-air marketplaces, and at times the vendor makes his way directly to customers by walking the streets hawking his wares. While this description befits one type of entrepreneurial venture, it is important to distinguish between this and other types of ventures. The street and marketplace vendors, as well as many others, can be classified as small-business entrepreneurs. These are self-employed entrepreneurs striving to make a living by developing a business that can be used to support his or her family. This is in contrast to a very different type of entrepreneurial venture—that of the scalable start-up, whose founder aims to grow the business into a large operation. This is often feasible because there is a novel idea behind the new venture, enabling it to grow eventually into a large business with significant core competencies and market share. However, capital investments are needed to transform a small business into a large operation that will in turn have to fulfill the expectations of investors with regard to return on investment. (The issue of private equity availability in Latin America is discussed later in this chapter.)

Latin America has both types of entrepreneurs—the small-business entrepreneur and the scalable start-up—but the opportunities and risks faced by these entrepreneurial types differ markedly. The GEM data are once again useful in identifying the differences across markets with regard to the types of entrepreneurial ventures that are prevalent in Latin American economies. Table 10.3 summarizes five key aspects of entrepreneurship for each of the Latin American markets: nascent entrepreneurship rate (a measure of starting new enterprises that are less than 3 months old); new-business owners (those who have been in business anywhere between 3 months and 3.5 years); early-stage entrepreneurial activity (a key measure in the GEM methodology, referred to as TEA; it is a total of the two previous measures and reflects the total level of early entrepreneurial activity); necessity-driven businesses (as a percentage of TEA); and improvement-driven opportunities (as a percentage of TEA). These data reveal some clear differences in the types of entrepreneurial ventures in the various economies. While the GEM terms do not align exactly with the two terms introduced earlier in this chapter, the small-business entrepreneur and the scalable start-up, the GEM measures can be viewed as proxies for these terms. In other words, one might expect that scalable start-ups are captured within improvement-driven opportunities, since these businesses are likely to have been in existence for more than 3 months or, even more likely, for several years. Since the cited time period agrees with the definition of improvement-driven opportunities, then it is assumed that scalable start-ups would be included under improvement-driven opportunities.

Table 10.3 leads to the following entrepreneurship-related observations for Latin America. The Latin American economies with higher GDP per capita (e.g., Chile) tend to have "improvement-driven opportunities" that account for a much larger percentage of the total level of early entrepreneurial activity (or TEA). Conversely, those economies with lower GDP per capita exhibit higher rates of TEA due to the prevalence of necessity-driven businesses. In other words, in countries where GDP per capita is higher, the larger, more well-established firms play a more significant role in the economy than they do in

Table 10.3 Entrepreneurial Activity by Latin American Country (2012)

Country	Nascent Entrepreneurship	New-Business Ownership	Early-Stage Entrepreneurial Activity (TEA)	Necessity-Driven Opportunity (% of TEA)	Improvement-Driven Opportunity (% of TEA)
Argentina	12	7	19	35	47
Barbados	10	7	17	12	63
Brazil	4	11	15	30	59
Chile	15	8	23	1	69
Colombia	14	7	20	12	48
Costa Rica	10	5	15	20	48
Ecuador	17	12	27	36	30
El Salvador	8	8	15	35	39
Mexico	8	4	12	13	52
Panama	7	3	9	19	57
Peru	15	6	20	23	53
Trinidad & Tobago	9	7	15	15	60
Uruguay	10	5	15	18	40
Average-unweighted	11	7	17	22	51

Source: Xavier et al. (2012).

markets with lower GDP per capita rates. This assertion is supported by other research that found that newly founded businesses tended to be very small operations that had little impact on a nation's overall economy (Kelly, Bosma, & Amoros, 2010).

10.3   Latin American Entrepreneurs and Technology Entrepreneurship

If one had to identify one of the most coveted start-ups by national governments given its potential to spur economic growth, then the "winner" would likely be technology start-ups (henceforth referred to by their more popular name, tech start-ups). If entrepreneurs thrive on fast-paced, rapidly changing, and highly uncertain environments, then Latin America is likely to appeal to them. Combine this with the fact that technology has been the gateway to entrepreneurship in Latin America in recent years, and one might then assume that Latin America is likely to (1) spawn its own breed of home-grown tech entrepreneurs and (2) attract entrepreneurs from other countries in search of its dynamic environment. The next two parts of this section focus on Latin American tech entrepreneurs in Latin America and on tech entrepreneurs from other world regions now working in Latin America. This discussion then leads to another subsection describing two other notable groups of tech entrepreneurs—those who left the region seeking more entrepreneurially focused or entrepreneurially friendly environments and Latin American female entrepreneurs.

Home-Grown Entrepreneurs in Latin America

The new tech entrepreneurs in Latin America are highly educated, highly skilled entrepreneurs. Many, for example are civil or aeronautical or systems engineers. Often, they have pursued additional graduate-level degrees such as a master's degree in business administration (MBA), from local, US-based, or European institutions. The tech entrepreneurs who studied outside Latin America generally did so with two motivations in mind: to broaden their exposure to a more entrepreneurially focused curriculum than might be available closer to home and to broaden their network of contacts that will be beneficial when establishing the business venture. See Box 10.1 for a focus on a Latin American entrepreneur.

Box 10.1—Focus: A Latin American Entrepreneur

QMagico, cofounded by Thiago Feijão, Mateus Oliveira, Vinicius Canaã, and Claudia Massei, is a Brazil–based startup (Sao Paulo) that plans to use Web technology to bring world-class education to Brazilian students in grades K–12. It won the award for best start-up in São Paulo in 2012. Massei is an aeronautics engineer who attended the University of Pennsylvania's Wharton School of Business (Way, 2012).

Importing Entrepreneurs into Latin America

Looking for a few good tech start-ups! That is the message that is implicitly heard time and time again from Latin American governments. Where local tech entrepreneurs are scarce or simply where "more is preferable," government recruitment programs have been implemented to attract them. Start-up Chile is among the region's most highly publicized programs aimed at attracting tech entrepreneurs to Chile.

In 2010, Chile began the program known as Start-up Chile, which aims to attract tech start-ups to Chile from all over the world through a highly competitive process, enticing them with $40,000 in seed money, office space, one-year temporary visas, and the promise of introductions to key business contacts and networks within the country. Chile has high expectations for Start-up Chile, as the goal is not simply to attract innovative tech start-ups and talent from the world over but rather to transform Chile into the innovation and entrepreneurship hub of Latin America. Start-up Chile capitalized upon Silicon Valley's weakness and immigration constraints to entice international entrepreneurs to Chile.

Three years after the program's inception, the organization has worked with more than 1,300 entrepreneurs and 700 projects from 65 countries. Chilean officials say that Start-up Chile has been a resounding success. Others are more cautious and argue that only a small percentage of the companies that came to Chile as participants in Start-up Chile have stayed much beyond one year, leading some to question whether Chile's transformation into the innovation capital of Latin America will in fact occur. This program has garnered so much media attention that other countries within Latin America, such as Brazil and, more recently, Colombia are seeking to replicate its mission to attract entrepreneurial talent within their borders. While both Colombia and Brazil have embraced Start-up Chile's ideals, the tactics used by each of these countries to attract entrepreneurs have been adapted to local needs and to local political realities. Brazil, for example, which has resorted to protectionist measures in the past to shield its domestic firms from foreign competition, is not as willing as Chile to use government funds in support of non-Brazilian entrepreneurial initiatives. Brazil, instead, has opted to strengthen its venture capital industry. Colombia, like Chile, is jockeying to become Latin America's next innovation hub and as a result, has invested in venture capital, established local accelerators, promoted role models and mentoring among entrepreneurs, created co-working spaces, and used government funds as seed money for laudable entrepreneurial initiatives.

Exporting Entrepreneurs from Latin America

Some of Latin America's tech entrepreneurs are quick to point to the unique challenges that the region's entrepreneurs face. In a lecture at Stanford University, Latin American serial entrepreneurs Wenceslao Cásares[3] and Meyer Malka[4] (cofounders of Bling Nation) discussed the difficult environment for entrepreneurs in Latin America. Cásares identifies several factors that weaken Latin America's entrepreneurial environment, including the region's economic fluctuations, weak institutions, and underdeveloped venture capital industry. On the positive side, he states that tech talent in Latin America is readily available (possibly exceeding its availability in the United States) and at a significantly lower cost than would be possible in the United States. However, Cásares argues that the negative factors weigh on entrepreneurs and distract them from the main task at hand—innovation. Meyer Malka contrasts Latin America's environment to the United States' entrepreneurial environment and indicates that there is a profound difference in perspective between the two. In Latin America, the credibility of an entrepreneur hinges upon his willingness to back a business venture with personal wealth, whereas in the United States credibility is derived from the level of venture capital that the entrepreneur attracts. Both entrepreneurs conclude that the advantages that Latin America offers over the United States, such as less competition and the availability and lower cost of highly skilled labor, is not sufficient to outweigh the heavy burden the region places on entrepreneurs (Cásares & Malka, 2011).

Harnessing Latin American Tech Talent

Universities in the United States—like those in other countries—are actively seeking to attract the highly skilled and highly educated Latin American talent pool through coursework, international alumni outreach programs, and online communities. Stanford University, for example, offers an array of tech-oriented entrepreneurship courses including Technology Venture Formation, Strategy in Technology-based Companies, Patent Law, & Strategy for Innovators and Entrepreneurs, among others. Columbia University offers coursework in a special program titled Entrepreneurship and Competitiveness in Latin America. This one-year certificate program targets Latin American entrepreneurs who wish to fine-tune their entrepreneurial skills and training. The University of Pennsylvania's Wharton School sponsors entrepreneur networking events in Latin America as part of its Global Alumni Forums. An online community was launched in spring 2013 in Cambridge, Massachusetts, specifically targeting Latin American entrepreneurs and professionals interested in business and/or economic development in Latin America.

There is clearly an effort under way to harness the tech talent in Latin America and link it with universities or other entrepreneurial ventures in the United States. It is important to note that Europe and its educational institutions are also active participants in this "competition." Some have referred to this as the "digital revolution of the techno-Latinas" (Keppel, 2012). The tech revolution is augmenting the cooperation between north and south and narrowing the psychological distance that has long existed between the Americas. US-based entrepreneurs are serving as mentors and investors for this group of highly talented entrepreneurs from the south.

How Do Female Entrepreneurs Fare in Latin America?

Chile, Peru, Colombia, and Mexico ranked as the top four countries for women entrepreneurs in Latin America, according to a study conducted by the Inter-American Development Bank's Multilateral Investment Fund (WEVenture-Scope, 2012). Table 10.4 shows the 20 countries that were assessed using the following five factors: security and stability (including macroeconomic risks, security, and corruption), business climate (including costs and regulatory requirements associated with starting businesses), access to finance (including the availability and use of financial services by women), capacity and skills (educational advancement by women), and social services (family support initiatives, including programs such child care).

Chile came in first because of its top ratings for security and stability, business climate, and social services. Mexico placed first in finance, thanks to the access to credit and loans it provides. Peru and Colombia came in second and third, respectively, for the excellent skills training programs they offer. However, Brazil (Latin America's largest market) ranked a disappointingly low 10th place in

Table 10.4 Ranking of Latin American & Caribbean Countries by Their Business Climate for Women Entrepreneurs (2013)

Rank	Country
1	Chile
2	Peru
3	Colombia
4	Mexico
5	Uruguay
6	Costa Rica
7	Argentina
8	Trinidad & Tobago
9	Panama
10	Brazil
11	Dominican Republic
12	Ecuador
13	Bolivia
14	Honduras
15	Nicaragua
16	Guatemala
17	El Salvador
18	Venezuela
19	Paraguay
20	Jamaica

Source: Multilateral Investment Fund (MIF), (2013), Inter-American Development Bank Group.

the region due largely to low scores on security (in the form of perceived high operating risks) and stability (high corruption levels).

Overall, funding for women's entrepreneurial ventures is weak in Latin America, with only 20% of the funding needed for the ventures provided by financial institutions. Another challenge cited by women entrepreneurs in Latin America is the lack of role models and networks that would otherwise provide support and advice to would-be entrepreneurs. This is slowly changing with new initiatives such as Ellas 2, which is an organization (started by a woman) that seeks to offer support, advice, networking opportunities, and even an annual competition, called WeXchange, in which winning tech start-ups founded by women are offered seed money to help jump start these promising new ventures.

10.4   Social Entrepreneurship in Latin America

There are organizations dedicated to solving Latin America's social and environmental challenges by applying business principles, and, despite various interpretations of what constitutes social entrepreneurship, they share the common thread of applying business principles to address a social issue (Tan, Williams, & Tan, 2005). Defining social entrepreneurship would be purely an academic pursuit if it were not for the fact that the definition has significant policy implications. The policy implications arise from the fact that in order for government to create an environment that is conducive to the development of social enterprises, policymakers must first understand what comprises social entrepreneurship. Tan et al. (2005) contend that social entrepreneurship consists of "altruistic businesses that are socially entrepreneurial in the sense that they attempt to profit a segment of society by innovation." However, Michael Porter would argue that a more sustainable approach to social entrepreneurship is to apply capitalist principles and seek to create shared value for the company and for the underserved segment of society. Porter (2012) says that the notion of shared value involves fine-tuning capitalist thinking because it offers a bigger opportunity that will lead to better outcomes for the segment of society that is the target of the firm's efforts and for the firm itself than the outcomes that philanthropic or purely corporate social responsibility initiatives would generate.

Great strides have been made in social entrepreneurship in Latin America in recent years. The creation in 2006 of an organization called Agora Partnerships is an example of social entrepreneurship initiatives that are consistent with Porter's concept of creating shared value. The organization's mission is "to accelerate the success of early-stage impact entrepreneurs who share our community's commitment to solving social and environmental challenges through business" (Agora Partnerships, 2013). Agora's partners range from women's agricultural cooperatives in Latin America or to organizations that employ marginalized youth in Nicaragua to those that provided postdisaster relief in Haiti. Agora initiatives aim to deliver positive change to some of the region's most challenging social ills by creating long-term value for shareholders and society.

Ashoka, a global NGO, is another example of a highly visible social entrepreneurship organization working to address some of Latin America's most pressing social and environmental issues. With nearly 3,000 members worldwide, the organization has a strong presence in Latin America, including Central America, Brazil, and Argentina. Ashoka provides support services, a global network of business and social contacts, and start-up financing to entrepreneurial ventures with a social impact component.

10.5   Summary

There is no doubt that the entrepreneurial climate in Latin America is being transformed, yet there is much work that remains before entrepreneurs in Latin America can say that the level of support they receive from the private sector in support of their initiatives is at par with that available in developed nations. One example of Latin America's accomplishments—and of the work that remains—is the availability of venture capital—or the lack thereof. Venture capital in Latin America as a percentage of the venture capital/private equity source of funding for entrepreneurial ventures is about 5%; the figure for the United States is about 25% (Haar, 2011).

While the sector continues to evolve and entrepreneurs continue to innovate, policymakers must continue their focus on several areas that can help foster the growth of entrepreneurship in the region. Policymakers must continue their push to build strong institutions that will allow for entrepreneurs and innovation to grow. Through regulation and taxation policies, for example, policymakers can enhance the entrepreneurial environment. National economic policies can also seek to facilitate contacts among entrepreneurs, scientists, established businesses, and government. This may require that governments revamp the promotional strategies of entrepreneurship opportunities, such as the methods used for dissemination of information and the strategies used to reach various target markets (including women entrepreneurs). Policymakers must continue to develop economic policies that, while adapted to local needs, will also create an environment conducive to enhancing the nation's innovative capacity. This may require a renewed commitment to new or improved infrastructure, including traditional infrastructure (to enhance efficiencies in distribution) but also a greater emphasis on development of technology infrastructure (such as improved Internet access).

One key area that continues to need the attention of policymakers in Latin America is education. Entrepreneurial skills can be developed through education in the sciences and technology but also through business skills and management training. Training in management and business skills for entrepreneurs should be as broadly accessible as possible and not limited to only certain demographic groups. Educators, particularly at the university level, might also play a role in this regard by considering curricular reforms that more suitably reflect the needs of entrepreneurs. Introduction of entrepreneurially oriented education programs at the university level might be one way to achieve this.

Finally, there is another issue that presents a potential risk to entrepreneurship, a nation's innovative capacity, and prospects for economic growth. It is the issue of changing political landscapes and political priorities. As mentioned earlier in this chapter, Latin America embraced capitalist ideals, but there are some leftist influences. The implications of this are as yet unclear for countries undergoing changes at the highest levels of government. Such is the case of Chile and its Start-up program. This is not an issue unique to Chile; other Latin American countries have also experienced shifts to the left and have in large part managed to keep a long-term view that recognizes the positive economic impact of supporting entrepreneurs, in particular tech entrepreneurs. However, with growth in the region slowing down or even leveling off in some countries, the fiscal reality is that governments will be forced to make some difficult choices. They may, in the short run, be forced to choose between funding social programs (such as poverty-alleviation initiatives) and funding entrepreneurial programs. In actuality, funding of entrepreneurial ventures could accomplish both ideals in the long run, but it is the inherent fear of the unknown and the high degree of uncertainty associated with entrepreneurial ventures that make this a very challenging decision for policymakers when faced with the need to rank funding priorities, especially in light of political realities.

Notes

1. GEM conducts the most expansive study of worldwide entrepreneurial activity and attitudes on an annual basis. The first study was done in 1999 as a joint effort between Babson College and the London Business School, and ever since then it has continuously expanded its global reach to the point where in 2013 it covered nations that account for 75% of the world's population and 89% of global GDP (www.gemconsortium.org/).
2. Juan Carlos García is vice-president of e-commerce at Wal-Mart de Mexico and Central America, a new division of Walmart, structured as a start-up.
3. An Argentine by birth and founder of Lemon.com (and Bling Nation, among other financial services ventures), Wenceslao Cásares opened more than 7,000 bank branches in marginalized neighborhoods in Brazil. Lemon.com has provided 15 million low-income customers with their first bank account.
4. A serial entrepreneur born in England and brought up in Venezuela, Meyer Malka is the chairman of Lemon.com. His entrepreneurial ventures focus on creating disruptive technology innovations in the financial services sector. For a look at the lecture, readers can go to http://stvp.stanford.edu/blog/?p=4347.

References

Agora Partnerships. (2013). Official website. Retrieved from http://agorapartnerships.org/accelerator-2/for-entrepreneurs.

Anchorena, J., & Ronconi, L. (2012). Entrepreneurship, entrepreneurial values and public policy in Argentina. *Inter-American Development Bank*. Working Paper Series No. 316.

Cásares, W., & Malka, M. (2011). *Challenges to entrepreneurship in Latin America*. Retrieved from http://stvp.stanford.edu/blog/?p=4347.

Castellani, F., & Lora, E. (2013). *Is entrepreneurship a channel of social mobility in Latin America?* Inter-American Development Bank. Working Paper Series No. 425.

Cromie, S. (1994). Entrepreneurship: The role of the individual in small business development. *IBAR, 15,* 62–76.

Díaz Casero, J. C., Almodóvar González, M., Sánchez Escobedo, M., Coduras Martínez, A., & Hernández Mogollón, R. (2013). Institutional variables, entrepreneurial activity and economic development. *Management Decision, 51*(2), 281–305.

Dodd, S. D., & Anderson, A. R. (2007). Mumpsimus and the mything of the individualistic entrepreneur. *International Small Business Journal, 25*(4), 341–360.

Ernst & Young. (2013). *Entrepreneurship and innovation: The path to growth in Latin America.* Retrieved from www.ey.com/GL/en/Issues/Driving-growth/Entrepreneurship-and-innovation—The-path-to-growth-in-Latin-America.

Haar, J. (2011). *Financing Latin America's entrepreneurs.* Retrieved from www.endeavor.org/blog/financing-latin-americas-entrepreneurs/#sthash.78LpvPfA.dpuf.

Kelly, D., Bosma, N., & Amoros, J. E. (2010). *Global entrepreneurship monitor—2010 executive report.* Retrieved from www.gemconsortium.org.

Keppel, S. (2012). *Startups in Latin America: The digital revolution heads south.* Retrieved from http://fusion.net/abc_univision/news/story/latin-america-tech-sector-rapidly-growing-16114.

King, R., & Levine, R. (1993). Finance, entrepreneurship, and growth. *Journal of Monetary Economics, 32,* 513–542.

Knowledge at Wharton. (2013). *Entrepreneurs in Latin America: A new mindset among a "rising tide."* Retrieved from https://knowledge.wharton.upenn.edu/article/entrepreneurs-in-latin-america-a-new-mindset-among-a-rising-tide/.

Larroulet, C., & Couyoumdjian, J. P. (2009). Entrepreneurship and growth: A Latin American paradox? *The Independent Review, 14*(1), 81–100.

Latin Business Chronicle. (2013). Latin Entrepreneur Index. Retrieved from www.latinbusinesschronicle.com/app/section.aspx?id=750&g=1.

Montealegre, O. (2012). *Innovation rising: A snapshot of entrepreneurship in Latin America.* Retrieved from www.diplomaticourier.com/news/regions/latin-america/407-innovation-rising-a-snapshot-of-entrepreneurship-in-latin-america.

Multilateral Investment Fund, Inter-American Development Bank Group. (2013). Retrieved from www.iadb.org/en/news/news-releases/2013-07-25/women-entrepreneurs-in-latin-america-and-the-caribbean,10518.html.

Porter, M. (2012). *Interview at the World Economic Forum, Davos, Switzerland.* Retrieved from www.huffingtonpost.com/2012/09/13/solo-sessions-2012-michael-porter_n_1878421.html.

Porter, M. E. (1990). *The competitive advantage of nations.* New York: Free Press.

Schmitz, J. (1989). Imitation, entrepreneurship, and long-run growth. *Journal of Political Economy, 97,* 721–739.

Schumpeter, J. (1934). *The theory of economic development: An inquiry into profits, capital, credit, interests, and the business cycle.* Cambridge, MA: Harvard University Press.

Tan, W.-L., Williams, J., & Tan, T-M. (2005). Defining the "social" in "social entrepreneurship": Altruism and entrepreneurship. *International Entrepreneurship and Management Journal, 1,* 353–365.

Turley, J. S. (2010). Innovation and growth—the Latin American opportunity. In Ernst & Young, *Entrepreneurship and innovation: The path to growth in Latin America.* Retrieved from http://c.ymcdn.com/sites/www.gbsnonline.org/resource/

collection/0C22350B-578A-4B69-9730-22A37ED43CFC/Entrepreneurship_and_innovation_-_The_path_to_growth_in_Latin_America.pdf.

Way, H. (2012). Thenextweb.com. http://thenextweb.com/la/2012/09/03/qmagico-crossfy-win-startup-world-brazil/.

Wennekers, S., & Thurik, R. (1999). Linking entrepreneurship and growth. *Small Business Economics, 13*, 27–56.

WEVentureScope. (2012). *Promoting entrepreneurship for women.* Retrieved from www.weventurescope.com/.

World Bank. (2013). *Doing business 2013: World Economic Forum, Global competitiveness report 2012–2013.* Retrieved from www.doingbusiness.org/~/media/GIAWB/Doing%20Business/Documents/Annual-Reports/English/DB13-full-report.pdf and www3.weforum.org/docs/WEF_GlobalCompetitivenessReport_2012-13.pdf.

Xavier, S. R., Kelley, D., Kew, J., Herrington, M., & Vorderwülbecke, A. (2012). Global Entrepreneurship Monitor: 2012 Global Report. *Global Entrepreneurship Research Association (GERA).* Retrieved from www.gemconsortium.org/.

Part IV

Challenges for the Future of Business in Latin America

11 Challenges for the Future of Business in Latin America

Introduction

Latin America has emerged as a growing and innovative region with large business and consumer markets that are willing and able to buy a wide range of goods and services. The region is now more politically stable, making headway in regulatory reforms, investing heavily in infrastructure, technology and education, and addressing the social and environmental problems that afflict it. This is a context that should invite forward-looking, long-term investments from businesses from inside and outside the region. Yet, challenges remain, primarily in the areas of corruption, natural resource management, and poverty alleviation.

The purpose of this chapter is to highlight the key challenges in Latin America's business environment and to identify windows of opportunity that these challenges may represent. The chapter covers three key topics. First, given the importance of natural resources to the region's competitiveness, issues related to sustainability and resource management will be of critical importance. This section assesses current efforts by firms and governments to address pressures related to responsible resource management and showcases sustainability as an area of business opportunity. Second, corruption and transparency are addressed. Corruption represents a significant risk to potential foreign investors and is a major deterrent to growth for firms already operating in the region. We therefore examine governmental and managerial responses to this challenge. Third, issues of income inequality and poverty continue to represent social and political risk, but they also represent significant opportunity. This section highlights business-based strategies for poverty alleviation in the region. We then focus on corporate social responsibility (CSR) as a strategic response to these three issues. The last section summarizes the main challenges and strategic recommendations identified.

11.1 Natural Resources and Sustainability

As discussed in chapter 3, natural resources are a significant driver of economic growth and organizational competitiveness in the region. Thus, issues related to sustainability and resource management will be of critical importance. For governments across the region, the key imperative will be extracting the most value from their resource-rich economies while minimizing resource depletion and environmental degradation, all of which is essential to ensuring long-term growth and development. For companies doing business in Latin America, the strategic imperative will be in identifying opportunities for independent or collaborative engagement in the natural resources sector, either directly or in industries that support the sector. Practices that demonstrate a commitment to environmental and social responsibility in the management of natural resources must be a critical component of any strategy.

It is estimated that by 2030, half of the world's countries could depend on natural resources for their economic growth. A recent report by the McKinsey Global Institute (MGI) also examined a new model for maximizing the potential value of resource-driven economies, particularly those with minerals, oil, and gas. It is not news that resource-driven economies have historically failed to turn their natural riches into long-lasting development; in fact, 69% of the poor live in resource-rich countries. The resource boom that has driven the economic growth of many countries around the world, including many in Latin America, could either be sustainable or ephemeral. If sustainable, almost half of the world's poor could be lifted out of poverty; proportionally, this has the potential to affect 70 million people in Latin America alone. Turning these natural-resource endowments into enduring development requires a new model, and the one proposed by MGI consists of six elements: "building the institutions and governance of the resource sector; developing infrastructure; ensuring robust fiscal policy and competitiveness; supporting local content; deciding how to spend a resources windfall wisely, and transforming resource wealth into broader economic development" (Dobbs, Oppenheim, Kendall, Thompson, Bratt, & van der Marel, 2013, p. 1).

Several Latin American countries are already engaging in the practices recommended in the MGI report. Chile and Brazil ranked 5th and 10th, respectively, in the quality of their sector governance and institutions, which includes a regulatory regime with clear and stable rules, open competition between state-owned enterprises and the private sector, and policies that attract and retain world-class talent. Chile, Mexico, Peru, Brazil and Colombia ranked 2nd, 5th, 8th, 9th, and 10th, respectively, in implementation of sound fiscal and competitiveness policies that allow them to capture the most value from their resource endowments through a focus on efficiency, productivity, and risk management. Finally, Brazil Colombia, and Chile ranked 5th, 8th, and 9th, respectively, in terms of spending their resources windfall wisely and transparently in ways that transform the revenue value of their resources into long-term development for the country as a whole (Dobbs et al., 2013).

Companies that commit to the sustainable management of natural resources and the social development of the communities where these resources are located can reap financially measurable gains. One of these benefits is a company's ability to secure a consistent, long-term supply of safe and high-quality raw materials. Another major benefit is the reduction of reputation risk. A firm's irresponsible actions will likely result in public and government resistance to the company's establishing or expanding operations; negative press that damages brands and sales; and the company's inability to attract and retain talent (Bonini, Koller, & Mirvis, 2009).

The most-feared risk for firms in natural resource–based industries is, of course, nationalization. Historically, the Latin American region has gone through waves of privatization and nationalization of their natural resource–based industries. This back and forth is the result of countries' attempts at balancing the productivity generated by privatized sectors with the need to ensure equitable distribution of benefits, which tend to be less equal with privatization. Nationalization is now a decreasing risk in Latin America, for a couple of reasons. First, some state-owned enterprises have adapted their ownership structures to attract private investment (e.g., Petrobras); second, some countries have found other ways to capture rents generated by this sector through royalties and taxation. For instance, in Chile more than 70% of copper production is in the hands of private firms, but the Chilean government imposes a royalty on copper production and uses this income in a transparent and responsible way (Sinnott, Dash, & de la Torre, 2010). This regulatory landscape is in line with our discussion regarding sound public management of resource-based sectors by countries in the region. However, companies that fail to behave in environmental and socially responsible ways are likely to attract, if not nationalization, at least governmental intervention; thus it is in the best interest of companies to implement environmentally responsible strategies.

The potential for countries in the region to leverage their resource endowments is significant; the business opportunities for firms willing to invest in natural resource extractive sectors across Latin America are even more so. MGI estimates that developing mineral, oil, and gas resources worldwide will require about US$17 trillion in investments, including $2 trillion in infrastructure, with at least half of that investment demanding collaboration between governments and the private sector (Dobbs et al., 2013).

One example of this collaborative approach is provided by Alcoa's sustainable-development initiative in the municipality of Juruti, on the banks of the Amazon River in the state of Pará in Brazil. In 2006, Alcoa received a license for a large-scale bauxite mining operation in Juruti that included, in addition to the mine, the construction of a beneficiation plant, a port, and a rail link. As a response to both the conditions of the licensing agreement and the company's well-established principles and values, Aloca entered into a collaborative agreement with the Center for Sustainability Studies of the Getulio Vargas Foundation and the Brazilian Biodiversity Fund to develop a long-term model of sustainable development for Juruti. The model includes the establishment of a multi-stakeholder council, the formulation of development indicators to measure the social and environmental impact of the project, and the creation of a sustainable development fund. In reflecting on the business rationale behind its ambitious approach to the mining operation in Juruti, Alcoa pointed to the long-term nature of mining operations (30–40 years) and to the company's long history operating in Brazil (more than 50 years). These conditions make it strategically imperative for the company to establish and nurture supporting relationships with local communities and governments (GVces/Alcoa/Funbio, 2008).

11.2　Corruption and Transparency

Corruption represents a significant risk to potential foreign investors and is a major deterrent to growth for firms already operating in the region; this section examines governmental and managerial responses to this challenge.

Corruption in Latin America is the result of a confluence of factors including bureaucratic and inefficient regulatory and judicial systems, poorly paid civil workers, and a certain degree of cultural acceptance for minor instances of corruption (the so-called grease payments). For many government employees in lower-level positions, a *mordida* (bite) or *propina* (tip) is expected for conducting everyday routine tasks, such as approving permits or licenses. Neither locals nor foreigners are happy paying these, but eradicating this behavior may be very difficult. These employees are not only used to these payments but believe they are entitled to them, and business people must tread lightly in refusing such payments. Obviously, this raises ethical and legal questions for managers and business owners, who must find a way to operate in this environment without violating the law or their personal and organizational ethical standards.

The situation is not hopeless, however. The presence of more democratic governments, the reduced prominence of state-owned enterprises in the economy, and greater access to information have made corruption, especially at higher levels of government, much less accepted and much more visible. Brazil, for instance, has embraced transparency and accountability through the establishment in 2004 of the "Transparency Portal of the Federal Government, which publishes a wide range of information, including the expenditures of federal agencies, the charges of elected officials on government-issued credit cards, and a list of companies banned from contracting with the government" (Cruz & Lazarow, 2012, p. 3). The general population across the region is also more vocal about protesting corrupt behavior among high-level government officials and powerful businesspeople. For businesses the question of bribery is a legal matter: these payments are prohibited and penalized by law in countries within the region and in others such as the United States (Foreign Corrupt Practices Act) and the United Kingdom (UK Bribery Law). Bribery is also discouraged by antibribery conventions such as those passed by the Organization for Economic Cooperation and Development and the United Nations.

Yet, corruption in Latin America is a widespread issue. The Corruption Perceptions Index measures the perceived levels of public-sector corruption. Table 11.1 summarizes the 2013 rankings and scores for selected Latin American countries.

Table 11.1 Corruption Perceptions Index (2013)

Country	Rank (1–177; 1= least corrupt)	2013 Score (0–100; 100 = least corrupt)
Uruguay	19	73
Chile	22	71
Costa Rica	49	53
Brazil	72	42
El Salvador	83	38
Peru	83	38
Colombia	94	36
Ecuador	102	35
Panama	102	35
Argentina	106	34
Bolivia	106	34
Mexico	106	34
Guatemala	123	29
Nicaragua	127	28
Honduras	140	26
Paraguay	150	24
Venezuela	160	20
Regional Average		39
Canada	9	81
United States	19	73

Source: Transparency International.

According to Alejandro Salas (2013), the Americas Director for Transparency International, many countries in Latin America have made good progress in setting up the infrastructure needed to prevent corruption: "21 countries in the Americas have access to information laws; 31 countries are signatories of the Organization of American States Convention Against Corruption; and 17 countries are participating in the Open Government Partnership." The latter requires participants to formulate an action plan for reducing corruption and to commit to independent progress reporting. Yet, the 2013 edition of the Corruption Perceptions Index shows very poor results for the region as a whole. The regional average score is 39 points, which is only slightly higher than that for the Middle East and North Africa (37) and for sub-Saharan Africa (33). As a comparison, the scores for Canada and the United States are 81 and 73, respectively. The region saw no gains in 2013; in fact, most countries either slipped or remained unchanged from the previous year. In Salas's opinion, the best corruption-preventing infrastructure in the region will do nothing to decrease corruption when you have "drugs and weapons worth millions of dollars crossing borders every month." Among the examples he cites are the paying of bribes to the police in Bolivia, the use of public resources for electoral purposes in Venezuela, and nepotism in government hiring in Paraguay (Salas, 2013).

Ports and customs remain two of the most problematic sectors for businesspeople in the region. In 2009, Mexico fired 700 of its customs inspectors and replaced them with more professionally trained personnel (Becker, 2011, p. 136). More recently, in November 2013, "federal police and military forces in Mexico seized control of the nation's largest cargo port, Lázaro Cárdenas, along the country's Pacific coast. The port had served as a major entry point for illicit goods into Mexico, and the seizure was part of a crackdown against the Los Caballeros Templarios cartel, which held sway over port officials thanks to bribes and extortion efforts" (Lindholm & Favaro, 2013). Although this type of government action is not common in the region, similar arrests of customs and port officials have happened in Venezuela, Brazil, Colombia, Mexico, and Panama. A main reason for the high levels of corruption in ports and customs is the inability of these facilities to efficiently handle the amount of trade traffic that goes through them. In the Brazilian port of Santos, it takes a container an average of 21 days to move through the port, and a ship can wait 16 hours to dock. Faced with delays in moving shipments through port or clearing customs, companies are willing to engage in payoffs in order to expedite the process (Lindholm & Favaro, 2013).

The prevalent landscape of corruption and unethical behavior experienced by firms in the region has prompted a variety of organizational actions to manage these risks. Ethical conduct in corporate governance has been one topic of interest—and action—for firms in the region for the past two decades. Several countries in the region have boards of corporate governance that promote best practices for their board members. The main issues of ethical conduct are related to the protection of minority shareholders' interest, disclosure, transparency, and internal and external accountability (Bedicks & Arruda, 2005).

Companies faced with corruption risks can also implement more direct measures to guide and monitor the behavior of their managers, employees, and business partners. Companies can adopt their own code of ethics and anticorruption policies so that managers doing business in the region know exactly what is and is not acceptable behavior. It is important that managers understand that engaging in corrupt behavior is against corporate values. Companies should also engage in careful vetting of third parties and should show due diligence in reviewing third-party contracts and fees (Lindholm & Favaro, 2013).

11.3   Income Inequality and Poverty

Since 2002, poverty in the region has decreased by 15.7% and extreme poverty by 8%. Yet, the sustained economic growth the region has experienced has not been sufficient to close the gap between the rich and the poor. In Latin America, income gaps are palpable: on average, 20% of households earn only about 5% of a country's income, while the richest 20% of the population controls 47% of the country's income (United Nations Economic Commission for Latin America and the Caribbean [ECLAC], 2013). Poverty is decreasing, but it is doing so at a slow pace, likely as a result of the global and regional economic downturn and delayed recovery. Issues of income inequality and poverty continue to represent social and political risk (e.g., recent social unrest in Brazil and a swing to the left in Honduran politics), but they also represent significant opportunity. In this section we identify key areas of business opportunity in sectors that represent unmet needs for consumers at the base of the pyramid and highlight some examples of business-based strategies for poverty alleviation in the region.

The base of the pyramid (BoP) in Latin America represents a market of about 165 million people (28% of the population), with the extreme poor amounting to 66 million (11%) of the total population (ECLAC, 2013). In Mexico alone, the BoP market is 37 million strong. This is a market with countless unmet needs, and firms ignore it at their own peril. As C. K. Prahalad and Stuart Hart (2002), and their colleagues (London and Hart, 2011) have come to superbly articulate over the past decade, there are significant and valuable opportunities for business development at the BoP. The broad scope of unmet needs in BoP markets offers firms the opportunity to generate growth and profitability while developing new technologies and new business models. Identifying and pursuing these opportunities will require long-term thinking, creativity, and deep collaborations with a wide array of stakeholders.

In order to identify windows of opportunity, we must first understand the main needs of BoP consumers. Primary needs include access to drinking water, health-care services and insurance, and housing. Other basic areas of spending include food, household durables, cars, recreation, telecommunications, and clothing. For instance, a recent report by ECLAC (2013), found that health-care insurance spending among the poor is increasing, thus confirming that there is a market for these products and services even among the very poor.

The demographic trends in Latin America indicate that the region's urban BoP market will be easiest to develop. Its needs are shaped by higher incomes, a higher degree of connectivity, and more direct contact with reference and aspirational groups than are available to the rural BoP. This market will demand more nuanced segmentation and targeting approaches, especially in terms of demographic and psychographic variables, such as household composition, level of education, occupation, values, attitudes, and lifestyles. These consumers place great importance on brand reputation and quality of services provided, and, if targeted with the appropriate mix, they are likely to become loyal customers. Urban consumers can be accessed through already established communication and distribution channels, and a multichannel strategy means more points of contact at a lower cost. Adapting pricing and financing schemes and localizing product portfolios will be essential, but accessing the urban BoP can be accomplished with lower transaction costs than can accessing the rural BoP.

Examples of companies that are already exploring and leveraging these opportunities can be found throughout Latin America. Several firms in the region, for instance, have adopted inclusive business models, which are commercially viable business initiatives that engage low-income communities as suppliers, distributors, or consumers. In Table 11.2 we summarize a few cases of companies that have successfully entered BoP markets in the region and highlight one such case here to provide perspective on the strategic elements required to engage low-income consumers and communities.

Table 11.2 Examples of Business Initiatives for BoP Markets in Latin America

Industry/Sector	Company	Country(ies)
Agribusiness	LATCO Intl. (sesame)	Bolivia
	Sabritas (sunflowers)	Mexico
	Agricorp (beans)	Nicaragua
	Delizia (diary)	Bolivia
	Dinant (Cohune palm nut)	Honduras
	Nestle	Peru
	Pronaca (corn)	Ecuador
Education	FINAE (educational loans)	Mexico
	Colegios Peruanos (private schools)	Peru
	PUPA (pre-school educational materials)	Brazil
Financial Services	Fopepro (agricultural loans)	El Salvador, Guatemala, Honduras, Nicaragua, Bolivia, Colombia, Ecuador, Peru, Paraguay
	Bancorp (agricultural loans)	Paraguay
	Microfin	Uruguay
	Alternative Insurance Company (micro-insurance)	Haiti
	PyMe Capital (business loans/ credit)	El Salvador, Guatemala, Honduras, Nicaragua, Dominican Republic, Bolivia, Colombia, Peru, Paraguay
	MiBanco (microfinancing)	Peru
	Banco Gerador (banking)	Brazil
Health	Ancalmo (pharmaceuticals)	El Salvador
	GlaxoSmithKline	Brazil
	Salud Facil (financing)	Mexico
	Cruzsalud (medical services)	Venezuela
Housing	Credifamilia (housing loans)	Colombia
	Patrimonio Hoy (home building)	Mexico, Costa Rica, Nicaragua, Dominican Republic, Colombia
	Vision Banco (housing loans)	Paraguay
Energy	Tecnosol (alternative energy)	Nicaragua, El Salvador, Honduras, Panama
Manufacturing	Masisa (wood/furniture)	Argentina, Chile, Brazil
Construction	GrupoNueva (construction)	Argentina, Guatemala

Source: Authors' elaboration based on data from Inter-America Development Bank (2013); SNV/ WBCSD (2011); and Corporate websites.

Cementos Mexicanos (CEMEX)

Cementos Mexicanos is the third largest cement producer in the world. In 2012, the company reported $15 billion in net sales, with net operating earnings of $1.3 billion and total assets of $37 billion. CEMEX's program Patrimonio Hoy is an example of a successful initiative by a multilatina to penetrate the low-income consumer market in Mexico. The first pillar to CEMEX's strategy was nontraditional marketing research. In order to gain deeper knowledge of consumer needs, the firm engaged in anthropological field research, embedding a team of managers in low-income communities for several months. Through this research, the firm was able to understand the constraints faced by low-income consumers and to realize that their needs went beyond cement. As London and Hart (2011) state, CEMEX illustrates the benefits of engaging low-income consumers with humility and with a mindset that allows listening and learning from them. The firm's response was to develop a holistic home-building solution that incorporated, among other things, fixed prices for construction materials, storage and delivery, technical design assistance, and access to credit. The second element of CEMEX's success lies in the firm's ability to build long-lasting relationships with stakeholders in the communities it hoped to serve. These relationships were essential for CEMEX's business development and implementation. The last element of CEMEX's strategy was its long-term orientation and commitment to the low-income segment. This long-term perspective allowed the firm to experiment and to continuously adapt and reinvent its business model to fit the needs of the market. Since its inception in 1998, Patrimonio Hoy has helped almost 400,000 low-income families build their homes, and it now operates through 100 offices in Mexico, Colombia, Costa Rica, Nicaragua, and the Dominican Republic (CEMEX, 2013a). Beyond the financial success, the program has enhanced CEMEX's image as a socially responsible and innovative company and has undoubtedly earned it brand loyalty in the countries it serves.

11.4   Corporate Social Responsibility

Corporate social responsibility is defined as the "practices that are part of the corporate strategy which complement and support the main business activities, explicitly seek to avoid damage and promote the well-being of stakeholders by complying with the law and voluntarily going beyond it." (Peinado Vara, 2006, p. 62). There are increasing pressures on companies from every part of globe to behave in ways that demonstrate their commitment to the social and environmental concerns of the communities in which they operate. Our discussion on the continued presence of corruption, expectations for sustainable management of natural resources, and space for developing market-based strategies that alleviate poverty all point to the importance of corporate social responsibility for businesses in Latin America. Developing a strong social leadership capability can give Latin American firms and foreign firms operating in the region a sustained competitive advantage. In this section, we discuss the state of corporate social responsibility in the region and identify some examples of companies that are committing resources and strategic capabilities to sound stakeholder management.

A 2009 report by McKinsey found that environmental, social, and governance programs can have measurable value in terms of firms' financial performance. The research identified the following areas of value creation:

1. Growth: through the development of new markets and new products; the increases to sales and market share resulting from enhanced reputation and differentiation; and the gains in innovation outcomes (e.g., patents, new business models).
2. Return on Capital: operational efficiency generated by cost reductions in energy and water usage, for instance; workforce efficiency, primarily through higher employee morale and retention; improved supply chain management; and price premiums that an enhanced brand image allows.
3. Risk Management: less regulatory risk by complying with local laws and expectations of local stakeholders; less operational risk, such as reduction of public resistance to company expansion; and less reputation risk, such as boycotts and negative publicity.
4. Management Quality: firms' ability to develop leaders and organizations that are more adaptable and agile; and a push to engage markets with a long-term strategic perspective. (Bonini, Koller, & Mirvis, 2009; Bonini & Görner, 2011)

Corporate social responsibility is neither a new concept nor a new practice among Latin American firms. The focus of CSR actions and programs has traditionally focused on social issues, as would be expected in a region where poverty, income inequalities, and poor health and education are daily concerns. This social orientation is also grounded in two cultural aspects. First, owners' and managers' sense of duty to society is influenced by the region's religious (particularly Catholic) traditions (Puppim de Oliveira, 2006). Second, as discussed in chapter 7, the feudal and collectivist nature of the region is translated in modern Latin American society into a form of "benevolence" from bosses and others in positions of power. The responsibilities of the haves with respect to the have-nots is fulfilled through philanthropic and/or corporate actions. Thus, CSR has taken the form of company-supported foundations, donations, direct subsidies for employees, and financing of community development projects such as clinics and schools.

One example of this is the Juan Bautista Gutierrez Foundation, the social branch of Multi-Inversiones (Gutierrez Group), which supports education and health initiatives in Guatemala. Its activities include supporting training programs for elementary school teachers; recognizing nongovernmental organizations (NGOs) that create projects related to education or health; offering university scholarships for low-income students; funding or subsidizing schools, education materials, and entrepreneurial programs; supporting health initiatives, hospitals, and health centers with equipment and physical improvements; and donating food, medicine, and transportation during natural disasters. In addition, its Ayudame a Vivir Foundation (AYUVI [Help Me to Live]) focuses on assisting children suffering from cancer by financing hospital equipment and subsidizing treatments. In the United States, the group has continued its philanthropic causes through its support of the Make-a-Wish foundation and St. Jude's Children's Hospital (Corporación Multi Inversiones, 2013).

The philanthropic approach common among Latin American firms has evolved into a more fully integrated CSR approach that is embedded into a company's overall strategy. There is abundant evidence that social and financial goals are not incompatible. CSR can help establish valuable networks with low-income consumers, community organizations, and local governments. Moreover, the economic gains to the community in the form of jobs and improved living conditions can in turn produce additional market benefits for the firm (Peinado Vara, 2006).

An example of corporate citizenship in the area of social development is provided by CEMEX. The firm's experimentation and eventual implementation of its successful Patrimonio Hoy program in the late 1990s led the company to develop additional programs that were socially oriented and that allowed it to build closer linkages with local governments, NGOs, and communities. Although the majority of these initiatives are concentrated in Mexico, the firm is seeking to replicate them in other Latin American countries. These social development programs are (1) ConstruApoyo, which was initially a program designed to help communities in Mexico rebuild quickly, efficiently, and transparently after natural disasters but now extends to other government-subsidized housing and community construction; (2) Lazos Familiares, which helps communities build and renovate community institutions and buildings, such as health centers, hospitals, orphanages, and schools; (3) Mejora tu Calle, which provides assistance to communities and local governments for neighborhood improvement projects and which unites the public and private sectors in providing a market-based solution to the paving of streets and sidewalk construction; and (4) Centro Productivos de Autoempleo (CPA), another collaboration among CEMEX, municipal authorities, and NGOs to establish community centers where low-income families can temporarily work producing concrete blocks and other precast products (CEMEX, 2013b).

More recently, firms doing business in the region have widened the scope of their CSR activity to focus not only on social problems but also on environmental sustainability. The World Business Council for Sustainable Development's (WBCSD) website lists national WBCSD councils in 17 countries in the region, with company members that include multinationals from outside the region, large domestic firms and family conglomerates, and medium-size businesses from a broad range of sectors. Some of these national councils were created as early as 1992, although the majority were established in the early 2000s.

These councils are actively engaged in a variety of programs and initiatives that include, among others, industrywide initiatives to identify and communicate best practices and assessment tools; facilitate dialogue and learning on sustainable business development among companies, governments, and NGOs; and introduce and monitor specific programs in the areas of energy efficiency, resource management, and inclusive business models (WBCSD, 2013). Furthermore, the KPMG International (2013) survey on corporate social responsibility reporting shows that reporting of CSR activity has increased in the region, with the percentage of companies reporting CSR programs ranging from 56% to 78% among the countries included in the survey (Brazil, Chile, Colombia, and Mexico).

Companies like LAN-TAM and Petrobras, for instance, have embarked in a variety of initiatives to "green" their operations. LAN-TAM, the airlines group, has a modern fleet (6.9 years on average, compared to 11 years for the industry worldwide) and policies and procedures aimed at reducing CO_2 emissions, fuel use, and noise pollution (LAN-TAM, 2013). Petrobras responded to a series of environmental disasters in 2000—and the corresponding bad press and damage to its bottom line—by overhauling and modernizing its operations to become one of the most sustainable energy companies in the world and a leader in renewable energy (Gabrielli de Azevedo, 2009).

11.5   Summary

In Latin America, where corruption is still rampant, poverty is real and visible, and overdependency and destruction of natural resources are growing concerns, companies and corporate leaders that can demonstrate a high level of ethics and environmental and social responsibility will have a measurable competitive advantage. In this chapter we summarized current efforts by firms and governments to address pressures related to responsible resource management and showcased social and environmental sustainability as a potential element of strategic opportunity. As mentioned earlier, the visibility of CSR actions and reporting in Latin America are increasing. In order to manage risks and generate growth and profitability, companies must formulate strategies and design value chains that incorporate the ethical, social, and environmental concerns of multiple stakeholders in the region.

References

Becker, T. (2011). *Doing business in the New Latin America*. 2nd ed. Santa Barbara, CA: Praeger.

Bedicks, H. B., & Arruda, M. C. (2005). Business ethics and corporate governance in Latin America. *Business and Society*, 44(2), 218–228.

Bonini, S., & Görner, S. (2011). *The business of sustainability: McKinsey global survey results*. Retrieved from www.mckinsey.com/insights/energy_resources_materials/the_business_of_sustainability_mckinsey_global_survey_results.

Bonini, S., Koller, T. M., & Mirvis, P. H. (2009, July). Valuing social responsibility programs. *McKinsey Quarterly*. Retrieved from www.mckinsey.com/insights/corporate_finance/valuing_social_responsibility_programs.

CEMEX. (2013a). *Annual report 2012*. Retrieved from www.cemex.com/InvestorCenter/files/2012/CemexAnnualReport2012.pdf.

CEMEX. (2013b). Official company website. Retrieved from www.cemex.com/Sustainable Development/HighImpactSocialPrograms.aspx.

Corporación Multi Inversiones (2013). Corporate website. Retrieved from http://corporacionmultiinversiones.com/responsabilidad-social.

Cruz, M., & Lazarow, A. (2012). *Innovation in government: Brazil*. Retrieved from www.mckinsey.com/insights/public_sector/innovation_in_government_brazil.

Dobbs, R., Oppenheim, J., Kendall, A., Thompson, F., Bratt, M., & van der Marel, F. (2013). Reverse the curse: Maximizing the potential of resource driven economies. *McKinsey Global Institute*. www.mckinsey.com/insights/energy_resources_materials/reverse_the_curse_maximizing_the_potential_of_resource_driven_economies

Gabrielli de Azevedo, J. S. (2009). The greening of Petrobras. *Harvard Business Review* (March), 43–47.

GVces/Alcoa/Funbio. (2008). *Sustainable Juruti: A proposed model for local development*.

Inter-American Development Bank. (2013). *Opportunities for the majority portfolio 2011 & 2012*. Retrieved from www.iadb.org/en/topics/opportunities-for-the-majority.

KPMG International. (2013). *KPMG survey of corporate responsibility reporting 2013*. Retrieved from www.kpmg.com/sustainability.

LAN-TAM. (2013). Corporate website. Retrieved from www.lan.com/en_us/sitio_personas/about_us/sostenibilidad_lan/trabajando_medio_ambiente/index.html.

Lindholm, N., & Favaro, T. (2013, December 9). Stuck in a bottleneck, Latin American ports breed corruption. *Forbes*. Retrieved from www.forbes.com/sites/riskmap/2013/12/09/stuck-in-a-bottleneck-latin-american-ports-breed-corruption/.

London, T., & Hart, S. L. (2011). *Next generation business strategies for the base of the pyramid: New approaches for building mutual value*. Upper Saddle River, New Jersey: FT Press.

Peinado Vara, E. (2006). Corporate social responsibility in Latin America. *Journal of Corporate Citizenship, 21*, 61–69.

Puppim de Oliveira, J. A. (2006). Corporate citizenship in Latin America: New challenges for business. *Journal of Corporate Citizenship, 21*, 17–20.

Salas, A. (2013). *CPI 2013: Traffic lights in the Americas—lifesavers or urban decorations?* Retrieved from http://blog.transparency.org/2013/12/03/traffic-lights-in-the-americas-lifesavers-or-urban-decoration/.

Sinnott, E., Dash, J., & de la Torre, A. (2010). *Natural resources in Latin America and the Caribbean: Beyond booms and busts?* Washington, DC: The World Bank.

SNV/WBCSD. (2011). *Inclusive business: Creating value in Latin America*.

Transparency International. (2013). *Corruption perceptions index*. Retrieved from http://transparencyinternational.org.

United Nations Economic Commission for Latin America and the Caribbean [ECLAC]. (2013). *Social Panorama of Latin America*. Retrieved from www.eclac.org/cgi-bin/getProd.asp?xml=/publicaciones/xml/8/51768/P51768.xml&xsl=/tpl-i/p9f.xsl&base=/tpl-i/top-bottom.xslt.

World Business Council for Sustainable Development. (2013). Official website. Retrieved from http://wbcsd.org/members-only/regional-network/members-list/latin-america/latinamericahome.aspx.

12 The Future of Business in Latin America

Introduction

In this book, we set out to look at Latin America's progress thus far in the 21st century. We are encouraged to find that the region has done well economically, socially, and politically. Our review finds a region that has made substantial progress in reducing poverty, reducing inequality, and increasing standards of living. The region's progress has been accomplished during a period character-ized largely by democratically elected leaders and during an era of social and technological progress. A poll of people in the region in 2013 found that about 77% of respondents were satisfied with life, a 23-point increase from the initial period of our review in 2000. In the same poll, the number of Latin Americans observing that their countries are making progress is also on the increase. In 2013, 37% of respondents mentioned progress, whereas only 27% did so in 2000 (Latinobarometro, 2013).

This long period of stability has allowed Latin Americans to become more confident and optimistic about the future. With a solid foundation, Latin America is at a turning point in its development and is ready to move onto a higher plateau. Nevertheless, progress in the economic, political, and social spheres has varied across the individual countries of the region. Some Latin American countries are at the forefront of economic and social development. Mexico and Chile joined the Organization for Economic Cooperation and Development (OECD), a group of first-world economies and societies, in 1994 and 2010, respectively (OECD, 2013). The door has been opened for Latin American countries, and other nations are likely to follow.

Progress and satisfaction with life are, however, uneven and polarized. Such polarization has led to the conclusion that there are two Latin Americas. One part of Latin America is enjoying progress, and the other one is being left behind (Latinobarometro, 2013). This polarization exists across and within countries. For instance, the top five countries indicating progress in 2013 were Ecuador, Panama, Nicaragua, Uruguay, and the Dominican Republic. On the issue of satisfaction with life, the top five countries that reported being satisfied were Panama, Costa Rica, Dominican Republic, Colombia, and Argentina. On the other end of the scale, the five countries with the lowest levels of satisfaction, in descending order, were Bolivia, Peru, Chile, Honduras, and Paraguay. The fact that Chile is one of the most prosperous economies in the region rules out the conclusion that poverty explains life dissatisfaction (Latinobarometro, 2013).

The challenge of reconciling the region's differences and lack of consistency on current opinion on life satisfaction and progress suggests more questions than answers. How might Latin America continue to advance its economic and social development? How might the region's historical accomplishments serve as the foundation of such progress? And what are the implications of these changes for doing business in the region?

In this chapter, we explore these questions and summarize what we have learned from our review of the region in the 21st century thus far.

12.1   Moving the Economies to the Next Level

Latin American economies are clearly moving into a period of low to medium economic growth, in the range of 3% to 4%, as noted in chapter 1. The heterogeneity in economic growth that was characteristic of the region in the first decade of the 21st century will likely continue, but with lower average annual growth rates. The two dominant countries in the region, Brazil and Mexico, are moving into a period of low to medium growth; of the other five core countries, Colombia, Chile, and Peru are expected to exhibit higher levels of growth, and Argentina and Venezuela are likely to exhibit slow growth accompanied by high levels of inflation. A similar scenario can be observed among the Central American countries. Panama, Costa Rica, and Nicaragua are poised for higher levels of growth and Guatemala and Honduras for medium levels of growth, and El Salvador will grow the slowest.

Chapter 1 reviewed how the region's economic growth relied on exports of natural resources, particularly to China. China has also been a large investor and lender in Latin America. In the future, Latin America will be better off reducing such dependence on a single trade and investment partner. Thus, another path after the inflection point would see increased export-market diversification and efforts to attract investors from other parts of the world. As chapter 1 mentions, too much commodity export concentration to a single destination (China) seems to hinder economic development or, at the very least, puts it at risk (BBVA, 2013e). There are many other market opportunities in South-South trade. Africa seems to be a natural market for Latin American exports due to geographic proximity and strong cultural ties with certain countries that were part of a shared colonial past and of the African diaspora. Brazilian and Chilean companies have begun to make inroads in the African continent through investment in infrastructure, natural resources, and technology, and we expect the success of these first movers to influence other Latin American firms to follow suit.

As chapter 3 mentioned, one of the key sources for future growth is improvement in productivity. Achieving such improvement will require greater investment in education and infrastructure and a more efficient government. Firms in Latin America may also join the quest for improved productivity at the micro level with the upgrading of their labor and capital inputs. This quest has already taken place in a few countries and economic sectors. Moreover, productivity gains will require that private firms allocate more resources to research and development, which in turn will allow Latin American countries and firms to diversify and move away from natural-resources extraction and toward value-added industries.

Some Latin American countries have already started to diversify their economies so as to minimize their reliance on natural resources. Countries seek to minimize the volatility in their economies that can arise when a nation is overly dependent upon revenues from natural and agricultural resources. Chile has recognized this and has been a leader in the region in its attempts to spur economic growth through technology start-ups.

Another example is Mexico's car industry, which is gradually moving from an assembly and car-manufacturing platform to one based on creating value through technological improvements in prototype development (A. T. Kearney, 2013). Such a shift requires advanced technical talent and industry specialization. Mexican universities have followed through with upgrading engineering programs and graduating larger numbers of qualified Mexicans who demand compensation rates that are a fraction of those in the United States. As a result, Mexico's car industry is producing more and innovating more and creating a solid middle class of mid-level, well-paid positions.

Improving government's efficiency can go a long way toward enhancing a country's economic performance and spurring the strength of its business sector. For example, Mexico ranked 53rd and Chile ranked 34th in the Ease of Doing Business index, while Brazil, the largest economy in the region, ranked 118th out of 189 countries (World Bank, 2013). Brazil's success in addressing some of its regulatory constraints will likely encourage growth in entrepreneurial ventures that ultimately can grow into small and medium-size firms and contribute in a meaningful way to economic growth.

The search for new paths to growth cannot be done without further improvements in the transparency and governance of governmental and social institutions. This will be the most difficult task for all Latin American countries. Many of the reasons for the failure to achieve basic levels of the conditions needed for business and society to function properly are deeply embedded in a culture that tolerates corruption and inefficiency. (Chapters 3 and 11 provide a discussion of the degree and scope of corruption and regulatory bureaucracy.) This attitude is changing, however, and thus we can expect governments and institutions to face increasing pressures for transparency and accountability. The street protests in Brazil mentioned in chapter 5 are an indication that Latin Americans are better off but discontent with their countries' progress on a number of fronts, and corruption is one visible target. Latin Americans will become more activist in the future, and this activism will likely include a reversal of their tolerance of corruption. According to one report, the mantra for the future is "listen to me" (*Economist*, 2013).

12.2 Further Regional Polarization

Our review also exposed the growing polarization of Latin America and examined the consequences for the strategic reconfigurations of the business environment in the region. In chapter 2, we argued that Latin America has mirrored the change of a global economic order wherein emerging economies have driven global economic growth while developed economies have stagnated. This has led to the polarization between two distinct economic clusters in Latin America. One group of economies is led by Brazil and is composed mostly of South American countries strongly aligned with Asian economies. Another group of economies is led by Mexico and is mostly represented by Central American and Caribbean countries more aligned with the advanced economies of the United States and Europe. This economic polarization presents different risks and challenges for the two groups. The Brazil-led cluster is vulnerable to overdependence on commodity specialization and deindustrialization of its members' economies. The Mexico-led group is vulnerable to the sluggish growth prospects of the advanced economies in the long term, and it is also threatened by the Asian economies' global competitiveness superiority in manufactured-goods export industries, although recent evidence suggests that over time Mexico could become a formidable global competitor in the manufacturing sector.

As the Asian economies have slowed down, the Brazil-led cluster has adjusted accordingly, particularly Brazil. Brazil's economy reached a low growth rate of 0.9% in 2012 with an expected economic growth in 2013 of barely 2.4% and 2% forecast for 2014 (Forbes, 2013; World Bank, 2013). Such sluggish results raise questions as to whether Brazil is faltering or is merely in a transition period. This period could propel Brazil to reinvent its economy, supporting innovation, sustainable environmental practices, and capitalization of its energy riches while dealing with stubborn moderate inflation and social unrest. The rest of the countries in the Brazil-led cluster continued to produce robust annual economic growth rates ranging from 4% to 5% in 2013, with Peru leading the way and Colombia and Chile following closely (BBVA, 2013a; 2013b; 2013c). Such disparity of results suggests a future of further polarization within the Brazil-led cluster, whose members seem to be decoupling from the powerful lead of the main economy in the cluster.

Contrary to Brazil's recent troubles, Mexico seems to be turning around and finding a renewed economic drive as the US economy slowly recovers from a deep recession. Mexico's economic growth in 2012 was 1.2% and was expected to reach 3.1% in 2014 (BBVA, 2013d). It is also expected that the newly reformed oil law in the country will contribute to increases in foreign direct investment and over the long term will increase Mexico's exports of oil and gas and lead to a more favorable position in Mexico's current account. The more promising prospects for Mexico are shared by the rest of the countries in the cluster, with Panama leading the way with 8.3% economic growth in 2013 (*Wall Street Journal*, 2013). In a similar fashion to what we observe in the Brazil-led cluster, some countries in the Mexico-led cluster seem to be decoupling from the largest economy in the group.

The recent economic developments described lead us to predict further polarization in the region rather than future convergence. If there is further polarization, we may have some guidance as to how these clusters will be structured from the study by Izquierdo and Talvi (2011), which identified four evolving clusters, defined as follows: (1) Brazil, Colombia, Argentina, and Paraguay; (2) Chile, Venezuela, Trinidad and Tobago, Peru, Uruguay, Bolivia, and Ecuador; (3) Mexico, Costa Rica, Honduras, Panama, Belize, Guyana, the Dominican Republic, and Suriname; and (4) Nicaragua, El Salvador, Bahamas, Barbados, and Jamaica (Izquierdo & Talvi, 2011). The shape and level of further regional polarization in Latin America is important for business strategies. In chapter 2, we advanced a contingency strategy model based on two regional economic clusters. A future of four or more clusters may require a more refined differentiation of regional strategy. Such differentiation will be based on how these clusters evolve.

12.3 Social Shifts and the Consumer Market in Latin America

The expansion of the middle class and the reduction in poverty have made a big impact on markets, as noted in chapters 1 and 4. Much of the sustained economic growth after the 2008 recession in Latin America can be attributed to the growth of strong domestic markets across the region. Will middle-class Latin Americans move up as they become more affluent? How would a large upper-middle-class market shape future consumer markets in the region? It is too early to say, but the process of upgrading living standards may be the natural evolution of Latin America's consumer markets.

As reviewed in chapters 4 and 5, today's Latin American consumers have a strong appetite for electronics, communications, and credit cards. The more affluent Latin American consumer may upgrade his or her lifestyle and be more interested in education and services than in consumer commodities.

Furthermore, demographic trends suggest Latin America will be aging fast. The number of children may peak in the next 10 years and then decline for all Latin American countries, while the number of elderly will triple by 2050 (Center for Strategic and International Studies [CSIS], 2013). This process will be most pronounced in Chile, Mexico, and Brazil.

The combination of middle-class migration to higher incomes and an aging population will create a Latin America different from the one we know today. Aside from the health and public-services challenges, firms may have to change their approach to reach a much older and more demanding consumer.

While great strides have certainly been made with regard to the creation of a large middle class, poverty alleviation remains a priority for many Latin American countries. The number of poor in Latin America was estimated to reach 164 million in 2012 (Economic Commission on Latin America and the Caribbean [ECLAC], 2013). The demographics in Latin America share the spatial concentration of poverty of other emerging markets in the sense that 79% of the poor are urban dwellers and 21% live in rural areas. Poverty alleviation programs are more likely to reach urban dwellers (United Nations Department of Economic and Social Affairs, 2013). Latin America is a vast continent, and many of these rural communities are found in remote areas with limited access to the basic services and amenities that we have discussed in chapters 4 and 5. This book has focused on documenting the urban population of Latin America rather than the conditions of rural dwellers. We acknowledge this deficit and realize not only that collectively the rural poor should be at the frontier of future research but that governments and firms must be more attuned to their needs and concerns.

From a business perspective, the need to attend to the needs of the poor—urban and rural—has received increasing attention from both academics and practitioners. Businesses from the region especially and some foreign firms have entered the lower-income segment in Latin America with innovative products and services and nontraditional business models. Successful base-of-the-pyramid ventures can be found across the region in energy, housing, and telecommunications, for example. Although real challenges remain (especially regarding distribution), meeting the unmet needs of low-income consumers represents a significant window of opportunity for companies willing to engage these markets with collaborative, innovative, and long-term strategic approaches.

12.4   Cultural Reaffirmation

Culture changes much more slowly than technology or the economy. In our review of Latin American culture (with an emphasis on the business culture), we portrayed Latin American culture as strongly relationship driven, one in which family and work relations are important. This cultural base will remain solid in the future. Perhaps the major change is in how those relationships will be maintained. In chapter 4, we discussed the deep penetration of communications technology in the region. Latin Americans are leveraging social technology to maintain their relations in a more hurried society. This process may intensify, and we would expect to see more Latin Americans connected to social networks. Thus, Latin American culture may have a more impersonal link—through technology—but with the same goal of keeping relationships alive. Such intensification opens up multiple opportunities to engage the Latin American consumer.

National cultural identity is on the rise and will continue to influence Latin Americans, as will economic polarization and a renewed interest in discovering one's own identity. Although curious to experience other cultures and visit neighboring countries, Latin Americans are becoming increasingly interested in and proud of their own national identity. As they explore their country's customs, folklore, and geography, they are more likely to prefer local products or work for firms owned by nationals. Such a trend is especially evident in food consumption. As chapter 5 illustrated, local operators have made large inroads into fast-food markets with appeals to local taste and ingredients.

No discussion on culture as it relates to Latin America can overlook the role of women in society. As a region, Latin America likely has the greatest percentage of political leaders who are women. Argentina, Brazil, Chile, and Costa Rica are all at present headed by women. This is not purely a 21st-century phenomenon, as in the 20th century Argentina, Nicaragua, and Panama were also headed by democratically elected female presidents. Does the visibility of women heads of state in traditionally patriarchal societies translate into greater strides for women in these countries or in the region overall? This question cannot be answered easily; however, to reframe the issue from a business perspective, this line of thinking gives rise to several business-related issues. Does the seemingly high number of women in politics translate to high(er) numbers of women heading up Latin American firms? The answer is, not yet. Although some women have taken the reins of their family business, the majority of top executive positions and board seats are still controlled by men. Latin American firms will be advised to take quick steps to remedy this situation, not only for top executive positions but across all levels within their organizations. The increasing labor and talent shortages in the region cannot be met without effectively incorporating more women into the workforce (Leutert, 2012). Flexible working conditions, fair wages, and developmental programs such as networking and mentoring will be essential to move women into middle and top managerial positions. Addressing gender imbalances is a potential source of competitive advantage for Latin American firms and a topic that will demand future attention from both researchers and managers.

12.5   Regional Strategy and Competition

The rivalry between the large multinationals and the rising multilatinas was a feature of the past decade. We believe that the multilatinas are not only holding their ground but winning the market. These multilatinas have upgraded their competencies and leveraged all of the advantages of being local. With global ambitions, many of these multilatinas are using their regional competencies to challenge developed-country multinationals in tertiary markets in Asia, Europe, and Africa. The future may be determined by sheer size or new competencies. It is clear that multilatinas will strive to enhance their current success. They may need to use mergers and acquisitions to grow and to invest much more in R&D. The failure to do the latter is perhaps the multilatinas' main weakness.

As competition for Latin American consumer markets moves to the next level of sophistication, the regional strategies of multinationals will become more innovative in the creation of consumer value. Multinationals from outside the region may narrow their strategic focus to large-country markets that make sense to keep in their business portfolio. As mentioned in chapter 5, three potential Latin American markets receiving the most attention could be Brazil and Mexico along with one midsize economy market such as Peru, Colombia or Chile. Deeper penetration of these markets will drive these multinationals to build national strategies to reach secondary and tertiary city markets. Clearly, the void created by the absence of the larger nonregional multinationals will be filled by the multilatinas as discussed in chapter 9. The success of these multilatinas will demand a deeper understanding of the cultural differences among country markets in the region, including differences in business cultures and business environments.

Small and medium-size businesses (SMEs) will continue to play an important role as well, as they continue to be the main generators of jobs (and, in some cases, innovation) in the region. The expansion and consolidation of multilatinas will be enhanced by the presence of strong SMEs that can be incorporated into their value chains. Thus, governments' support of SMEs through improvements to the business environment and firm-level competencies will be critical in this development. In addition, reducing the size of the informal sector, another major competitive constraint faced by SMEs, will likely have an overall positive impact on the region's economies and its competitive environment.

12.6   Entrepreneurship

Latin American countries have long recognized that entrepreneurial activities can lead to innovation and business growth. Our discussion identified two important issues to consider. First, policymakers play a key role in creating an environment that nurtures the entrepreneurial spirit and allows entrepreneurial ventures to grow and develop into competitive businesses. Second, we find that not all entrepreneurial ventures lead to the same outcomes. Some ventures will have a more profound economic impact, and, therefore, policymakers must attempt to identify high-impact start-ups. The complexity of this task cannot be overstated. In essence, policymakers are being asked to look into the entrepreneurial crystal ball to try to identify which entrepreneurial ventures might offer the greatest impact in the future and to provide the support that is needed to allow those ventures to prosper.

The earlier discussion would suggest that, as Latin American countries position themselves for further growth, they might benefit from the implementation of an entrepreneurial learning initiative for impact analysis and knowledge exchange (as other world regions have proposed). This type of program could be implemented on a national or possibly on a pan-regional level. As indicated in chapter 10, the strengthening of national institutions is another key to creating an entrepreneurially friendly environment. Latin American officials—in politics and in academia—have also recognized that the curriculum at several levels in their educational systems may need to be restructured to incorporate a greater focus on management, leadership, finance, and other business-related topics. Finally, there is a need for the creation of entrepreneurial networks where aspiring entrepreneurs can be exposed to role models, identify suitable mentors, and connect with potential investors. Some nonprofit groups have also stepped in to sponsor these kinds of exchanges, with a particular focus on female entrepreneurs in Latin America.

12.7   Corporate Social Responsibility

In Latin America, corruption is still rampant, poverty is real and visible, and overdependence on and destruction of natural resources are growing concerns. Companies and corporate leaders who can demonstrate a high level of ethics and environmental and social responsibility will have a measurable competitive advantage in the years to come.

There are increasing pressures on companies from every part of globe to behave in ways that demonstrate their commitment to the social and environmental concerns of the communities in which they operate. These pressures are increasingly observed in Latin America. One such instance is the growing concern over the impact that multinationals and even regional firms have on the environment and on indigenous communities. In Latin America, respect for the land is often engrained in the psyche, stemming from long-held indigenous traditions in which the land is to be respected and preserved for future generations. This is a concern being faced time and time again in rural areas, where extractive industries are often based. Indigenous people in remote areas must be given the opportunity to voice their opposition to organizations that fail to respect the environment, particularly when "modernization" threatens such people's livelihoods and traditions. Firms that can integrate the social and environmental concerns of indigenous communities into their strategies will be better positioned for long-term growth in Latin America.

Corporate social responsibility (CSR) is neither a new concept nor a new practice among Latin American firms. The focus of CSR actions and programs has traditionally focused on social issues, as would be expected in a region where poverty, income inequalities, and poor health and education are daily concerns. More recently the scope of CSR has expanded to include environmental sustainability, especially regarding the management of natural resources. Latin American firms that recognize the value creation potential of socially and environmentally responsible strategies will reap the benefits of a more favorable company and brand reputation, lower regulatory and operational risks, greater efficiencies, and new product and market opportunities. Developing a strong social leadership capability can give Latin American firms and foreign firms operating in the region a unique competitive advantage, one that can be leveraged in other emerging regions such as Asia and Africa.

12.8   Concluding Remarks

The overall conclusion of our review of Latin America in the past decade is positive. We found the region progressing and full of economic and social energy. The region's accomplishments are based on the efforts of many to build better societies with democratic participation. Latin American societies not only have moved forward in economic progress but seem to be content with life. Satisfaction with life is not purely based on economic progress. Some of the Latin American countries that have made substantial economic progress in the past decade at the national level have societies whose members indicate a low level of satisfaction with life. Achieving a more even distribution of the benefits of economic progress among everyone in society will be a major challenge for the region.

Adoption of technology throughout the region also has had a positive impact on business and consumer markets and has the potential to be a major driver of future growth and productivity. Technology is changing how people interact with family and friends and is increasing points of contact between firms and consumers. Technology also offers the promise of innovative approaches to the long-standing needs of the poor, including improvements to food production systems and increased access to health, education, and energy.

The business environment is difficult and challenging. Regulatory inefficiencies and poor infrastructure are the main challenges countries and firms will have to overcome. Yet, the region is now more affluent, competitive, and integrated into the rest of the world. There is reason to believe that the winners of this emerging market will be companies, both foreign and domestic, that have worked hard to gain the trust of Latin American consumers. Thus far, the prospects are good for multilatinas and national champions that have effectively leveraged their competencies and their deep knowledge of local markets to meet the changing needs and expectations of Latin American consumers.

Cultural identities will remain a strong differentiating factor in the region, and although Latin Americans are embracing new values (e.g., individualism), their connections to family and their national culture will shape both market and managerial approaches. Firms' responses to the needs of women and low-income consumers will be two primary areas of opportunity.

The future of the region will be markedly different from the conditions that prevailed during the past decade. Latin America may resemble the profile of a mature and advanced society, with all of the problems and characteristics of the developing world. Moreover, it will be a region where social content and discontent coexist with increasing economic progress. The challenge of managing the problems of a developing country that is embedded into an advanced economy will not be easy, but the region offers enormous promise—for its people, domestic firms, foreign investors, and the globalized economy as a whole.

References

A. T. Kearney (2013). *Reigniting Mexico's automotive industry.* Retrieved from www.atkearney.com/documents/10192/d8efd180–9af1–48c0–8111-defaaebb8c75.

BBVA. (2013a). *Colombia economic outlook fourth quarter 2013.* Retrieved www.bbvaresearch.com/KETD/fbin/mult/1302_ColombiaOutlook_1Q13_tcm348–373665.pdf?ts=28112013.

BBVA. (2013b). *Peru economic outlook fourth quarter 2013.* Retrieved from http://servi ciodeestudios.bbva.com/KETD/fbin/mult/1311_PeruEconomicOutlook_eng_ tcm348–411937.pdf?ts=12122013.

BBVA. (2013c). *Chile economic outlook fourth quarter 2013.* Retrieved from http://servi ciodeestudios.bbva.com/KETD/ketd/bin/ing/publi/chile/noveddes/detalle/ Nove348_198728.jsp?id=tcm:348–183559–64.

BBVA. (2013d). *Mexico economic outlook fourth quarter 2013.* Retrieved from http://servi ciodeestudios.bbva.com/KETD/fbin/mult/1311_MexicoOutlook_4Q13_tcm348– 411638.pdf?ts=12122013.

BBVA. (2013e). *Latin American export commodity concentration: Is there a China effect?* Retrieved from www.bbvaresearch.com/KETD/fbin/mult/WP_1306_tcm348–370671.pdf.

Center for Strategic and International Studies (2013). *Latin America's aging challenge.* Retrieved from http://csis.org/files/media/csis/pubs/090324_gai_english.pdf.

CSIS. (2013). *See* Center for Strategic and Independent Studies.

Economic Commission on Latin America and the Caribbean. (2013). *Reduction of poverty slows down in Latin America.* Retrieved from http://lacreport.com/eclac-report-reduction-poverty-slows-down-latin-america#sthash.A6q6h3JZ.dpuf.

Economist. (2013). Listen to me. Retrieved from www.economist.com/news/americas/2158 8886-slightly-brighter-picture-democracy-not-liberal-freedoms-listen-me.

Forbes. (2013). J. P. Morgan radically cuts Brazil's 3Q growth forecast. Retrieved from www.forbes.com/sites/kenrapoza/2013/08/18/j-p-morgan-radically-cuts-brazils-3q-growth-forecast/.

Izquierdo, T., & Talvi, E. (2011). *One region, two speeds? Challenges of the new global economic Order for Latin America and the Caribbean.* Washington, DC: Inter-American Development Bank.

Latinobarometro. (2103). *Informe 2013.* Retrieved from www.latinobarometro.org/doc umentos/LATBD_INFORME_LB_2013.pdf.

Leutert, S. (2012). *Women key to Latin America economic progress.* Retrieved from http://global publicsquare.blogs.cnn.com/2012/11/13/women-key-to-latin-america-economic-progress/.

Organization for Economic Cooperation and Development. (2013). *List of OECD member countries.* Retrieved from www.oecd.org/general/listofoecdmembercountries-ratificationoftheconventionontheoecd.htm.

United Nations Department of Economic and Social Affairs. (2013). *World urbanization prospects, the 2011 revision.* Retrieved from http://esa.un.org/unup/Analytical-Figures/Fig_1.htm.

Wall Street Journal. (2013). Panama's economy to extend strong economic growth. Retrieved from http://online.wsj.com/news/articles/SB100014241278873245320045 78364710313021902.

World Bank. (2013). *Brazil Overview.* Retrieved from www.worldbank.org/en/country/ brazil/overview.

Index

Page numbers in italics indicate that the term is found in either a figure or table